"HOME IS A NAME,

A WORD,

IT IS A STRONG ONE;

STRONGER THAN A MAGICIAN EVER SPOKE,

OR A SPIRIT EVER ANSWERED TO,

IN THE STRONGEST CONJURATION."

Charles Dickens

Design by **Kent Thompson, Architect and Sullivan Bruck Architects**
Photo by **Janet Adams – Business First**

CENTRAL OHIO HOME BOOK

A COMPREHENSIVE HANDS-ON DESIGN SOURCEBOOK FOR BUILDING, REMODELING, DECORATING, FURNISHING AND LANDSCAPING A LUXURY HOME IN CENTRAL OHIO

Photo courtesy of **Ralph Fallon Builder, Inc.**
Photo by **Will Shively**

PUBLISHED BY

THE
ASHLEY
GROUP

Chicago New York Los Angeles

Las Vegas Philadelphia Atlanta Detroit

Arizona Southeast Florida Washington D.C. Colorado

San Francisco North Carolina Dallas/Fort Worth

San Diego Houston Boston Seattle Kansas City

Orange County Central Ohio Connecticut/Westchester County

Published By
The Ashley Group
7654 Crosswoods Dr.
Columbus, OH 43235
614.431.2950 FAX 614.431.2052

Reed Business Information.
Reed Business Information
A Division of Reed Elsevier Inc

ISBN 1-58862-111-1

CENTRAL OHIO HOME BOOK

Publisher *Adam Trabitz*
Editor-in-Chief *Dana Felmly*
Managing Editor *Laurence P. Maloney*
Senior Editor *James Scalzitti*
Assistant Editor *Alison M. Ishihara*
Office Manager *Amanda Weinbrecht*
Account Executive *Aaron Bass*
Production Director *Paul Ojeda*
Production Manager *Michael Patten*
Creative Director *Bill Weaver*
Senior Graphic Designer *Kristin Bashaar*
Ad Service Coordinator *Tommy Kusmierz*
Graphic Designers *Rozalia Singh, Andrew Stamm*
Marketing & Book Sales Coordinator *Tracy Potocki*
Circulation Manager *Christine Kurgan*
Prepress *Cahners Prepress*
Printed in Hong Kong by *Everbest Printing Company*

THE ASHLEY GROUP

Group Publisher *Paul A. Casper*
Director of Publications *N. David Shiba*
Regional Director *J.D. Webster*
Group Controller *Patricia Lavigne*
Group Administration *Nicole Port, Kimberly Spizzirri*

REED BUSINESS INFORMATION

Chief Executive Officer *James Casella*
Chief Financial Officer *John Poulin*
Executive Vice President *Ronald C. Andriani*
Vice President, Finance *David Lench*

Front Cover *Kevin Knight and Company*
Photo by Leslee Kass

Back Cover *Sullivan Bruck Architects*
Photo by Bill Tijerina

Note

The premier edition of *The Central Ohio Home Book* was created like most other successful products and brands are – out of need. The *Home Book* concept was originally conceived by Paul Casper, currently Group Publisher of The Ashley Group. Paul, a resident of Chicago's North Shore, at one time was planning the renovation of his home. However, he quickly discovered problems locating credible professionals to help his dream become a reality. Well, Paul's dream did become a reality – it just happens to be a different dream now! Instead of Paul simply finishing his new home, he saw the need by consumers nationwide to have a complete home resource guide at their disposal. Thus, he created the distinct *Home Book* to fulfill consumers' needs for reliable and accessible home improvement information.

After three successful years, the Home Book drew the attention of Reed Business Information. In April 1999, Reed purchased it, and since then, the *Home Book* network has grown rapidly. By the end of 2001 there were Home Books in 14 markets nationwide. In addition to Central Ohio and Chicago, Home Books are available in Washington D.C., Detroit, South Florida, Colorado, Dallas/Fort Worth, Houston, Los Angeles, Atlanta, San Diego, Philadelphia, Arizona, Las Vegas and North Carolina. Within the next year, Home Books will be published in San Francisco, Seattle and Kansas City, among other cities.

Public demand for quality home improvement services continues to increase. The Ashley Group recognizes this trend, which is why we exact the same amount of dedication and hard work from ourselves that we expect from our *Home Book* advertisers. We hope our hard work rewards you with the quality craftsmanship you deserve, turning your dream house into a reality.

Congratulations on purchasing a *Home Book*. Now reward yourself by kicking back and delving through its pages. We hope you enjoy the inspiring ideas within.

Dana Felmly *Editor-in-Chief*

James Scalzitti *Senior Editor*

Why You Should Use This Book

Why You'll Want to Use the Central Ohio Home Book

At times, in this high-speed information-driven culture, we can easily become lost and disoriented. Where we find information, how we find it, and how credible this information is, has become critical to consumers everywhere.

The Central Ohio Home Book recognizes and addresses these concerns, and provides ease of use and comfort to consumers looking to build, renovate or enhance their home. As a consumer, the anxiety of searching for trustworthy, experienced housing professionals can be overwhelming.

Relief is in Sight

The Central Ohio Home Book puts an end to this stress. It offers you, the reader, a comprehensive, hands-on guide to building, remodeling, decorating, furnishing and landscaping a home in Central Ohio. The book also offers readers convenience and comfort.

Convenience

The Central Ohio Home Book compiles the area's top home service providers with easy-to-read listings by trade. It also dissuades readers' fears of unreliable service providers by featuring many of the finest professionals available, specialists who rank among the top 10 of their respective fields in Central Ohio. Their outstanding work has netted them many awards in their fields. The other listings are recommendations made by these advertisers.

The goal of the Central Ohio Home Book creators is to provide a high quality product that goes well beyond the scope of mere Yellow Pages. Its focus is to provide consumers with credible, reliable, and experienced professionals, accompanied by photographic examples of their work.

This crucial resource was unavailable to the founders of the Central Ohio Home Book when they were working on their own home improvement projects. This lack of information spurred them on to create the book, and to assist other consumers in finding the proper professionals that suit their specific needs. Now, thanks to the team's entrepreneurial spirit, you have the Central Ohio Home Book at your fingertips, to guide you on your home enhancement journey.

Comfort

Embrace this book, enjoy it and relish it, because at one time it didn't exist; but now, someone has done your homework for you. Instead of running all over town, you'll find in these pages:

• More than 700 listings of professionals, specializing in 40 different trades.
• Instructional information for choosing and working with architects, contractors, landscapers and interior designers.
    • More than 1,000 photos inspiring innovative interior and exterior modeling ideas.
      • A compilation of the area's top home enhancement service providers with easy-to-read listings by trade.

Excitement...The Central Ohio Home Book can turn your dream into a reality!

Adam Trabitz

Adam Trabitz, *Publisher*

The premier resource provider for the luxury home market

Central Ohio Home Book

About the Front Cover:
Warmth and an elegant style radiate
from this home by Kevin Knight
and Company.

Photo by **Studio Ohio**

Contents

Continued

46

102

57

470

253

485

About the Back Cover:
A home that is stately yet responsive to today's families, by Sullivan Bruck Architects.

Photo by **Bill Tijerina**

Contents

117

217

292

90

How To Use

TABLE OF CONTENTS

Start here for an at-a-glance guide to the 12 tabbed categories and numerous subcategories. The book is organized for quick, easy access to the information you want, when you want it. The Table of Contents provides an introduction to the comprehensive selection of information.

INTERIOR DESIGN SPOTLIGHT

Dedicated to showcasing the elegance and vitality of some of the most beautiful residences in the area.

DESIGN UPDATE

Read what top home industry professionals think are the most exciting new styles, future trends and best ideas in their fields as we continue into the millennium. See even more inspiring photos of some of Central Ohio's most beautiful, up-to-date luxury homes and landscapes. It's a visual feast, full of great ideas.

"HOW-TO" ARTICLES

Each tabbed section begins with a locally researched article on how to achieve the best possible result in your home building, remodeling, decorating or landscape project. These pages help take the fear and trepidation out of the process. You'll receive the kind of information you need to communicate effectively with professionals and to be prepared for the nature of the process. Each article is a step-by-step guide, aiding you in finding the materials you need in the order you'll need them.

This Book

DIVIDER TABS

Use the sturdy tabs to go directly to the section of the book you're interested in. A table of contents for each section's subcategories is printed on the front of each tab. Quick, easy, convenient.

LISTINGS

Culled from current, comprehensive data and qualified through careful local research, the listings are a valuable resource as you assemble the team of experts and top quality suppliers for your home project. We have included references to their ad pages throughout the book.

FEATURES

From Interior Design Spotlight to New in the Showroom, we've devoted attention to specific areas within the various sections. We've also gone in-depth, with feature articles in the Architects and Home Builders sections.

INDEXES

This extensive cross reference system allows easy access to the information on the pages of the book. You can check by alphabetical order or individual profession.

BEAUTIFUL VISUALS

The most beautiful, inspiring and comprehensive collections of homes and materials of distinction in Central Ohio. On these pages, our advertisers present exceptional examples of their finest work. Use these visuals for ideas as well as resources.

Design

*What are the hot ideas and attitudes that are shaping new
Update, where top local professionals tell what's happening*

THE EXPANDING KITCHEN

Bob Webb Builders: "The kitchen has always been
a home's gathering place. Today, our clients are
expanding their kitchens into their family rooms
and dining rooms, creating one big, open space for
entertaining. Careful planning and design creates
an ideal space for entertaining while keeping an
environment of formality and comfort."

Update

homes, interiors and landscapes in your area? Read Design
now in their businesses, and what's coming in the future.

21

Photo by **Leslee Kass**

WARM, COMFORTABLE SANCTUARIES

Fry Contracting Co.:"People want their homes to be sanctuaries, a place to find warmth and comfort. Things that last are most important in remodeling - the character of a particular wood, the grace of a staircase, the way the light fills a room ... these are the things that matter. The only way to achieve them is to focus on quality."

23

AT THE HEART OF THE HOME

Cooley Custom Cabinetry, Inc.: "Function and style are what a homeowner wants. Custom cabinetry can address the practical needs while expressing the owner's personal style. Custom storage elements such as appliances behind designed cabinet interiors ensure a well-organized kitchen. And flair can be added to either traditional or contemporary kitchens by mixing old antique pieces such as islands and hutches."

Photo by **J.E. Evans**

FINELY FURNISHED KITCHENS

Miller Cabinet Company: "Nothing is standard in custom cabinetry today. People want their kitchen and bath cabinetry to be unique. A more specialized look in finishes is popular, with glazing, distressing on stained or painted wood, and two-color finishes in big demand. People are mixing finishes for effect, so that the island or the cabinets around the range may be stained while the rest of the cabinetry is painted. They also want furniture detailing – feet, onlays, corbels, fluting, post details – that make the cabinetry look more like fine furniture. The effect is to make the kitchen look and feel as finely designed and 'furnished' as the rest of the home."

Photo by **H.R. Croghan**

LETTING IN LIGHT

Romanelli & Hughes: "Our clients love wide-open kitchen areas with lots of workspace and light. One of the main features they want is an abundance of natural light, especially in the common areas. By letting in natural light, we are able to bring the beauty of the outdoors in, where it can be enjoyed year-round."

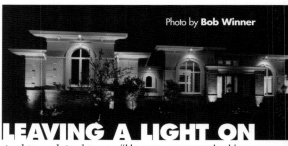

Photo by **Bob Winner**

LEAVING A LIGHT ON

Architrend Architects: "Homeowners are looking to enhance the visual impact of their home, creating a warm, secure environment after dark. Architectural and landscape lighting not only enhances the architectural elements of their home, but is the best to create natural and sophisticated lighting design, for pathways, terraces and garden areas."

TELLING A STORY IN GLASS

Franklin Art Glass Studios, Inc.: "Over the years, stained glass has been used to tell a story with a leaded glass panel. Today this practice is as strong as ever, with the use of stained glass to tell the story of one's culture or a family history."

FINDING YOUR "NICHE"

Brian Wiland & Associates, Inc: "Home designs of the past were very formal and stiff. The floor plans of these homes make it difficult to provide for the functions of current lifestyles without major remodeling. One way to achieve more flexibility is to design open spaces with less load-bearing walls. The incorporation of niche spaces that can also be used for a variety of functions will enable these homes to adapt."

UP-TO-DATE TRADITIONAL

Larry Folk - Architect: "**A large percentage of today's homebuyers are looking for designs that reflect traditional values. They want the kind of house that they or their parents may have grown up in, but with up-to-date floorplans and all of the modern conveniences. This design style makes it easy to come home to and comfortable to live in.**"

25

BEAUTIFUL COMPLEXITY

Urban Environments, Inc.: "The increasing appreciation for estate gardening services in Central Ohio has been dramatic. Estate gardening draws on the storied landscape history of European estates that are valued as much for their gardens as for the treasures contained within. The estate gardens developed in Central Ohio over the past few years have increased in complexity and variety as more homeowners are truly using their outdoor spaces as extensions of their interior living areas."

OUTSIDE THINKING

Behal/Sampson/ Dietz Building Design: "Conceptualizing exterior space at the earliest design stages can be as important as conceptualizing the interior space. Creating exterior spaces, such as terraces, porches and trellised patios, to their best functional advantage, convenient access and carefully planned views, can meld exterior space with interior space to create the best homes."

Photo by **Al Teufen Photography**

TIME-TESTED DESIGNS

Kevin Knight & Company: "Our clients have realized that 'trends' in design can be fleeting. They have learned that what might seem avant-garde today will become dated after only a few years. They are now embracing architecture that has been proven to be ageless. This is true throughout America; clients are looking to the established, time-tested neighborhoods for design inspiration and are measuring quality and value against these existing homes."

THE SENSE OF TOUCH

Meyers-Welsh architecture + design: "A design trend that has never gone out of style is the tactile quality of materials. The sense of an exceptionally designed space has a lot to do with the things you feel and the way materials are presented. The feel of materials throughout is what impacts the perception of the overall space. Whether it is the finish of a stone counter, the grain of a wood floor or the visual quality of lighting, the impact on the senses is what creates comfort in a custom home."

"OPENING UP" THE KITCHEN

J.S. Brown & Co., Inc.: "People want to make changes to their homes that will open up the rooms and create a warm, more spacious gathering place for family and friends. One example is the kitchen. Although more people are eating out today, there is still a strong desire to have a well-equipped kitchen, with the latest conveniences at their fingertips."

Photo by **Studio Ohio**

Photo by **Bryan Barr**

A WARM FEELING

Grand Design Group: "In designing kitchens today, we often incorporate cabinetry that resembles furniture. We are also using a mix of finishes such as paint and stain, and glazes to add more definition and detail. Into this we sometimes add elements such as chandeliers that are larger than normal, to draw attention to a kitchen island and make the space feel warmer."

Photo by **Better Image:** **Greg Bartram**

HIDING THE REMOTES

Newcome Electronic Systems: "Ease of use and integration with home interiors are two important features for custom home audio/video consumers today. The ability to control the home's systems, such as home theater, whole house audio, lighting controls, intercom, and security from a touch-screen panel is appealing to our clients. Most homeowners also want the system components blended into the architecture. This is done with hidden speaker treatments, in-wall component modules and keypads, and wireless remote control circuitry."

BACK TO BASICS

Buck & Sons Landscape Service, Inc.: "The last decade of landscape design has predominantly been geared toward low maintenance plantings, dictated by today's busy lifestyles. We are seeing, however, a resurgence of people requesting herbs, perennial and cut flower gardens. Typically, these types of gardens are not considered low maintenance. However, gardening overall is becoming viewed as more of an outdoor activity for fun and relaxation than a chore. This new century has made everyone rethink their priorities. The 'back to basics' of home gardening seems to reflect the rekindled spirit of the American lifestyle and home."

ON THE WATERFRONT

Sullivan Bruck Architects: "Waterfront architecture presents different challenges than standard view-oriented designs. The architect must design for the obvious vistas to the water, but must also be cognizant of prevailing winds, direct and reflected sun, outdoor living and entertaining needs. The architect must be able to combine all these considerations to create both a street-front and water-front entry ◄ to the house."

MULTI-FUNCTIONAL WALLS

Timberwood Landscape Company, Inc.: **"Over the past five years, people have been spending more time at home and in their yards. Our clients have been requesting a variety of wall systems for their outdoor spaces - from enclosures that define yard space to free-standing structures that serve as benches, allowing the homeowners to relax and enjoy their surroundings."**

PERSONALITY REFLECTIONS

Mull & Weithman Architects, Inc.: **"Today's homes are being designed to be interpretations of the lifestyles and personalities of their owners. High quality, uniquely detailed and charismatic spaces are preferred over large quantities of space. The custom home market trends continue to eliminate more traditional formal spaces in favor of a more casual, comfortable living environment."**

TRUST YOUR INSTINCTS

A Muse Gallery: "In building a fine collection of artwork, a more eclectic form of collecting is not only popular now, but perfectly acceptable. A contemporary abstract can easily show in the same room as a traditional landscape, a steel sculpture, an African mask, and a fine blown glass bowl. Be true to your instincts – if you like one piece of artwork, it will probably work with another piece you react to."

TRADITIONAL STYLE

Thomas Beery Architects, Inc.: "In the custom home market, people are turning to stylized, traditional structures. In order to create an accurate representation of a particular style, the details become very important. Homeowners, we have found, are willing to spend a little more to achieve this effect."

A FOUNDATION FOR FURNITURE

Amish Originals: "Durability, functionality and flexibility are key components of what today's consumers see as value. The use of solid hardwoods reflects a desire to bring natural elements inside, and provides a durable foundation for furniture that will withstand the test of time. We see solid cherry as closing the gap on oak as the most popular wood choice. Additionally, a resurgence in Shaker and Mission furniture reflect a desire to maintain flexibility. The simple lines allow for consumers to change the 'feel' of a room through the use of specialty hardware and decorative accessories."

Photo by Feinknopf Photography

UNIQUE RECLAIMED MATERIALS

Jonathan Barnes Architecture and Design: "For those looking for a personalized, one-of-a-kind space, there are a great number of materials and fixtures available to help achieve a unique look. From concrete counters to glass tiles, riverstone flooring to European lighting, there are a multitude of opportunities for expressing individual tastes. Some products, such as reconstituted wood veneer, in which the grain is actually designed, are the result of advanced technologies. Others, such as reclaimed Jerusalem stone tiles and mosaics, are literally thousands of years old and carry individual certification numbers."

DISTINCTIVE WALLCOVERINGS

Regency Wallcraft: "We are seeing an increase in wall space devoted to wallcoverings, especially with 'showroom' papers and distinctive contract wallcoverings. Contract materials that are first introduced in the corporate environment are finding their way home."

THE SCULPTURE WITHIN

Baker Henning: "We often encounter clients who expect themselves to achieve perfection in their residences. Sometimes, though, when they don't have sympathetic and encouraging guidance, the homeowners can become paralyzed with the fear of making 'incorrect' design decisions. Builders must remain stylistically neutral, as well as dispell any misconceptions that there are 'correct' and 'incorrect' designs. It is in this way that the core aesthetic values of the homeowner can emerge and be expressed and understood by everyone involved in the process. Through a careful and gradual process of discovery, the surface trends of the moment can be cut away to reveal the one fully formed, undeniably 'correct' design, which truly resonates with the client."

ADDITION, NOT DISTRACTION

Kinman Associates, Inc.: "Landscape design at its highest level becomes an integral part of a larger whole. Landscape designs must add to, instead of take from, a property and all of its elements."

A NATURAL FLOW

The Pagura Co., Inc.: "A natural look, whether seen in water features, brick paver driveways or retaining walls, is popular among our clients. Homeowners want their water features to look as though Mother Nature created them. Often, the water features include indigenous limestone slabs, which hide the water source, so it looks as though the water is gently meandering over the stone, as it may have done for hundreds of years. These features can end in a rock-edged swimming pool, which has a natural, lagoon-like look, rather than just looking like a manmade swimming pool. Homeowners want the outside of their homes to flow with the existing architecture."

REFINED, UPDATED KITCHENS

Clive Christian, Columbus: "The European influence continues to remain strong in upscale kitchen design. Especially popular with our clients is the combination of traditional English styling with contemporary stainless steel appliances and sleek finishes. Details that create warmth and reflect the English style include the use of paneled doors with stylish metal knobs, cornices, traditional pullout baskets and natural stone and wood used on counter surfaces. Accessorizing with fine china and silver complete the picture, creating the elegance and refinement reminiscent of a country estate."

TIMELESS ELEGANCE ►

Footprints Rug Co., Inc.: "As designers, architects and builders turn toward more classic interiors, they seek the resources that convey a look of timeless elegance. Many are finding that in handcrafted Old World-styled hardwood flooring. Genuine hand-finished woods age gracefully with a patina that increases the flooring's beauty over time."

WARMING WOOD

Arched Casings, Inc.: "Whether in new home construction or remodels, homeowners are finding that curved wood provides a timetested classic design. When curves are used in the design concept of the project, they become the focal point of the room. Either stained or painted, the warmth of curves has been a mainstay in the architectural design world."

THE GREAT OUTDOORS

M. J. Design Associates, Inc.: "Homeowners want to enjoy their outdoor space as an extension of their indoor living space. Patios and porches become dining rooms and living rooms. 'Decorating' these outdoor spaces is as important as decorating indoors. Ever-changing color throughout the seasons and beautiful views from all vantage points allow family and friends to relax and enjoy themselves, and never run out of scenery."

KITCHEN CONVENIENCE

Showcase Homes: "We're seeing a real push for upgraded kitchens and appliances. When it comes to designing their kitchens, our clients want roll-out shelving, larger center islands and upgraded cabinetry, for starters. Wider refrigerators, quieter dishwashers and space-saving microhoods are all popular as well, due to their convenience, elegance and accessibility."

MORE MEANINGFUL GARDENS

Finlandscape Inc.: "During the last three decades, we have seen major changes in Central Ohio landscapes. Improved technology, better equipment, more efficient installation methods and an ever-changing supply of new plant materials and improved consumer knowledge in gardening are some of the major factors. People are becoming aware of more meaningful design themes with authentic garden styles. There is a great desire, appreciation and knowledge in America today of how to build stylish homes with great architectural details, including interior decorating. A big challenge still lies ahead, in creating better outdoor environments, in order to 'complete the picture.'"

SAFE AND SECURE

Golden Bear Lock & Safe, Inc.: "Home security has become increasingly important to today's homeowner, from a simple safe to a high-tech security access system. Our clients want their safes to either complement their decorating scheme or to discreetly fit in with the home. To accommodate these desires, a variety of styles and finishes are available, or the safe can be built into a wall, floor or piece of furniture."

COMFORTING COLORS

Elegant Reflections: "Recent color trends have resurfaced in a similar yet unique way to reflect colors of the past. These new colors are used to create earthy, relaxed and serene atmospheres, and are displayed in a variety of applications, including wall treatments, window treatments and bedding. To further add to the earthy and relaxed tone of a room, light and airy sheer screens allow the outdoors to be enjoyed by those inside."

OLD WORLD CRAFTSMANSHIP

Ralph Fallon Builders, Inc.: "The hallmark of individually crafted custom homes is the Old World craftsmanship of wood throughout the home. This includes handcrafting architecturally designed doors, cabinetry and millwork profiles, as well as tables and doors."

Photo by **Photog**

COMFORTABLE EXPRESSIONS

Damron Design: "In today's fast-paced society, clients more than ever desire to be surrounded by comfort. Whether it be formal or informal, home-owners find solace in environments that express their own personal tastes for elegance and relaxation."

TIMELESS SIMPLICITY

Amish Country Furnishings: "As people look to decorate their homes in a manner that fits the way they live, Mission style furniture continues to be strong. There is a trend toward natural, warm colors on the wood, which help to keep the furniture from feeling too formal. Many Mission pieces are strict reproductions of turn-of-the century originals, while other pieces can be characterized as being influenced by the Mission or Arts and Crafts styles but with some contemporary liberties taken in their execution."

Photo by **Kevin Fitzsimons**

COLORFUL EXPRESSIONS

Christy Romoser Interiors: "**Don't be afraid to express yourself. In today's environment of bold expression, a vibrant and clear color palette can introduce a daring element to a room. Mixing stripes, polka dots and diamonds can balance the combination of bold hues and sumptuous textures. Add a dramatic oil painting, and you have completed your room's statement.**"

Photo by **Brad Simmons Photography**

ENVIRONMENTAL ENHANCEMENTS

Designed Illumination: "Today's home-owners are searching for lighting that enhances their environment by revealing the beauty of their homes. Decorative fixtures such as pendants and chandeliers with adjustable con-cealed lighting add another layer of interest, flexi-bility and ele-gance. Today's multi-functional rooms require lighting that can change with the owner's mood or needs."

"TIMELESS" TIMEPIECES

Clock Warehouse: "New clocks, antique clocks, traditional clocks, contemporary clocks: today's trend is not to be 'trendy.' Rather, it is to have, what one might call a 'timeless' piece of art that will also tell time. Style and selection is most important to consumers, whether they are choosing a clock or a fine table or chair as that spe-cial accent piece in their homes."

SOOTHING SOUNDS

Drake's Landscaping: "More people are choosing water features to add peace and tranquility to their backyards. A natural-looking, cascading stream and the soothing sound of the water can take one far away from a busy life, if only for a short time."

Photo by **Bryan Barr**

RENAISSANCE OF CLASSIC STYLES

Franco & Miriello Builders, Ltd.: "The high-end custom home market has been experiencing a ren-aissance of more classic architectural styles. These designs include Shingle Style, French Country, English Cottage, New England Colonial, and Georgian. This approach manifests itself through interior and exterior detailing, resulting in the maintenance of architectural purity over the project's entire composi-tion. Architecture isn't the only element that recalls the home in its traditional sense. Bringing family and friends into the home is also influencing interior architecture. Hearth rooms combined with bigger eat-in kitchens drive this concept. These areas are becoming the heart of the home, where family and friends can congregate and socialize."

IN HARMONY WITH NATURE

Riverbend Timber Framing: "The greatest trend in custom home building today is the creation of a haven from busy, frantic lives, a place of retreat and rejuvenation from the outside world, yet a place very much in harmony with nature. Natural wood has long been a favorite of homeowners, and timbers add historic reference, timeless beauty, warm tones, and strength unmatched by other materials. Dramatic architectural features have always been created by the ancient art of timber framing, and today's great rooms and spacious living areas are no exception."

COLORFUL EASY-CARE LANDSCAPES

Better Way Gardening: "Homeowners want landscapes that are low maintenance and that have bountiful color. By using shrubs with blooms or colorful foliage, seasonal and season-long perennials and evergreens, this type of landscape is achievable. In order to finish the look, plants of varying textures and heights should be blended in. Multi-level patios are also in high demand. These patios allow the homeowner to separate the eating area from the entertaining area."

Photo courtesy of **Roger Wade**

NON-TRADITIONAL ELEMENTS

Reed Arts: "One of the most interesting trends in framing today is the use of non-traditional materials to create an overall effect. For example, to enhance a photo of one's family's original homestead (a log cabin), a frame can be created using actual pieces of wood siding salvaged from the cabin itself."

THE GROWTH OF STONE

Coffman Stone: "Stone has traditionally been the material of choice for landscapers and homebuilders alike. When you look at stone, you see quality and longevity. Recently, with new technologies available for cutting and processing stone, it has become much more readily available. The increased popularity and affordability of stone is evident in communities all over the country."

RECOLLECTIONS OF THE PAST

archignition studio: "We find that people love the heavy timber framing of barn houses and their honest materials like natural vertical wood siding and standing seam metal roofing. So many people today are looking for larger homes with voluminous great rooms, and most historical styles end up looking like a house on steroids, even when increased to 4,000 sq. ft. But a barn house just comes into its own realm at the larger house sizes of today. Whether new or renovated, barn houses are cost effective, because of their modest materials, simple rectilinear massing and gable roofs. They are a true recollection of the past for all of us - especially in the Midwest."

38

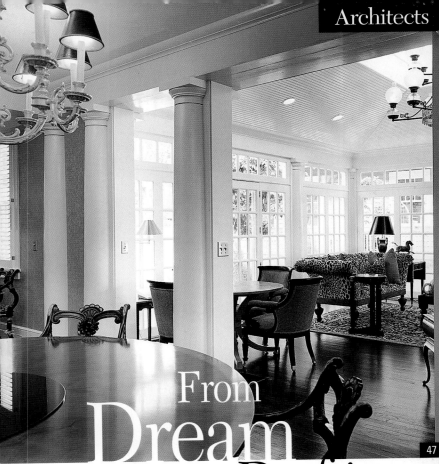

From Dream to Drafting Table

Architects are at once artists and engineers. At their best, they are dreamers of extraordinary vision. They pride themselves on knowing how their clients want to live, even when that vision may be hard to articulate. An architect's art is supported by strong grounding in technical knowledge: mechanical engineering, materials, finishes, and environmental awareness.

When you hire an architect, you hire a professional who will see the building process through from start to finish. Site checks are standard operating procedure for architects; you won't have to worry about a design that looks great in blueprints, but is ruined in the execution. We have the privilege of featuring the finest of these creative, technically proficient problem solvers to help you bring your ultimate home to life.

Photo courtesy of **Baker Henning Productions, Inc.**

WHY YOU SHOULD WORK WITH A TOP ARCHITECT

1. They are expert problem solvers. A talented architect can create solutions to your design problems, and solve the problems that stand in the way of achieving your dream.

2. They have creative ideas. You may see a two-story addition strictly in terms of its function - a great room with a master suite upstairs. An architect immediately applies a creative eye to the possibilities.

3. They provide a priceless product and service. A popular misconception about architects is that their fees make their services an extravagance. In reality, an architect's fee represents a small percentage of the overall building cost.

YOUR OWN DREAM TEAM

Whether you're building your dream home in the city, a second vacation home, or remodeling your home in the suburbs, it takes a team to design and build a high quality residential project. A team of an architect, builder, interior designer, kitchen and bath designer, and landscape architect/designer should be assembled very early in the process. When these five professionals have the opportunity to collaborate before ground is broken, you'll reap the rewards for years to come. Their blend of experience and ideas can give you insights into the fabulous possibilities of your home and site you never considered. Their association will surely save you time, money and eventually frustration.

THE ARCHITECT – MAKING THE DREAM REAL

Licensed architects provide three basic, easily defined tasks. First, they design, taking into account budget, site, owner's needs and existing house style. Second, they produce the necessary technical drawings and specifications to accomplish the desires of their clients, and explain to a contractor in adequate detail what work needs to be done. Lastly, architects participate in the construction process. This straightforward mission requires more than education.

It requires listening. The best architects have gained their status by giving their clients exactly what they want – even when those clients have difficulty articulating what that is. How? By creatively interpreting word pictures into real pictures. By eliciting the spirit of the project and following that spirit responsibly as they develop an unparalleled design.

It requires experience. Significant architects, such as those included in your Home Book, maintain a reputation for superiority because their buildings are stunningly conceived, properly designed and technically sound. If a unique, steeply pitched roof was custom-designed for you by a licensed architect with an established reputation, you can be confident that it is buildable.

Suggestions by an experienced architect can add value and interest to your new home or remodeling project. He or she may suggest you wire your home for the technology of the future, frame up an attic for future use as a second floor, or build your countertops at varying levels to accommodate people of different heights.

This area is blessed with many talented architects. It's not uncommon for any number of them to be working on a luxury vacation retreat in another country or a unique second home in another state. Their vision and devotion to design set a standard of excellence for dynamic and uncompromising quality.

WORKING WITH AN ARCHITECT

The best relationships are characterized by close collaborative communication. The architect is the person you're relying on to take your ideas, elevate them to the highest level, and bring them to life in a custom design that's never been built before. So take your time in selecting the architect. It's not unusual for clients to spend two or three months interviewing prospective architects.

In preparation for the interview process, spend time fine-tuning your ideas. Put together an Idea Notebook (See the sidebar 'Compile an Idea Notebook'). Make a wish list that includes every absolute requirement and every fantasy you've ever wanted in a home. Visit builders' models to discover what 3,000 sq. ft. looks like in comparison to 6,000 sq. ft., how volume ceilings impact you or what loft living feels like. Look at established and new neighborhoods to get ideas about the relationship between landscaping and homes, and what level of landscaping you want.

GOOD COMMUNICATION SETS THE TONE

The first meeting is the time to communicate all of your desires for your new home or remodeling project, from the abstract to the concrete. You're creating something new, so be creative in imprinting your spirit and personality on the project. Be bold in expressing your ideas, even if they are not fully developed or seem unrealistic. Share your Idea Notebook and allow the architect to keep it as plans are being developed. Be prepared to talk about your lifestyle, because the architect will be trying to soak up as much information about you and your wishes as possible.

• Be frank about your budget. Although some clients are unrestricted by budgetary concerns, most must put some control on costs, and good architects expect and respect this. Great ideas can be achieved on a budget, and the architect will tell you what can be achieved for your budget.

• However, sticking to your budget requires tremendous self-discipline. If there's a luxury you really want, (a second laundry room, a built-in aquarium) it's probably just as practical to build it into your design from the outset, instead of paying for it in a change order once building has begun.

WHAT'S YOUR LIFESTYLE?

(Your architect will want to know.)
• Who lives in your house now?
• Who will live there in the future?
• Who visits and for how long?
• Do you like traditional, contemporary or eclectic design?
• Why are you moving or remodeling?
• What aspects of your current home need to be improved upon?
• Do you like functional, minimalist design, or embellishments and lots of style?
• Do you entertain formally or informally?
• How much time will you spend in the master bedroom? Is it spent reading, watching TV, working or exercising?
• What are the primary functions of the kitchen?
• Do you need a home office?
• Do you like lots of open space or little nooks and crannies?
• What kind of storage do you need?

COMPILE AN IDEA NOTEBOOK

It's hard to put an idea into words, but so easy to show with a picture. Fill a good-sized notebook with plain white paper, tuck a roll of clear tape and a pair of scissors into the front flap, and you've got an Idea Notebook. Fill it with pictures, snapshots of homes you like, sketches of your own, little bits of paper that show a color you love, notes to yourself on your priorities and wishes. Circle the parts of the pictures and make spontaneous notes: "Love the finish on the cabinets," "Great rug," "Don't want windows this big." Show this to your architect, and other team members. Not only will it help keep ideas in the front of your mind, but will spark the creativity and increase understanding of the entire team.

• Ask lots of questions. Architects of luxury homes in the area are committed to providing their clients with information up front about the design process, the building process and their fees. These architects respect the sophistication and intelligence of their clientele, but do not necessarily expect them to have a high level of design experience or architectural expertise. Educating you is on their agenda.

• What is the breadth of services? Although this information is in your contract, it's important to know the level of services a firm will provide. There is no set standard and you need to be sure if an architect will provide the kind of services you want – from basic "no-frills" through "full service."

• Find out who you will be working with. Will you be working with one person or a team? Who will execute your drawings?

• Ask for references. Speak to past and current clients who built projects similar to yours. Ask for references from contractors with whom the architect works.

• Does the architect carry liability insurance?

• Ask to see examples of the architect's work – finished homes, job sites, and architectural plans. Does the work look and feel like what you want?

• Find out how many projects the architect has in progress. Will you get the attention you deserve?

• Decide if you like the architect. For successful collaboration, there must be a good personal connection. As you both suggest, reject, and refine ideas, a shared sense of humor and good communication will be what makes the process workable and enjoyable. Ask yourself, "Do I trust this person to deliver my dream and take care of business in the process?" If the answer is anything less than a strong and sure, "yes!," keep looking.

UNDERSTANDING ARCHITECTS' FEES AND CONTRACTS

Fees and fee structures vary greatly among architects, and comparing them can be confusing, even for the experienced client. Architects, like licensed professionals in other fields, are prohibited from setting fees as a group and agreeing on rates. They arrive at their fees based on:

  (A) an hourly rate
  (B) lump sum total
  (C) percentage of construction cost
  (D) dollars per square foot
  (E) size of the job
  (F) a combination of the above

The final quoted fee will include a set of services that may vary greatly from architect to architect. From a "no frills" to a "full service" bid, services are vastly different. For example, a no frills agreement budgets the architect's fee at two to seven percent of the construction cost; a full service contract budgets the architect's fee at 12 to 18 percent. Some firms include contractor's selection, bid procurement, field inspections, interior cabinetry, plumbing and lighting design, and punch list. Others don't.

One concrete basis for comparison is the architectural drawings. There can be a vast difference in the number of pages of drawings, the layers of drawings and the detail level of the specifications. Some include extra sketchbooks with drawings of all the construction details and in-depth written specs which call out every doorknob and fixture. Some offer impressive three-dimensional scale models to help you better visualize the end result, and computerized virtual walk throughs.

The benefit of a more detailed set of drawings is a more accurate, cost-effective construction bid. The more details noted in the drawings and text, the fewer contingencies a contractor will have to speculate on. The drawings are the sum total of what your contract with a builder is based upon. If a detail isn't included in the drawings, then it's not part of the project and you'll be billed extra for it.

Services should be clearly outlined in your contract. Many local architects use a standard American Institute of Architects (AIA) contract, in a long or short form. Some use a letter of agreement.

Have your attorney read the contract. Be clear that the level of service you desire is what the architect is prepared to deliver.

THE DESIGN PHASE

The architect will be in communication with you as your project progresses through the phases of schematic design, design development, preparation of construction documents, bidding and negotiating with a contractor, and contract administration (monitoring the construction). If any of these services will not be supplied, you should find out at your initial meeting.

The creativity belongs in the first phases. This is when you move walls, add windows, change your mind about the two-person whirlpool tub in favor of a shower surround, and see how far your budget will take you.

The time involved in the design process varies depending on the size of the project, your individual availability, and coordinating schedules.

ADD MORE LIVING SPACE

What might it cost to add a 15 x 20 ft. family room and rehab a kitchen and powder room? Here is a typical breakdown, incorporating a brick and stone exterior, classical frieze board, with copper gutters and cedar shingles or slate roofing. The family room's interior features 5/8 in. drywall with poplar base and crown moldings and herringbone clear oak flooring.

Family Room:
- **Exterior and Interior: $90,000**
- **Entertainment cabinetry: $10,000**

Kitchen & Powder Room Rehab:
- **Cabinetry, custom: $47,500**
- **Appliances: $18,000**
- **Stone countertops, backsplash & tilework: $15,000**
- **Plumbing, Electrical & HVAC: $26,000**
- **Demolition & construction: $18,000**

- **Contingency (10%): $ 22,450**
- **Architectural fees (15%): $ 33,675**

Total: $280,625

AMERICAN
INSTITUTE OF
ARCHITECTS

**American Institute
of Architects**

**1735 New York
Ave., NW
Washington, DC
20006
800.AIA.3837
Fax:
202.626.7547
www.aia.org**

AIA is a profes-
sional association
of licensed archi-
tects, with a
strong commit-
ment to educating
and serving the
general public. It
frequently spon-
sors free seminars
called, "Working
with an
Architect," which
feature local
architects speak-
ing on home
design and build-
ing. AIA has also
produced an edu-
cational package
including a video
entitled,
"Investing in a
Dream," and a
brochure, "You
and Your
Architect." It's
available at many
local libraries
throughout the
area.

Think practically. Consider what you don't like about your current home. If noise from the dishwasher bothers you at night, tell your architect you want a quiet bedroom, and a quiet dishwasher. Think about the nature of your future needs. Architects note that their clients are beginning to ask for "barrier-free" and ergonomic designs for more comfortable living as they age or as their parents move in with them.

A key role architects can play is in the planning for a secure home. Your architect can perform a security assessment, which will determine what is to be protected, what is the risk level and nature of the potential threat, what are the property's vulnerabilities, and what can be done to achieve the desired level of protection.

BUILDING BEGINS: BIDDING AND NEGOTIATION

If your contract includes it, your architect will bid your project to contractors he or she considers appropriate for your project, and any contractor you wish to consider. You may want to include a contractor to provide a "control" bid. If you wish to hire a specific contractor, you needn't go through the bidding process, unless you're simply curious about the range of responses you may receive. After the architect has analyzed the bids and the field is narrowed, you will want to meet the contractors to see if you're compatible, if you're able to communicate clearly, and if you sense a genuine interest in your project. These meetings can take place as a contractor walks through a home to be remodeled, or on a tour of a previously built project if you're building a new home.

If your plans come in over budget, the architect is responsible for bringing the costs down, except, of course, if the excess is caused by some item the architect had previously cautioned you would be prohibitive.

Not all people select an architect first. It's not uncommon for the builder to help in the selection of an architect, or for a builder to offer "design/build" services with architects on staff, just as an architectural firm may have interior designers on staff. ∎

Finally...
Central Ohio's Own
Home & Design
Sourcebook

The **Central Ohio Home Book** is your final destination when searching for home remodeling, building and decorating resources. This comprehensive, hands-on sourcebook to building, remodeling, decorating, furnishing, and landscaping a luxury home is required reading for the serious and discriminating homeowner. With more than 500 full-color, beautiful pages, the **Central Ohio Home Book** is the most complete and well-organized reference to the home industry. This hardcover volume covers all aspects of the process, includes listings of hundreds of industry professionals, and is accompanied by informative and valuable editorial discussing the most recent trends. Ordering your copy of the **Central Ohio Home Book** now can ensure that you have the blueprints to your dream home, in your hand, today.

Order your copy now!

CENTRAL OHIO
HOME BOOK

Published by
The Ashley Group
7654 Crosswoods Drive, Columbus, OH 43235
614-431-2950 fax 614-431-2052
E-mail: ashleybooksales@reedbusiness.com

Architects

ARCHATAS, INC. ....**(614) 885–0600**
6797 North High Street, Suite 129, Worthington   Fax:(614) 885–1221
See ad on page: 85
Principal/Owner: James S. Luckino, AIA, C.S.I.
Website: www.archatas.com   e-mail: jsl@archatas.com

ARCHIGNITION STUDIO ....**(614) 481–9707**
1469 Roxbury Road, Columbus
See ad on page: 94
Principal/Owner: Kent V. Thompson, AIA
e-mail: kvtarchignition@aol.com   Additional Information: Houses are the greatest challenge in architecture today and I strive for archignition studio's to fit their context, site and owners like a glove. We want to design houses that clearly reflect their owners and offer a true spirit of place – houses that are a gift to the street. My favorite projects are sizzling collaborations between builder, architect and owner.

ARCHITECTURAL RESOURCE GROUP, INC. ....**(614) 888–9600**
65 East Wilson Bridge Road, Suite, Worthington   Fax:(614) 888–9618
See ad on page: 166, 167
Principal/Owner: Bill Pepperney

ARCHITETTURA SERRAGLIO, INC. ....**(614) 759–6070**
7404 East Main Street, Reynoldsburg   Fax:(614) 759–6986
See ad on page: 84
Principal/Owner: Mario Serraglio
Website: www.architettura.com   e-mail: mario@iwaynet.net

ARCHITREND ARCHITECTS ....**(937) 832–1150**
55 Hillside Court, Englewood   Fax:(937) 832–1590
See ad on page: 82
Principal/Owner: Jim Bauman
e-mail: atrend2000@aol.com   Additional Information: 25 years experience in residential design. Projects in Ohio, Indiana and Virginia. Design awards: Professional Builder and Custom Home Magazines.

JONATHAN BARNES ARCHITECTURE AND DESIGN ....**(614) 228–7311**
399 East Main Street, Columbus   Fax:(614) 228–7552
See ad on page: 62, 63
Principal/Owner: Jonathan Barnes
Website: www.jbadusa.com   e-mail: info@jbadusa.com   Additional Information: Jonathan Barnes, Masters of Architecture Harvard, leads JBAD as a specialized, design–focused firm that provides unique, high–quality design solutions.

THOMAS BEERY ARCHITECTS, INC. ....**(614) 442–7580**
2929 Kenny Road, Suite 235, Columbus   Fax:(614) 442–7581
See ad on page: 68
Principal/Owner: Tom Beery
e-mail: tbeery@beeryarch.com

BEHAL SAMPSON DIETZ ....**(614) 464–1933**
990 West Third Avenue, Columbus   Fax:(614) 298–2149
See ad on page: 90, 91
Principal/Owner: John Behal, Thomas Sampson,
Website: www.bsdarchitects.com   e-mail: mfournier@bsdarchitects.com

BRIAN KENT JONES ARCHITECT ....**(614) 358–3729**
150 East Broad Street, Suite 600, Columbus   Fax:(614) 224–0990
See ad on page: 64, 65
Principal/Owner: Brian Kent Jones
Website: e-mail: Additional Information: *

BRICE ARCHITECTS ....**(614) 486–4100**
2074 Arlington Avenue, Columbus   Fax:(614) 486–2900
See ad on page: 97
Principal/Owner: Rider Brice

Platinum Award: Architectural Design
Platinum Award: Formal Entry
Platinum Award: Study
Platinum Award: Great Room
Platinum Award: Master Bedroom
Platinum Award: Living Room

Gold Award: Master Bathroom
Gold Award: Exterior / Curb Appeal

Silver Award: Interior Decor
Silver Award: Outdoor Living

MILHOAN Architects LLC

milhoanarchitects.com
614.222.0001

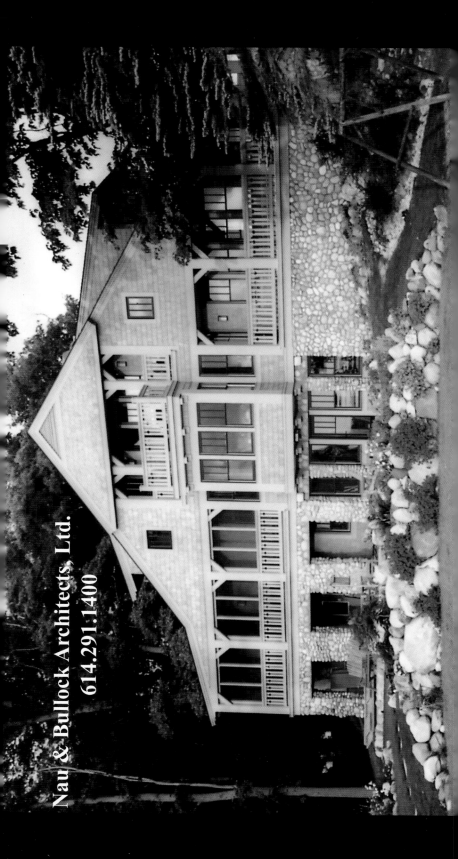

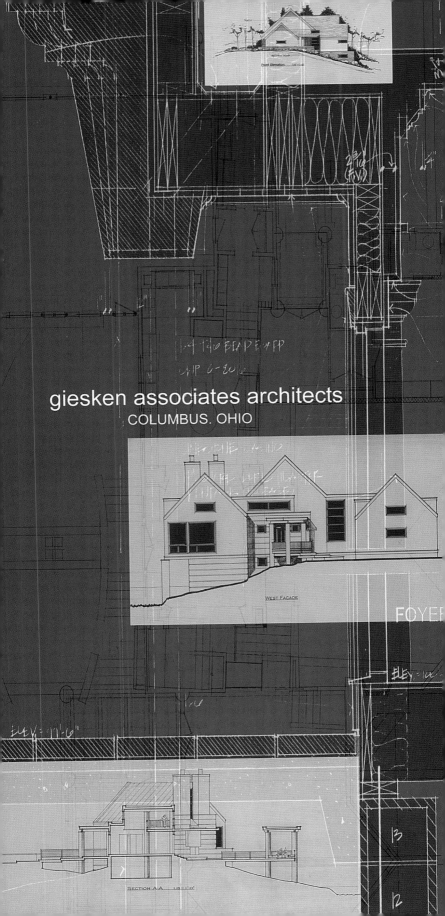

giesken associates architects
COLUMBUS. OHIO

WEST FAÇADE

FOYER

SECTION A-A 1/8"=1'-0"

© feinknopf photography

M&W

mull & weithman architects, inc.

614-267-6960 tel • 614-267-6978 fax

info@mw-architects.com • www.mw-architects.com

JONATHAN BARNES

JB
AD

ARCHITECTURE
AND DESIGN

JONATHAN BARNES
ARCHITECTURE AND DESIGN

399 East Main Street Suite 210
Columbus, Ohio 43215
614 228 7311 jbarnes@jbadusa.com

A.D.

ARCHITECTURAL DESIGN

BRIAN KENT JONES

614.358.3729 · briankentjones.com

JEANNE CABRAL ARCHITECTS...**(614) 239–9484**
2939 Bexley Park Road, Columbus   Fax:(614) 239–6993
See ad on page: 55
Principal/Owner: Jeanne M. Cabral
Website: www.jeannecabral.com e-mail: jeannecabral@aol.com
Additional Information: Award winning firm specializing in custom & luxury homes.
Attention to detail & personal service. Expertise in light commercial services.

GEORGE PARKER & ASSOCIATES ....**(614) 476–3600**
106 Short Street, Gahanna   Fax:(614) 476–2253
See ad on page: 92, 93
Principal/Owner: George Parker, AIA
e-mail: gepj106@aol.com

GIESKEN ASSOCIATES ARCHITECTS...**(614) 262–7555**
3763 North High Street, Columbus   Fax:(614) 262–7556
See ad on page: 59
Principal/Owner: Robert J. Giesken
e-mail: gieskenaia@aol.com

GLAVAN FEHER ARCHITECTS INC. ....**(614) 228–3400**
2 Miranova Place, Columbus   Fax:(614) 228–3337
See ad on page: 80, 81
Principal/Owner: Jeffery L. Glavan, J. Edward Feher
Website: www.glavan.com e-mail: edfeher@glavan.com

DAVID JOHNSON ARCHITECTS...**(614) 890–7001**
5636 Highland Lakes Avenue, Westerville   Fax:(614) 890–7608
See ad on page: 88
Principal/Owner: David Johnson

KSH ARCHITECTS...**(614) 221–5181**
300 Marconi Boulevard, Suite300, Columbus   Fax:(614) 221–5081
See ad on page: 83
Principal/Owner: Kevin Hoffman

LARRY FOLK ARCHITECT ....**(614) 864–2814**
13055 Silverbrook Drive, Pickerington   Fax:(614) 864–3102
See ad on page: 89
Principal/Owner: Larry Folk
e-mail: lfolk@insight.rr.com

MANLEY AND HARPER, INC. ....**(614) 447–3277**
3828 North High Street, Columbus   Fax:(614) 447–3279
See ad on page: 96
Principal/Owner: Patrick W. Manley, Scott R.
Website: www.manleyandharper.net e-mail: home@manleyandharper.net
Additional Information: Individually designed contemporary and site–specific homes by
experienced award–winning architects. Energy efficiency, passive solar and
sustainable architecture.

MEYERS WELSH ARCHITECTURE & DESIGN ....**(614) 221–9433**
22 East Gay Street, Suite 301, Columbus   Fax:(614) 221–9441
See ad on page: 70, 71
Principal/Owner: Christopher Meyers, AIA ,
Website: www.meyerswelsh.com e-mail: cmeyers@meyerswelsh.com
Additional Information: Residential, Retail, Commercial and Office Architecture & Design.

MILHOAN ARCHITECTS, LLC ....**(614) 222–0001**
300 East Long Street, Columbus   Fax:(614) 222–0033
See ad on page: 56, 57
Principal/Owner: Gene R. Milhoan, AIA
Website: www.milhoanarchitects.com e-mail: architecture@milhoanarchitects.co

MULL & WEITHMAN ARCHITECTS INC. ....**(614) 267–6960**
4525 Indianola Avenue, Columbus   Fax:(614) 267–6978
See ad on page: 60, 61
Principal/Owner: Joseph C. Weithman, AIA
Website: www.mw–architects.com e-mail: info@mw–architects.com

NAU & BULLOCK ARCHITECTS, LTD. ....**(614) 291–1400**
996–B West Third Avenue, Columbus   Fax:(614) 291–1401
See ad on page: 58
Principal/Owner: Thomas Nau, David Bullock

THOMAS
BEERY
ARCHITECTS, INC.

2929 Kenny Rd. • Suite 235 • Columbus, OH 43221 • 614.442.7580 • FAX.614.442.7581

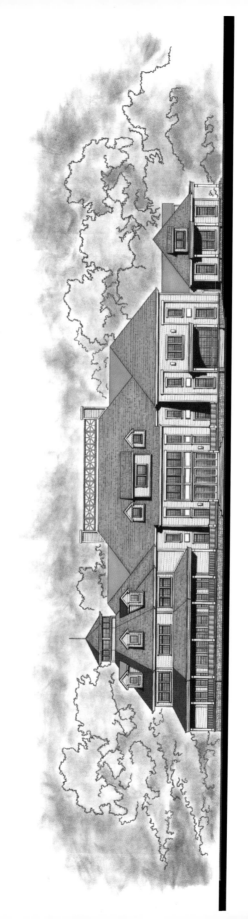

DESIGNING
Dreams

Whether it is a detailed historic home or a daring modern abode on the side of a cliff, the way a home looks from the outside isn't of much value if the space within isn't sufficient.

Each home must share one important factor in order to make the space work for those inside – the guiding hand of a professional architect.

Since every project has its own challenges and solutions, we asked a few of Central Ohio's premier architects to discuss projects where they've had to think outside the typical "box" to make interior spaces truly feel like home.

Archi

When architect, client, builder, designers and craftspeople share a vision and their unique talents, the result are homes with timeless character.

73

Photo courtesy of **Brian Kent Jones Architect**
Photo by **Leslee Kass**

itects

Climb Every Mountain

Doug Stone, principal architect at Stock and Stone Architects, recalled one very unique site he was presented with; the edge of a cliff. The visual effect would be pretty dramatic, since the home would share the cliff's edge with a waterfall, which led into a stream.

The client's office hangs off the cliff and looks down into the stream, according to Stone, but the center of the home is the library. On the first floor one will find a library table, and the space around it doubles as a formal dining room. The second floor of the home extends the library, with a bookcase-lined balcony. A spiral staircase leads to the third floor, where the owner can seek solace in a multi-windowed tower, allowing a view onto the waterfall and stream. "It's a very exciting room," Stone said. The home's master bedroom, on one side of the home, connects to the other side of the home via a 192 ft. long bridge, which stretches over a ravine.

"The most unique sites generally create the most unique homes," said Stone. "It forces you to think outside the typical lot."

Tree Houses For Grown Ups

"Unexpected" and "atypical" solutions to space design challenges are what Jonathan Barnes pursues when opening up homes for their owners.

Barnes, principal, Jonathan Barnes Architecture and Design, explained that "Too often, people live in houses they didn't build." In many instances these homes were not built with large windows or large groups of windows, both features that are popular with homeowners these days. So Barnes will implement a design that includes greater fenestration, and since the roofs in these homes are often low as well, part of this includes lifting the roof top to accommodate the new windows.

In this way, the role of the home is changed from a space that the inhabitants must adjust to, to a place that adapts to their lifestyles.

History Lessons

There may be times when a person's home needs to reflect their current lifestyle as well as his or her past. Brian Kent Jones, president, Brian Kent Jones, Architect, created an Ohio home for a couple with family roots in Louisiana. They wanted a historical yet functional home that recalled their southern experiences, said Jones.

"The kitchen and 'keeping room' (an adjacent pantry area) is the focus of the informal living area in this antebellum-inspired home," said Jones. While much of the home echoes more formal spaces associated with the couple's lives in the south, "It is this informal space that anchors the practical heart of the residence."

Affectionately referred to as "the tree room," this reading room created by Jonathan Barnes gives the homeowners a bird's eye view of the area around their home.

Photo courtesy of **Jonathan Barnes Architecture and Design, Ltd.**

itects

Doug Stone has also had to tangle with serving both historic concerns and contemporary family life. He explained that a Georgian home he designed for a family in Indianapolis, had to have a historic appearance. "They were trying to have very historically correct rooms," he said. The design of the

Archi

QUALITY OVER SIZE

Kenric Fine Homes: "With today's sophisticated clients, we are seeing much more emphasis being put on quality rather than size. People are willing to decrease the size of their new home in order to achieve the amenities they demand. They want quality finishes, which include extravagant custom woodwork, custom cabinets, media rooms and gourmet kitchens with high-end appliances. They want homes with an overwhelming attention to detail, while combining today's latest construction techniques and technological advances."

LOOKS AND FEELS REAL

Bellallusions: "Clients are moving away from the traditional white ceiling by including the ceiling in the overall décor of the room with faux finishing. The wonderful thing about faux finishing is that it reflects the personality of the homeowner. One of the current trends is to incorporate elements of texture into finish. With the range of products available today, it is possible to achieve the three-dimensional look and feel of actual stone blocks, bricks or aged plaster on top of existing surfaces."

GRANITE MADE ACCESSIBLE

Marble & Granite Works: "New custom fabrication technology has given granite countertops a competitive pricing edge lately, so that homeowners who like the look of natural stone can have the deep iridescent colors and elusive one-of-a-kind type of beauty that only nature can create. They also appreciate the incredible durability of granite, as well as its elegance."

Photo by **William Reuter**

RESPONSIVE ARCHITECTURE

Roy Yoder Architect: "In the current climate of contractor-lead development and 'custom' home building, there remains a large need for organic architecture that grows from a client's behavior, lifestyle and value system. The architect must make a number of studies of clients, to determine who they are behaviorally and how their lives will play out in this structure. The questions posed by the architect will determine how aspects of the home will play out, from the size of kitchens to sun angles to the selection of appliances and fixtures. The 'organic' nature of this approach requires the ability of the architect to synthesize all of the studies and produce a true home that is aesthetically natural, beautiful, and utilitarian."

FREEDOM AND FLEXIBILITY

Heninger Homes, Ltd.: "Gourmet kitchens, luxurious bathrooms and professionally designed entertainment areas are the focus of today's custom home buyers. With so many construction materials and products available today, clients feel free to create each and every room to be a personal retreat and a design statement."

Photo by **Chris Merriman/Soho Studio Co.**

INTELLECT AND IMAGINATION

Archatäs Inc.: "Today, the trend is to create a style based on a client's needs, habits and intellect. A good design stems from one's imagination. A great design is a product of the intellect. So one must go outside the box for answers."

PROFESSIONAL KITCHENS, IN-HOME CONVENIENCE

Ferguson Bath & Kitchen Gallery: "Today, more homeowners are filling their kitchens with fixtures that offer innovative features that not only increase efficiency, but also enhance décor. They want the features of a professional kitchen, to achieve stress-free entertaining."

NOT YOUR FATHER'S REC ROOM

Billiards Plus: "The trend toward home remodeling and the inclusion of elaborate family play spaces continues to rise in popularity. The 'rec' rooms of the past have evolved into the gaming rooms of today and feature much electronic wizardry. Interestingly, billiards, which requires no electricity to play and no wild special effects, is among the more popular pieces in today's family play spaces."

46

Photo courtesy of **Brian Kent Jones Architect**
Photo by **Leslee Kass**

ARCHITECTS

brian wiland

DESIGN/BUILD ARCHITECTS

38 West Bridge Street
Dublin, Ohio 43017

Baker Henning

47 EAST LINCOLN STREET

COLUMBUS, OHIO 43215

614/280-8900   fax/280-9015

www.bakerhenning.com

home adhered to historic details, but in his words, "it didn't go too far." The site lines in the home were "a little more open" than would have been found in a typical Georgian, "so you feel as if you're not shut off from people in other spaces (in the home)."

Architects creating homes of a classic, historic nature, must also take into consideration the needs of modern-day homeowners.

Photo courtesy of **Stock & Stone**

itects

Archi

Homeowners today want the views and natural light that come with large numbers of windows and one way an architect can accommodate this desire is to raise the roof and add skylights.

Photo courtesy of **Jonathan Barnes Architecture and Design, Ltd.**

Jonathan Barnes noted that, when adding on to an existing home, he likes the new space to differ from the old, yet the change should not be a shocking one. "We take a lot of care in how these shapes meet the rest of the house," he said. He noted that the newer area should gently reveal itself as one moves closer to it.

"The average person pays more attention to design and quality of space than his or her parents did," said Barnes. They want the spaces to be more individual in nature, to reflect their personalities and lifestyles more than homes once did.

Every person connected to a project must have an active hand in the proceedings, said Brian Kent Jones. "The best buildings result from a process that thoroughly engages the client, architect, builder, interior designer and talented craftspeople." When everyone is brought together in this way, the result, he said, are "functional buildings with timeless character." ■

While architects often seek to bring the outdoors inside, elements such as this pavilion in New Albany, OH, can set the stage for those coming to a home from the outdoors, announcing the entrance.

Photo courtesy of **Brian Kent Jones Architect**
Photo by **Leslee Kass**

tects

GLAVAN FEHÉR ARCHITECTS INC.
2 MIRANOVA PLACE
COLUMBUS, OHIO 43215
TEL 614.228.3400
FAX 614.228.3337
WWW.GLAVAN.COM

ARCHITREND
A R C H I T E C T S

JIM BAUMAN | SHAWN DUNCAN
9 3 7 . 8 3 2 . 1 1 5 0
55 HILLSIDE COURT, ENGLEWOOD, OHIO 45322

THE SPECTRUM OF GLASS

Glass Hill Designs: "Little has changed in the medium of stained glass over the past 900 years. But with its multitude of colors and textures available today, glass can be used to create just the right atmosphere to suit any home's space. The 'new' thing about glass is that every leaded art glass commission is a unique, never-before-seen work of art."

EVERYDAY ROOMS

Aurora Industries: "With more time being spent in the home these days, homeowners want their dwellings to be convenient and versatile. They want every room of the home to be a daily-use room. An example of how these desires are accommodated is when the traditional living room and dining room are incorporated into an open, flowing floorplan."

SMALL, PRETTY GARDENS

Greenscapes Landscape Company, Inc.: "Homeowners may be downsizing their homes, but they still want to have nice gardens. They are looking for beautiful gardens with elements of water, stone and pavers. With technology today, we are able to create waterfalls and small ornamental ponds complete with Koi and wetland plants. Imported or cast fountains and statuary are also very popular for customizing a small space. Homeowners are entertaining more outdoors, and to accommodate this, they are adding paver areas with grills."

SIMPLIFY, SIMPLIFY

Genesis Audio: "Today there is a wide array of choices in programming a home theater or media room. Satellite and cable TV offer hundreds of channels. Even more options are available with DVD, High Definition Television (HDTV) and Digital Television (DTV). New control systems offer a level of simplicity and reliability not possible before. They function as a system integrator, making different formats all work as one. Software programming does all the legwork behind the scenes. In short, it makes things easy."

BAR-RAISERS

Riverstone Construction, Inc.: "Customers are raising the bar of professionalism that they require from contractors and suppliers. Computer technology allows better communication for scheduling service and estimating job cost accounting. Many of our customers are using the World Wide Web to further their product knowledge, while creative design remains a high priority for them."

FILLING THE GRANDEST SPACES

Andy's Frame Setting:
"Homeowners want grand interiors! They want the vaulted ceilings, large walls and a lot of open space. Galleries are providing large double- or triple-stacked framed pieces to fill those large spaces. The art styles that clients like seem to be moving more toward a soft contemporary feel, with a touch of modern flair. Still, there are some homeowners who long for a splash of vivid color."

Photo by **Thomas Keever**

KEEP IT SIMPLE

Progressive Audio:
"The audio/video industry has evolved from basic stereo systems to whole house integration of audio, home theater and lighting control. Simplicity of use, facilitated by the latest technology, is what our clients want. The ability to control virtually all of the technology-based systems in the modern home with the ease of pushing a button on a remote control or touch panel is fast becoming the top priority on the wish list."

QUALITY OVER QUANTITY

Wyndfield Custom Homes: "Today's clients desire quality over quantity. The quality of details throughout the home is more important than the size of the home or the number of things inside. Clients require homes designed with the utmost function and use of creative space, with quality craftsmanship."

STAIRWAY SENSITIVITY

Glavan Fehér Architects, Inc.: "Residential new build and renovation clients have become more knowledgeable in recent years. One of the many areas this has impacted has been the foyer, or main hall, of the home, which in our region often includes a staircase. Many of our clients express a high degree of sensitivity to how the stair functions, its comfort and the quality it expresses."

Photo by **William McCarthy**

CONCRETE CANVASES

Design Crete: "New techniques now allow skilled professionals, artists and craftsmen to color, shape, texture, sandblast, cut and polish concrete. Colored sands, decorative aggregates and even colored glass can be embedded or incorporated into the surface of the concrete to create dynamic and distinctive effects."

WHAT ART SAYS

Artistically Bent, Ltd.: "When a piece of art is displayed in the home, its owner, and what the owner sees in the art, is represented to all. Art also brings another dimension to the home, that of the passion of the artist."

44

REFLECTIONS IN STONE

DelTedesco Tile & Construction Corp.: "The use of natural stone products in the home has been gaining in popularity. Today's natural stone, such as granite, marble, limestone, slate and travertine offer an electrifying range of colors that allow interior designers and homeowners to create the expression of personal taste that reflects a unique style of living."

THE DIMENSIONS OF GLASS

Classic Glass & Mirror, Inc.: "The use of interior glass with decorators, architects and homeowners has evolved tremendously. We have seen so many different uses of these elements, including large glass shower enclosures, glass handrails, room dividers, and decorative mirrors. The varieties of glass available today, including clear, obscure, fluted, and antique, are being used today to satisfy a variety of decorative tastes."

ANOTHER LEVEL

Big 8 Remodeling Company: "For families who don't want to move, but require more space, adding a second floor is becoming a more common option. Building up, instead of out, does have its advantages. Homeowners do not have to worry about property lines, landscaping or the grade of the lot. Oftentimes, adding a story costs roughly the same as adding a room, and the homeowner does not have to alter or add on to the existing foundation."

SOUND CONSTRUCTION

Graves Piano & Organ, Inc.: "The demand for traditional ebony grand pianos remains strong because of their ability to blend with many types of décor. An increasing number of customers, however, are interested in high-quality natural wood finishes and handmade pianos with intricate wood inlay. Automatic disc player pianos, utilizing both CDs and floppy discs, continue to be very popular with both new and existing pianos."

KIDS ROOMS, GROWN-UP STYLE

My Own Room: "Parents and their children no longer view 'kids' rooms' as temporary or transitional. They insist on the same style and quality as the rest of the home. They also look to include study, storage and sleep-over options."

SIMPLE, ELEGANT BEAUTY

Miller's Furniture: "With life becoming ever more complicated by the day, many people are looking for furniture with simple, elegant beauty. This trend has sparked a re-emergence in Mission-style furniture, and the Amish rank among the world's best craftsmen of this furniture type. Characterized by simple lines with little or no intricate detail, Mission-style furniture can be used in every room of the house."

KEVIN S HOFFMAN ASSOCIATES

K S H

architects

300 Marconi Blvd Suite 300
Columbus Ohio 43215
telephone   614.221.5181
fax   614.221.5081

7404 East Main Street
Reynoldsburg, Ohio 43068
614.759.6070

Photography by SOHO Studio Co.

The DiBenedetto Res
Powell, Ohio

Photography by Soho Studio Co.

A R C H A T Ä S
a professional design company

6797 N. High Street · Suite 129

Worthington · Ohio · 43085

Tel. · 614.885.0600   Fax. · 614.885.1221

Architects

STOCK & STONE ARCHITECTS, LLC ....**(614) 261–5810**
3686 North High Street, Columbus   Fax:(614) 261–5813
See ad on page: 69
Principal/Owner: David Stock, Douglas Stone
e-mail: ssarchite@aol.com Additional Information: Proper execution of design and detail is
essential. We have specialized in custom residential design for 12 years.

SULLIVAN BRUCK ARCHITECTS, INC. ....**(614) 464–9800**
309 South Fourth Street, 5th Floor, Columbus   Fax:(614) 464–9809
See ad on page: 95
Principal/Owner: Joseph W. Sullivan, Gary A. Bruck
Website: www.sbarch.com e-mail: info@sbarch.com Additional Information: Founded in 1983;
specializing in refined, vernacular custom luxury residential design, including resort, remodel
and interior architecture.

DEAN A. WENZ ARCHITECTS, INC. ....**(614) 239–6868**
2463 East Main Street, Bexley   Fax:(614) 239–9868
See ad on page: 87
Principal/Owner: Dean A. Wenz
Website: www.wenz–architects.com e-mail: dwenz@wenz–architects.com

BRIAN WILAND AND ASSOCIATES INC. ....**(614) 798–0234**
38 West Bridge Street, Dublin   Fax:(614) 798–0636
See ad on page: 46b, 46c, 171
Principal/Owner: Brian Wiland
Additional Information: Brian Wiland and Associates is a design/build architectural firm
specializing in the design and construction of single family homes and remodeling.

ROY J. YODER ARCHITECT, INC. ....**(614) 794–7320**
4111 Executive Parkway, Suite 303, Westerville   Fax:(614) 794–7327
See ad on page: 67
Principal/Owner: Roy J. Yoder
Website: www.ryoder.com e-mail: ryoder@ryoder.com Additional Information: RYA is a
full–service firm with a 20 year history of quality service and long–term client relationships.
Residential Design

2463 E. Main Street, Bexley, Ohio 43209
614 239 6868

Larry Folk
Architect

Residential Architecture
Planning + Design/Build

13055 Silverbrook Drive
Pickerington, Ohio 43147
Telephone - 614.864.2814
Fax. - 614.864.3102
E-mail - lfolk@insight.rr.com

"Fine Homes - by Design"

Photo by Jeffrey A. Rycus, Rycus Associates Photography

Photo by Jeffrey A. Rycus, Rycus Associates Photography

Photo By Al Teufen Photography

Photo by Jeffrey A. Rycus,
Rycus Associates Photography

BEHAL SAMPSON DIETZ

BUILDING DESIGN

614.464.1933
www.bsdarchitects.com

Photo by R&C Photography

Architecture

Interiors

Landscape

Ecological Site Planning

Residential Development

George Parker & Associates
106 Short Street
Gahanna, OH 43230
614.476.3600

Through our "Interactive Design" process, we ensure that your new home will reflect your unique tastes and our professional touch.

Kent V. Thompson Limited

architect

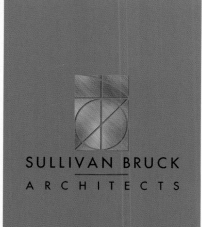

Manley and Harper, Inc

Architecture

MH

3820 North High Street Columbus, Ohio 43214 614 447 3277

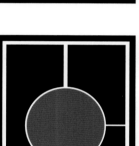

RIDER BRICE
ARCHITECTS & BUILDERS

2074 Arlington Ave.
Columbus, OH 43221
614.486.4100
Fax: 614.486.2900

Residential
Designers

BAKER HENNING ....**(614) 280–8900**
47 East Lincoln Street, Columbus　　　　　　　　Fax:(614) 280–9015
See ad on page: 46d, 100, 102d, 172
Principal/Owner: Damon Baker, Todd Henning
Website: www.bakerhenning.com e-mail: damonb@netwalk.com
Additional Information: Established in 1986. Began in historic renovation. Today does a mix of design/build and build with outside architects on major renovation and new custom home projects.

DAMRON DESIGN & DRAFTING ....**(614) 855–0280**
6790 Harlem Road, Westerville　　　　　　　　Fax:(614) 855–0280
See ad on page: 99
Principal/Owner: Jim Damron
e-mail: damrdezine@aol.com Additional Information: Thirteen years in custom building and design. Over 600 custom residences in Central Ohio from 106K– 1 million +.

DAMRON

DESIGN & DRAFTING

Member Of
The American Institute
of Building Design

A | **I**
B | **D** ®

6790 Harlem Road   Phone/Fax 614.855.0280
Westerville, Ohio   Email: damrdezine@aol.com

BAKER HENNING

PRODUCTIONS, INC.

47 EAST LINCOLN STREET

COLUMBUS, OHIO 43215

614/280-8900 fax/280-9015

www.bakerhenning.com

Finally...
Central Ohio's Own
Home & Design
Sourcebook

The **Central Ohio Home Book** is your final destination
when searching for home remodeling, building and decorating
resources. This comprehensive, hands-on sourcebook to building,
remodeling, decorating, furnishing and landscaping a luxury home
is required reading for the serious and discriminating homeowner.
With more than 500 full-color, beautiful pages, the **Central Ohio
Home Book** is the most complete and well-organized reference
to the home industry. This hardcover volume covers all aspects of
the process, includes listings of hundreds of industry professionals,
and is accompanied by informative and valuable editorial discussing
the most recent trends. Ordering your copy of the **Central Ohio
Home Book** now can ensure that you have the blueprints to
your dream home, in your hand, today.

O R D E R   F O R M

The Ashley Group Luxury Home Resource Collection

The **Ashley Group (www.theashleygroup.com)** is pleased to offer as your final destination when searching for home improvement and luxury resources the following **Home Books** in your local market. Available now: *Chicago, Washington D.C., South Florida, Los Angeles, Dallas/Fort Worth, Detroit, Colorado, New York, Atlanta, Arizona, Philadelphia, San Diego, North Carolina, Boston, Houston, Las Vegas, Connecticut/Westchester County, Central Ohio and Kansas City.* These comprehensive, hands-on guides to building, remodeling, decorating, furnishing, and landscaping a luxury home, are required reading for the serious and selective homeowner. With over 700 full-color, beautiful pages, the **Home Book** series in each market covers all aspects of the building and remodeling process, including listings of hundreds of local industry professionals, accompanied by informative and valuable editorial discussing the most recent trends.

Order your copies today and make your dream come true!

CUSTOM HOME BUILDERS

&

REMODELERS

Breathtaking

Locations • Quality • Value

SHOWCASE

HOMES ®

A DIVISION OF M/I SCHOTTENSTEIN HOMES, INC.

www.showcase-homes.com

614-418-8800

BAKER HENNING

47 EAST LINCOLN STREET

COLUMBUS, OHIO 43215

614/280-8900 fax/280-9015

www.bakerhenning.com

Bringing It Together

Once you've envisioned your dream home, you need a builder in order to turn that dream into a place you can live. Builders create new realities. They can take your ideas and turn them into the house that you will call home.

While design/build teams of architects and builders are becoming increasingly popular, the home in which you will be living will be the direct result of your contractor's efforts and expertise. Depending on the breadth of your project, you and your builder will be in a working relationship that could last as long as a year or two. Therefore, it is essential to choose a company or individual with whom you have a good rapport, who has excellent references as well as experience with your type of project. Seek out a builder whose attention to quality detail, willingness to listen to your concerns, and in-depth knowledge of the trades assures you a smooth road on the way to your new home.

Photo courtesy of **Baker Henning Productions, Inc.**

WHICH COMES FIRST – THE ARCHITECT OR THE BUILDER?

Answering this question can seem like the "chicken or the egg" riddle: Do you hire the builder first, the architect first, or choose a design/build firm, where both functions are under the same roof?

If you work first with an architect, his or her firm will recommend builders they know have a track record in building homes of the same caliber you desire. Most likely, your architect contract will include bidding and negotiation services with these builders, and you may expect help in analyzing bids and making your selection. Your architect contract also may include construction administration, in which the architect makes site visits to observe construction, review the builder's applications for payment, and help make sure the home is built according to the plans.

Perhaps you've seen previous work or know satisfied clients of a custom home builder, and wish to work with him. In this scenario, the builder will recommend architects who are experienced in successfully designing homes and/or additions similar to what you want. The builder will support you, and the architect will cost-control information through realistic cost figures, before products are integrated into the house.

If you like the idea of working with one firm for both the architectural design and building, consider a design/build firm. Design/build firms offer an arrangement that can improve time management and efficient communication, simply by virtue of having both professional functions under the same roof. There is also added flexibility as the project develops. If you decide you want to add a feature, the design/build firm handles the design process and communicates the changes internally to the builder. When you interview a design/builder firm, it's important to ascertain that the firm has a strong architectural background, with experienced custom home architects on staff.

All scenarios work and no one way is always better than the other. Make your choice by finding professionals you trust and with whom you feel comfortable. Look for vision and integrity and let the creative process begin.

FINDING THE RIGHT CHEMISTRY

The selection of a builder or remodeler is a major decision, and should be approached in a thoughtful, unhurried manner. Allow plenty of time to interview and research at least two candidates before making your choice. Hours invested at this point can save months of time later on.

TEN GOOD QUESTIONS TO ASK A BUILDER'S PAST CLIENTS

1. Are you happy with your home?
2. Was the house built on schedule?
3. Did the builder respect the budget and give an honest appraisal of costs early on?
4. Did the builder bring creativity to your project?
5. Were you well informed so you properly understood each phase of the project?
6. Was the builder accessible and on-site?
7. Does the builder provide good service now that the project is complete?
8. How much help did you get from the builder in choosing the products in your home?
9. Is the house well built?
10. Would you hire the builder again?

At the initial interview, the most important information you'll get is not from brochures, portfolios, or a sales pitch, but from your own intuition. Ask yourself: Can we trust this person to execute plans for our dream home, likely the biggest expenditure of our lifetime? Is there a natural two-way communication, mutual respect, and creative energy? Does he have the vision to make our home unique and important? Is his sense of the project similar to ours? Will we have any fun together? Can we work together for at least a year?

If you answer "Yes!" you've found the most valuable asset – the right chemistry.

CHECK REFERENCES, GET INVOLVED

The most distinguished builders in the area expect, even want, you to check their references. More luxury home clients are taking the time to do this research as the move toward quality workmanship continues to grow.

Talk to clients. Get a list of clients spanning the last three to five years, some of whom are owners of projects similar to yours. Call them and go visit their homes or building sites. Satisfied customers are only too happy to show you around and praise the builder who did the work. If you can, speak with a past client not on the builder's referral list. Finding one unhappy customer is not cause for concern, but if you unearth a number of them, cross that builder off your list.

Visit a construction site. Clients who get the best results appreciate the importance of the sub-contractors. Their commitment to quality is at the heart of the job. Do the subcontractors appear to be professional? Are they taking their time in doing their work? Is the site clean and neat?

Contact subcontractors with whom the builder has worked. If they vouch for the builder's integrity and ability, you'll know the firm has earned a good professional reputation. Meeting subcontractors also provides a good measure for the quality of workmanship you'll receive.

Visit the builder's office. Is it well-staffed and organized? Does this person offer the technology for virtual walk-throughs? Do you feel welcome there?

Find out how long the builder has been in business. Experienced custom builders have strong relationships with top quality subcontractors and architects, a comprehensive knowledge of products and materials, and skills to provide the best service before, during and after construction.

Ask how many homes are currently being built and how your project will be serviced. Some builders work on several homes at once; some limit their total to 10 or 12 a year.

CAN YOU TELL THE DIFFERENCE?

Manufactured stone (also called cast stone, since the product is poured into molds in a liquid form) can provide the same look and feel of natural stone. In some instances, such as in driveways and walkways, manu-factured stone or concrete cast in the shape of say, cobblestone, can be the better alter-native, due to its uniformity. Natural stone shapes have to be cut and carved by hand, which involves a great deal of labor and expense. The price of cast stone varies depending on the style and level of detail, but it generally costs about half as much as natural products.

105

LAYING A FOUNDATION FOR SUCCESS

Two documents, the contract and the timeline, define your building experience. The contract lays down the requirements of the relationship and the timeline delineates the order in which the work is done. While the contract is negotiated once at the beginning of the relationship, the timeline continues to be updated and revised as the project develops.

THE CONTRACT

The American Institute of Architects (AIA) provides a standard neutral contract which is widely used in the area, but some firms write their own contracts. As with any contract, get legal advice, read carefully, and assume nothing. If landscaping is not mentioned, then landscaping will not be provided. Pay careful attention to:

• Payment schedules. When and how does the builder get paid? How much is the deposit (depends on the total cost of the project but $10,000 to $25,000 is not uncommon) and will it be applied against the first phase of the work? Do you have the right to withhold any payment until your punch list is completed? Will you write checks to the builder (if so, insist on sworn waivers) or only to the title company? Remodeling contracts typically use a payment schedule broken into thirds – one-third up front, one-third half-way through the project, and one-third at completion. You may withhold a negotiated percentage of the contract price until you're satisfied that the terms of the contract have been met and the work has been inspected. This should be stipulated in the contract. Ten percent is the average amount to be held back, but is negotiable based on the overall size of the project.

Builders and remodeling specialists who attract a quality-minded, high-end custom home client are contacted by institutions offering attractive construction or bridge and end loan packages. Ask your contractor for referrals if you want to do some comparative shopping.

• The total cost – breakdown of labor and materials expenses.

• Change order procedures. Change orders on the average add seven to 10 percent to the cost of a custom home. Be clear on how these orders are charged and the impact they eventually will have on the timetable.

• The basic work description. This should be extremely detailed, including everything from installing phone jacks to the final cleaning of your

CREATE A RECORD

You have a team of highly qualified professionals building your home, but the ultimate responsibility is on your shoulders. So keep track of the project. Organize a binder to keep all of your samples, change orders and documents together. Make copies for yourself of all communication with your suppliers and contractor. Take notes from conversations and send them to the contractor. This can help eliminate confusion before a problem occurs.

TRUTH ABOUT CHANGE ORDERS

The building process demands an environment that allows for changes as plans move from paper to reality. Although you can control changes through careful planning in the preliminary stages of design and bidding, budget an extra seven to 10 percent of the cost of the home to cover change orders. Changes are made by talking to the contractor, not someone working at the site.

home. A comprehensive list of specified materials should be given, if it hasn't already been provided by your architect.

• Allowances. Are they realistic? This is one place where discrepancies will be evident. Is Contractor A estimating $75,000 for cabinets while Contractor B is stating $150,000?

• Warranty. A one-year warranty, effective the date you move in, is standard in this area.

THE TIMELINE

This changeable document will give you a good indication if and when things will go wrong.

Go to the site often enough to keep track of the progress according to the timeline. Do what you need to do to keep the project on schedule. One of the main causes of delays and problems is late decision-making by the homeowner. If you wait until three weeks prior to cabinet installation to order your cabinets, you can count on holding up the entire process by at least a month. (You'll also limit your options to cabinets that can be delivered quickly.)

BUILDING SUPPLIER: EARTH

Some of the most popular materials around today are those that have been here forever. While our homes may contain the modern technology and up-to-date amenities, natural materials, such as marble, granite, stone and rich woods, provide the backbone for these homes. Italian tile can bring you a piece of that Tuscan villa you dream about, granite surfaces or heavy wood cabinetry can bring a bit of nature into your otherwise sleek and modern kitchen, and the visible use of certain types of stone throughout your home can pay tribute to the architectural heritage of the area.

Keep in mind, though, that whatever materials you are using, different times of the year dictate different prices. The cost of lumber, for example, traditionally goes up in late spring to mid-summer. Good builders might also be able to predict when there will be occasional shortages in such products as drywall and brick, and plan accordingly. They will also know when to buy certain items in bulk to decrease your overall costs. Also ask your builder about new products, such as manufactured, or faux, stone, which yield many of the same benefits of its natural counterpart, but at a reduced cost.

CREATING A CUSTOM HOME

While every home project is different, here's one example of some of the costs involved in building a custom home. This one is for construction of a 10,000 sq. ft. home with brick and stone veneer and a slate roof.

• Rough Lumber and Exterior Trim: $110,000
• Carpentry: $100,000
• Steel and Ornamental Iron: $12,500
• Windows: Skylight, $1,500 Windows and doors, $75,000
• Slate Roof: $140,000
• Radiant Heat: $12,500
• Security System: $5,000
• Masonry Veneer: $215,000
• Wood floors: $30,000
• Tile: Ceramic tile, $30,000 Hearth and surround, $10,500
• Cabinets and Vanities: $125,000
• Interior trim: Mantel, $10,900 Wine rack, $3,000 Closets, $8,000

SOURCE FOR HISTORIC PROPERTIES

**The National Trust for Historic Preservation
1785 Massachusetts Avenue, N.W. Washington, DC 20036
202.588.6000**

Having a home listed on the National Register doesn't restrict homeowners from demolishing or making changes (local restrictions do that), but offers possible financial assistance and tax credits for renovations, and limited protection against federal 'takings.' The organization sponsors programs, publishes newsletters and books, and advocates preservation.

THE TEAR-DOWN TREND

Land for new residential construction is getting harder to find, and "tear-down" renovations are becoming more common. There are often mixed emotions in an existing neighborhood as old structures come down. If you are considering a "tear-down" property, be sure you work with a builder and architect who are sensitive to the character of the neighborhood, and will help you build a home that fits in.

THE SECOND TIME'S A CHARM

Renovating a home offers the unique excitement of reinventing an old space to serve a new, enhanced purpose. It's an evolutionary process, charged with creative thinking and bold ideas. If you enjoy a stimulating environment of problem solving and decision making, and you're prepared to dedicate the needed time and resources, remodeling will result in a home which lives up to all of your expectations. You'll be living in the neighborhood you love, in a home that fits your needs.

A WORD ABOUT FINANCING OF REMODELING PROJECTS

Payment schedules in remodeling contracts typically require a deposit or a first payment at the start of the project, with subsequent payments due monthly or in conjunction with the progress of the work.

It is within your rights to withhold a negotiated percentage of the contract price until you're satisfied that the terms of the contract have been met and the work has been inspected. This should be stipulated in the written contract. Ten percent is the average amount to be held back, but is negotiated based on the overall size of the project.

Remodeling specialists who attract a quality-minded clientele are kept abreast of the most attractive remodeling loans on the market by lenders who specialize in these products. Ask your remodeler for referrals to these financial institutions.

RESTORE, RENEW

Many homeowners at the beginning of the new century are attracted to the historic architecture in older neighborhoods. Maturity and classicism are factors that persuade homeowners to make an investment in an old home and restore, renovate or preserve it, depending on what level of involvement interests them and the significance of the house. Renovations include additions and updating or replacing systems in the house. Restorations involve restoring the building to the specifications original to the house. Preservation efforts preserve what's there.

Like any remodeling project, it's an emotional and personal experience, only more so. Staying within the confines of a certain period or style is difficult and time consuming. That's why it's crucial to find an experienced architect and builder who share a reverence for tradition and craftsmanship. At your interview, determine if his or her portfolio shows competence in this specialty. It's vital to find a professional who understands historic projects and knows experienced and qualified contractors and/or subcontractors who will do the work for you. Ask if he or she knows experienced contractors who work in historic districts and have relationships with knowledgeable, experienced craftsmen. If you want exterior features, like period gardens or terraces, ask if they will be included in the overall plan. Make sure he or she has sources for you to find period furnishings, sconce shades or chimney pots.

There are many construction and design issues particular to old homes. The historic renovation and preservation experts featured in the following pages bring experience, creativity and responsibility to each project.

THESE OLD HOUSES

Before you fall in love with an old house, get a professional opinion. Find out how much is salvageable before you make the investment. Can the wood be restored? Have the casings been painted too many times? Is the plaster wavy and buckled? Can the house support ductwork for central air conditioning or additional light sources?

Notable remodelers are often contacted for their expert advice prior to a real estate purchase, and realtors maintain relationships with qualified remodelers for this purpose. They also keep remodelers informed of special properties suitable for custom renovations as they become available.

LEAVING HOME

Remodelers overwhelmingly agree their clients are happier if they move to a temporary residence during all, or the most intensive part, of the renovation. The sight of the roof and walls being torn out, the constant banging and buzzing of tools, and the invasion of privacy quickly take their toll on children and adults who are trying to carry on family life in a house full of dust. Homeowners who are well-rested from living in clean, well-lighted temporary quarters enjoy better relationships with each other, their remodeler and subcontractors.

Common hideaways are rental homes, suite-type hotels, the unoccupied home of a relative, or a long vacation trip. ■

HOME BUILDER SOURCES

The Ohio Home Builders Association
17 S. High St.
7th Floor
Columbus, OH
43215
614.228.6647
www.ohiohba.com

National Association of the Remodeling Industry (NARI)
847.298.9200
www.nari.org

CLEAN UP TIME: Now or Later?

109

Your remodeling contract should be specific about clean-up. Will the site be cleaned up every day, or at the end of the project? Everyday clean-up may add to the price, but is well worth the extra expenditure.

Custom
Homebuilders

ANDREAS BUILDING INC. ....**(614) 332–3532**
Post Office Box 985, Powell   Fax:(614) 635–0182
See ad on page: 146
Principal/Owner: Thomas A. Sakis
e-mail: tsakis1@columbus.rr.com

ARLINGTON BUILDERS ....**(614) 766–4304**
6333 Post Road, Dublin   Fax:(614) 766–2215
See ad on page: 164
Principal/Owner: Robert & Francie Grden

BARRETT CONSTRUCTION COMPANY ....**(614) 766–5545**
9494 Wedgewood Boulevard, Powell   Fax:(614) 865–3294
See ad on page: 136, 137
Principal/Owner: Edward M. Klekotka
Website: www.barretthomes.com e-mail: emk@barretthomes.com
Additional Information: Specializing in design/build residences throughout central Ohio
in all price ranges. We provide all financing through our mortgage company.

BETLEY VISTAIN BUILDERS, INC. ....**(614) 451–3201**
3366 Riverside Drive, Suite 204, Columbus   Fax:(614) 451–3237
See ad on page: 117
Principal/Owner: Walt Betley, Jeff Vistain

BOB WEBB BUILDERS ....**(740) 548–5577**
7662 North Central Drive, Lewis Center   Fax:(740) 548–6113
See ad on page: 135
Principal/Owner: Bob Webb
Website: www.bobwebb.com e-mail: build@bobwebb.com
Additional Information: Founded in 1960, Bob Webb has earned an impeccable reputation
for building a full line of homes around Central Ohio.

CANINI & PELLECCHIA, INC. ....**(614) 855–4545**
430 Beecher Road, Gahanna   Fax:(614) 939–1692
See ad on page: 147
Principal/Owner: Loreto V. Canini

CUGINI & CAPOCCIA BUILDERS, INC. ....**(614) 846–0052**
155 Green Meadows Drive, Westerville   Fax:(614) 846–0060
See ad on page: 168
Principal/Owner: Paul Cugini

110

RALPH

FALLON
BUILDER, INC.
614.436.5005

Individually Crafted Homes Since 1926

KEVIN KNIGHT
& COMPANY

KEVIN KNIGHT
& COMPANY
DESIGNERS • BUILDERS

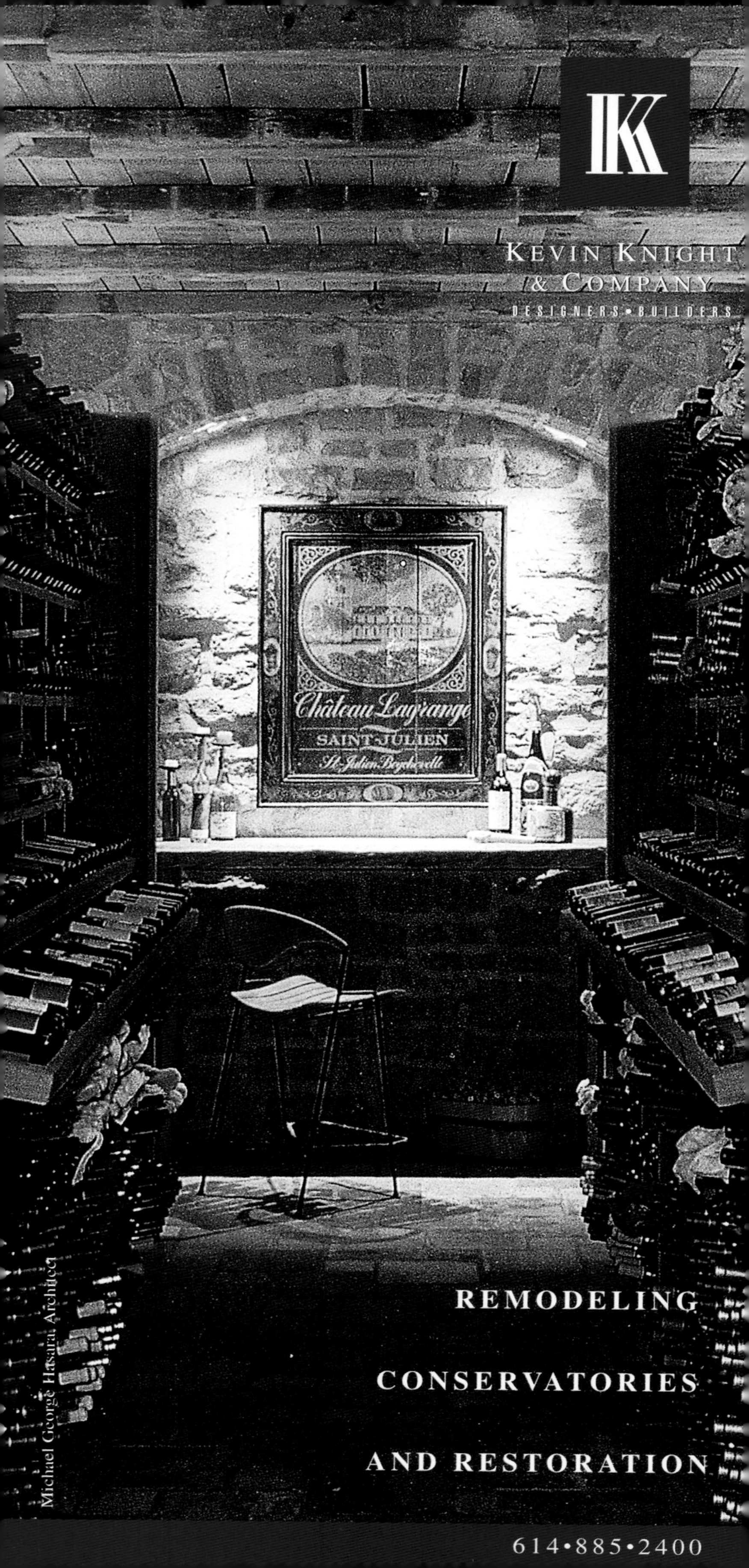

KK

KEVIN KNIGHT
& COMPANY
DESIGNERS • BUILDERS

Michael George Hasara, Architect

REMODELING

CONSERVATORIES

AND RESTORATION

614•885•2400

3366 Riverside Drive
Columbus, Ohio 43221
Tel: (614) 451-3201
Fax: (614) 451-3237
jvistain@columbus.rr.com

FRANCO & MIRIELLO
BUILDERS, LTD.

614.825.0954
www.franco-miriello.com

The Distinction of Architectural Design & Quality

Village Homes in Highland Village

Resort Style Living–
lawn care association, swimming,
dining and the Tartan Fields
Golf Club designed by Arnold Palmer

Choose plans with first floor Master Suites

Jimenez Haid–
Exclusive Custom Home Builder in

Highland Village

at Tartan Fields

Custom Homes built to your plan

JIMENEZ HAID
BUILDERS

(614) 540-2300

Featured Custom Home Builder in

TARTAN FIELDS

**Also building in New Albany and many
other fine communities and on your home site.**

TEALE
HOMES

Custom Builders and Renovators of Fine Homes

Subscribing to the highest professional standards, using some of the area's best architects, designers and craftsmen, giving you the attention *you* expect to make your project extraordinary.

30 West Olentangy Street in historic Powell
(614) 436-1808

HEINLEN FOLLMER, INC
3941 DUBLIN RD.
POWELL, OH 43065
(614) 889-9415

126

Besides the rustic touches they like indoors, homeowners in Central Ohio also have an appreciation for "natural" style landscaping.

HomeB

MATERIAL Matters

Our homes these days are more technologically advanced than they have ever been. They are wired so that they instinctively know what rooms we will be in at what times, and what we'd like the lighting and temperature to be as we enter. The technology within can bring the world into our living rooms.

Still, while homeowners are enjoying a degree of comfort, control and convenience in their homes never before heard of, they are looking to the craftsmanship, materials and rituals of the past to truly make them feel at home. They want their homes to have character, and they are turning to their builders to bridge that gap between the past and the future.

127

Photo courtesy of **Heinlen-Follmer, Inc.**

uilders

Perfectly Imperfect

Owners of Central Ohio's luxury homes don't mind if the wood in their homes looks imperfect – in fact, they prefer it. "Clients want a more rustic look to their homes," said Brain Jimenez, president of Jimenez-Haid Builders. He added that beams culled from old structures may come with the original peg and tenon holes in them, and these holes are kept unmodified, to showcase the character of the wood.

"I've noticed it in the last couple of years and more since last fall," said Kevin Knight, president and owner of Kevin Knight and Company, people want their homes to say something about them, and are accomplishing this with pieces of the past.

Hands-On Homeowners

Jimenez built a home for a couple who wanted a rustic, French Country feeling, but also some of Ohio's history incorporated into their dwelling. "We canvassed the state for wood that had the look they wanted as well as a history," Jimenez said. They found what they wanted at a farm in Delaware County. One of the farm's barns was about to be burned down, but Jimenez and his clients got there before the wood would be lost forever. The wood they recovered from the barn found a prominent place in the beams, flooring and mantel of the home's two-story great room/grand hall.

Jimenez's clients reveled in climbing through the barn, over farm machinery and debris, to pick out wood that would later be part of their own home. "It's kind of special when the families can actually participate in the search," he said.

They also came across an old plank door that was incorporated into the clients' new home as the entrance to their kitchen pantry. The old skeleton key to that door was never found, but that didn't matter, Jimenez said. The family felt "there's no need to lock the door; it's always open to their family," both literally and symbolically.

Steve Heinlen, president and co-owner of Heinlen-Follmer, Inc., recalled a client of his, a doctor, "who was looking for irregular, aged woods, the type that would be unlike anything anyone would find in any other house. He asked if we knew anything about wormy chestnut." Heinlen knew that the heavy, oak-like wood was pretty scarce; much of the species he wanted was wiped out by disease between 1910 and 1920.

But Heinlen found the wood his client was looking for in the remnants of several barns that had been dismantled in Pennsylvania and New York. "We ended up buying hand-hewn timbers that were roughly a century old," he said. After the timber had been kiln-dried, it was used for floor planks, doors, cabinets, ceiling, handrails and other accents throughout the nearly 7,000 sq. ft. home. Heinlen said logistically getting the timber to the home was "a great challenge," but it paid off, as it has given the home "a really special, unique look."

Elegance and natural elements can reside side-by-side in today's luxury homes, for a space that is refined, yet comforting.

129

Photo courtesy of **Heinlen-Follmer, Inc.**

uilders

Knight uses wood brokers to find this scarce material, and about three years ago, one of his brokers told him about some wood barns, built in the 1800s and 1820s, that were destined to be burned by the fire department. Knight got to the wood before it was lost forever, and he used it for the flooring in a home project.

130

Coffered ceilings are an element that builders can incorporate into a space to give a greater sense of depth to the room and an added dimension to the space above.

HomeB

Out of Uniform

And it's not only historic wood that is desired by homeowners. Oversized, imperfect brick, made as it was centuries ago, is also popular for Central Ohio's luxury homes, according to Knight. The color and shape of the bricks are not entirely uniform in appearance, but that is why homeowners love them. These bricks "have more of a natural character that's only achieved by (the handmade process)," said Knight.

Photo courtesy of **Kevin Knight and Company**

uilders

Simple, yet tasteful, furnishings in even the smallest spaces can only heighten the sense of style in a home's entryway.

Photo courtesy of **Kevin Knight and Company**
Photo by **Leslee Kass**

HomeB

Homeowners today want their rooms to be multifunctional, as is this hearth room. The floor is tumbled marble, the wood beams are pickled oak, the cabinets are wormy chestnut and the fireplace is of cut Kansas limestone.

Photo courtesy of **Kevin Knight and Company**
Photo by **Leslee Kass**

A sense of warmth and comfort can be instilled in a home by a varied spectrum of materials. For Heinlen, a current project of his involves putting a coffered ceiling with leather inset panels in a billiard room. With the pine beams running in a criss-cross pattern, 30 panels will be created on the ceiling. Once the panels are inlayed, the leather, imported from Italy, will be added. Like the elements in the other homes discussed here, this dyed leather does not have an artificial look of newness to it. The creases in the leather hold on to the room's shadows and create comfort. Combined with the inlaying of leather on the room's various wood countertops, the overall effect of the room is bold and masculine.

These dwellings have been given the type of respect one would have for a dwelling built for the ages. "The home now," said Knight, "is almost like an heirloom. Homeowners want some things that have some history and heritage." Looking to the future and what it may hold may be easier when one can be reminded of this connection to the past. ■

uilders

RALPH FALLON BUILDERS, INC. ....**(614) 436–5005**
533 Schrock Road, Columbus   Fax:(614) 436–3485
See ad on page: 111
Principal/Owner: Ralph W. Fallon
Website: www.ralphfallonbuilder.com e-mail: rfallon@ralphfallonbuilder.com

FRANCO & MIRIELLO BUILDERS LTD. ....**(614) 825–0954**
9 West Olentangy Street, Suite 2, Powell   Fax:(614) 825–0956
See ad on page: 118, 119
Principal/Owner: Peter Franco, Marc Miriello
Website: www.franco–miriello.com e-mail: info@franco–miriello.com

GIULIANI BUILDERS ....**(740) 965–4240**
5031 Red Bank Road, Galena   Fax:(740) 965–8480
See ad on page: 143
Principal/Owner: Robert S. Giuliani
Website: www.giulianibuilders.com e-mail: rsgiuliani@msn.com
Additional Information: Giuliani Builders provides quality, custom built homes
and individualized attention.

HEINLEN FOLLMER INC...**(614) 889–9415**
8941 Dublin Road, Powell   Fax:(614) 889–2974
See ad on page: 124, 125
Principal/Owner: Steve Heinlen, Todd Follmer
e-mail: tfollmer@columbus.rr.com

HENINGER HOMES LTD. ....**(614) 890–0160**
8601 Button Bush Lane, Westerville   Fax:(614) 890–0160
See ad on page: 149
Principal/Owner: John G. and Deborah J. Heninger
e-mail: heningerg.d@aol.com

HOMECRAFTERS OF OHIO ....**(740) 362–9595**
1147 Columbus Pike, #188, Delaware   Fax:(740) 362–5020
See ad on page: 144a, 144b, 144c, 144d, 144e, 144f, 144g, 144h
Principal/Owner: Jennifer Beam

JIMENEZ–HAID BUILDERS ....**(614) 540–2300**
941 Chatham Lane, #100, Columbus   Fax:(614) 457–7295
See ad on page: 120, 121
Principal/Owner: Brian Jimenez

Luxury for all lifestyles.

commitment · craftsmanship · reputation · integrity

Regardless of your price range, visit a Bob Webb home and experience luxury for all lifestyles.

Barrett

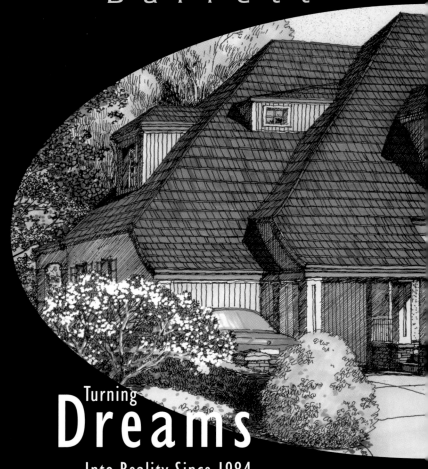

Turning
Dreams
Into Reality Since 1984.

What's Your Dream Home?

Financing Made Easy.
Affiliated with Barrett Mortgage Services
of Ohio, we'll make your dream come true
with competitive construction/permanent,
variable, and fixed loans.

Barrett

POWELL / WESTERVILLE / UPPER ARLINGTON

Barrett Construction Company
9494 Wedgewood Blvd.,
Powell, OH 43065
614.206.2988
www.barretthomes.com

4644 Aberdeen Avenue
Dublin, OH 43016
tel: 614.336.9004
fax: 614.336.7794

KENRIC
FINE HOMES

2728 Jewett Road • Powell, Ohio 43065
Tel: 614.846.3175 • Fax: 614.846.1404
www.kenricfinehomes.com

*Kenric Fine Homes is known for providing excellent service
and uncompromising value in each home they build.*

Welcome To Elegant Living Created By Romanelli & Hughes

Let us create an elegant home for you. Call for information regarding new home locations nearest where you want to live.

Romanelli & Hughes
BUILDING COMPANY
614/891-2042

GIULIANI
BUILDERS

5031 Red Bank Road

Galena, OH 43021

P: 740.965.4240

F: 740.965.8480

www.giulianibuilders.com

83 W. CAMPUS VIEW BLVD. | COLUMBUS, OH 43235
614.846.1030 | FAX: 614.436.8058 | WWW.TEMPESTABUILDERS.COM

Building Your **Dream** Home

This timetable is included to support you in transforming your dream into reality. The sections of this book include specific categories to help you find the best quality craftsmanship available. This timeline will help you to understand the process from start to finish. How long might it take for you from designing the house to making it your own home? It could take from one year to a year and a half. Eighteen months is not unusual for a completely custom-built home. It can take four to six months to receive design approval and city permits alone. So be patient and plan ahead. Often delays occur because of a lack of communication. Take the initiative to keep in touch with all parties necessary. We hope this timeline will help give you an indication of how that dream home of yours will become a reality!

Breaking Ground

What a joy to see that construction of your new home is underway!

Foundation Work

This will include footings and dampproofing. The cement will need a few days to solidify.

MONTH 5

Framing Begins

Rough framing of the house begins. At the end of this phase the structure will be in place, and you'll be able to see the rooms as they're going to look. This phase will take two to three months.

MONTH 6

Roofing Begins

Since the time you broke ground until the time you get to this stage, probably four months have lapsed. With the exterior framing of the house completed, the contractor can start working on the interior (mechanical elements).

MONTH 9

Inspecting the Progress

At various times throughout the process, there will be building/municipal inspections to make sure the house meets all city codes and zoning issues. Often, a builder will insist on a six-month, follow-up courtesy inspection.

• **Choosing a contractor**: The builder is usually considered the general contractor for the job. The general contractor will line up the subcontractors and enter into an agreement with the vendors. The general contractor will be solely responsible for construction methods, techniques, schedules and procedures. The key is that teams need to be in place.

• **Seasonal costs**: The builder will keep in mind that different times of the year require different costs. The cost of lumber, for example, traditionally goes up in late spring to mid-summer. Good builders might also be able to figure when there will be occasional shortages in such items as drywall and brick. They might also know when to buy certain items in bulk to decrease your overall costs.

Building a **Custom** House

Interview and Select an Interior Designer

A skilled designer will collaborate with the architect on matters such as windows and door location, appropriate room size and lighting plans

Interview and Select an Architect and Builder

This is the time to test the fit between what you want, what you need and what you can spend. It is advisable to interview two or three architects and builders and check their references before making a firm decision.

Site Selection

If you don't already own the land, meet with a realtor of your choice to describe the parameters of your future house. Also discuss future sites with your architect and builder.

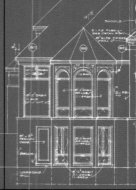

MONTH 1   MONTH 4

Design/Build Firms

A design/build firm is a company that employs architects, builders, estimators and sometimes interior designers and realtors. Read more about them in the Architects section.

• **Your architect and builder must work together.** The architect and contractor must be continually matching their budget and timelines. The architect converts the vision into buildable drawings. The contractor uses the drawings to make the plan work.

• **Final decisions:** Once you've received the initial drawings for the front, back and both sides of your house plus floor plans, you must make final decisions. You must decide on the exact footage of every level of your house and decide what unique elements you may want to include. For example, do you want your own home theater and entertainment center? Home automation and lighting?

Project
Description

Building an upscale, one-acre property, single-family home. This work includes planning the project (selecting an architect and builder), executing the project (the steps from breaking the ground to finishing the interior work) and finishing the project (closing on your new home).

FINISHED PROJECT

Final Inspection
Independent appraisals take place at this time.

Final Close
Representatives for both the builder and the client will attend, along with a staff person from the closing company.

Releasing the contractor
The client does a walk-through inspection and provides a "punch list"— a list of miscellaneous items the contractor needs to do to finish the work.

MONTH 16

• There are certain laws that protect the client. Experts other than independent appraisers may be called upon to ensure that all agreements and building codes have been met. The client can, of course, make notes and have miscellaneous details taken care of.

• **Warranty:** Most states provide warranty protection for the client. The builder's warranty is typically one year for construction. Specific manufacturer warranties can last as long as five to 10 years.

Additional Information
For more information, contact the National Association of Home Builders (NAHB) 1201 15th St. NW Washington, DC 20005-2800 202-266-8111.

SPONSORED BY:

HomeCrafters
351 W Central Avenue
Delaware, Ohio 43015
Toll Free 866.362.9595
www.HomeCraftersOhio.com

The Home Builders

"Making the dream real"

ANDREAS BUILDING INC.

Design • Build

P : 6 1 4 . 3 3 2 . 3 5 3 2

F : 6 1 4 . 6 3 5 . 0 1 8 2

KENRIC FINE HOMES ....**(614) 846–3175**
2728 Jewett Road, Powell　　　　　　　　　　　　　　Fax:(614) 846–1404
See ad on page: 140, 141
Principal/Owner: Ken Brengartner
Website: www.kenricfinehomes.com　e-mail: kbrengartner@kenricfinehomes.co

KEVIN KNIGHT & COMPANY ....**(614) 885–2400**
70 West Olentangy Street, Powell　　　　　　　　　　Fax:(614) 885–1610
See ad on page: 112, 113, 114, 115, 116, 178
Principal/Owner: Kevin Knight
e-mail: kk2400@aol.com　Additional Information: Kevin Knight & company can custom design your home, or work with your design team to create a home of unmistakable quality & enduring beauty.

L & R CONSTRUCTION COMPANY, INC. ....**(614) 891–0960**
5223 South Old 3C Highway, Westerville　　　　　　Fax:(614) 891–1488
See ad on page: 166, 167
Principal/Owner: Stephen Roof

M.A. TRUCCO BUILDERS, INC. ....**(740) 881–4663**
4415 Millwater Drive, Powell　　　　　　　　　　　　Fax:(740) 881–0009
See ad on page: 161
Principal/Owner: Matthew A. Trucco
e-mail: matrucco@mbusa.net
Additional Information: Building and Remodeling Fine Homes since 1984.

MARHILL BUILDERS, INC. ....**(614) 336–9004**
4644 Aberdeen Avenue, Dublin
See ad on page: 138, 139
Principal/Owner: Marvin L. Hill
Additional Information: Over 25 years of building custom quality homes, offering timeless functional floor plans with understated elegance.

MCVEY CUSTOM HOMES ....**(614) 538–1227**
3923 Tarrington Lane, Columbus　　　　　　　　　　Fax:(614) 538–1310
See ad on page: 122
Principal/Owner: Keith McVey

M–E BUILDING CONSULTANTS...**(614) 818–4918**
635 Brooksedge Boulevard, Westerville　　　　　　Fax:(614) 818–4901
See ad on page: 154, 155
Principal/Owner: Timothy R. Foley
Website: www.mebuildingconsultants.com Additional Information: M–E Building Consultants' residential construction managers provide: quality, value and an expedited schedule for your new home or remodeling projects.

145

In
Conclusion

Your new house started as a dream with a piece of land. Now your custom-designed home has become a reality. It's time to start living in the special place you've created. Enjoy!

Produced by The Ashley Group
847.390.2882
www.theashleygroup.com

Mechanical Work Begins

This includes the rough plumbing, HVAC, electrical and low-voltage work. Allow two to three weeks each for the mechanical steps.

Interior Work Begins

Once the rough mechanical work is completed, the insulation and drywall can be installed. The hardwood floors and tile can be worked on concurrently. Next up are the stairs and the cabinets. Then the millwork (trim around the doors and windows) takes shape. The painting of trim, walls and ceilings follows. Then the mechanical work can be finalized.

Finishing the Work

Final sanding, sealing, carpeting and closet shelving complete the job. Allow three to four months for the interior work and final items to take place.

MONTH 10   MONTH 11   MONTH 15

• Environmental and energy concerns:

Of course, you will want to save on energy consumption, so make sure the builder doesn't forget these issues. Consider the selection of furnaces and water heaters. Ask your builder what their standard efficiency ratings are. Your initial investment might be more, but you could reap the benefit of lower energy costs in the long run. Where the sun rises and sets may seem inconsequential. But you'll want to make sure some key rooms allow natural light at particular times (for example, the greenhouse effect).

Also, as you build your house, you may want to ask your builder about different ways to protect the outside of the house using some sort of protective covering or wrap. That helps address your concerns about water intrusion.

Keeping on Schedule

Make sure the builder provides you with a schedule and completion date. The duration of the project should be clearly defined in the contract. However, you can almost depend on the schedule changing due to unforeseen delays such as weather-related items. But the homeowner can also affect the schedule by making late selections and desiring personal changes.

CANINI & PELLECCHIA

430 Beecher Road, Gahanna, Ohio 43230 • (614) 855-4545

Building Beautifully Crafted Homes for Three Generations

xwyndfield
Custom Homes

765 Grindstone St. Westerville, Ohio 43082
614-523-2020

Heninger Homes LTD

Office: 614.890.0160 Cell: 614.306.3890

Builder of Fine Custom Homes

*LUXURY BASEMENTS & ADDITIONS   *SUPERIOR CRAFTSMANSHIP

*UNSURPASSED QUALITY & SERVICE   *ARCHITECTURAL SERVICES AVAILABLE

*Make your dream home a reality with HENINGER HOMES, LTD.

5067 CANTERBURY
POWELL, OH 43065
PH: 614.798.1036
MOBILE: 614.206.1968

MUSGRAVE CONSTRUCTION COMPANY, INC...**(740) 548–6622**
3050 Waterford Drive, Lewis Center   Fax:(740) 549–1255
See ad on page: 157
Principal/Owner: Dan Musgrave
e-mail: dsmusgrave@midohio.net

NEWCASTLE HOMES ....**(614) 206–5301**
134 Liberty Ridge Avenue, Powell   Fax:(614) 781–1803
See ad on page: 158, 159
Principal/Owner: Ed White

PIERCE CONSTRUCTION INC. ....**(614) 855–9494**
5201 Morse Road, Columbus   Fax:(614) 855–1222
See ad on page: 156
Principal/Owner: Rex Michael Pierce
Website: piercecompany@insight.rr.com e-mail: www.pierceconstructioninc.com
Additional Information: We specialize in high–end custom home building and remodeling and
have completed over 30 homes in the New Albany Communities.

ROMANELLI & HUGHES ....**(614) 891–2042**
Columbus
See ad on page: 142
Principal/Owner: Vince Romanelli , Dave Hughes
Additional Information: Since 1970 we have been building custom homes in the Columbus and
Delaware areas. Our custom homes range from 350,000 to wherever your imagination
and creativity leads you.

SHOWCASE HOMES ....**(614) 418–8800**
3 Easton Oval, Suite 240, Columbus   Fax:(614) 418–8889
See ad on page: 102b, 102c, 150
Principal/Owner: Irving E. Schottenstein, CEO
Website: www.showcase–homes.com e-mail: mgordon@showcase–homes.com

STONECRAFT BUILDERS, INC. ....**(614) 792–9701**
2715 Sawbury Boulevard, Columbus   Fax:(614) 792–9702
See ad on page: 153
Principal/Owner: Bill Antonick, David Bricker
Additional Information: Stonecraft Builders, Inc., a custom homebuilder and renovation
specialist, provides the finest quality custom designed homes tailored to meet the individual
tastes of its discriminating clients.

SWAIN BUILDERS ....**(614) 451–9207**
788 Lauraland Drive, Columbus   Fax:(614) 457–7992
See ad on page: 165
Principal/Owner: Thomas Swain
e-mail: tswainl@ameritech.net

Stonecraft Builders, Inc.

Custom Homes ✦ Renovations

2715 Sawbury Blvd
Columbus, OH 43235
Tel: 614.792.9701
Fax: 614.792.9702

PIERCE
Construction Inc.

5201 Morse Road
Columbus, Ohio 43230
614-855-9494
www.pierceconstructioninc.com

Musgrave Construction

Custom Home Builder
Dan Musgrave President
3050 Waterford Drive • Lewis Center Ohio 43035
Phone (740) 548-6622 • Fax (740) 549-1255

Distinction

Quality

Workmanship

Photos by Imagemakers Photographic

Custom Homebuilders

TEALE HOMES, INC. ....**(614) 436–1808**
30 West Olentangy Street, Powell   Fax:(614) 436–4760
See ad on page: 123
Principal/Owner: Lew Teale, Jerry Keyser
Additional Information: Founded in 1989, the two company principals have over 6 decades of building experience. Our specialties are custom homes, major additions and renovations.

TEMPESTA BUILDERS ....**(614) 846–1030**
83 W. Campus View Boulevard, Columbus   Fax:(614) 436–8058
See ad on page: 144
Principal/Owner: Armando, Roberto & Anthony
Website: www.tempestabuilders.com e-mail: tempestabuilders@columbus.rr.com
Additional Information: A family business since 1989, specializing in working with clients on how their dreams and ideas can become a reality.

TEUTSCH BUILDERS, INC. ....**(614) 798–1036**
5061 Canterbury Drive, Powell   Fax:(614) 798–1036
See ad on page: 151
Principal/Owner: Bill Teutsch

WOODSMEN BUILDERS, INC. ....**(740) 862–5609**
12755 Heimberger Road, NW, Baltimore   Fax:(740) 862–5609
See ad on page: 162, 163
Principal/Owner: Thomas A. Snider
Additional Information: Woodsmen Builders, Inc. is committed to building homes of the highest quality at a fair cost.

WYNDFIELD HOMES ....**(614) 523–2020**
765 Grindstone Street, Westerville   Fax:(614) 895–8853
See ad on page: 148
Principal/Owner: Dan Frutiger
e-mail: wyndfield_homes2001@yahoo.com
Additional Information: "The difference you deserve; The quality you can be proud of"

M.A. TRUCCO
BUILDERS, INC.

Trucco Builders
*
Designers,
Builders
of
Distinctive Homes

Trucco Builders
*
Combining
Quality
and
Integrity
to
Make Dreams
Reality

4415 Millwater Dr.
Powell, OH 43065
Tel: 740.881.4663
Fax: 740.881.0009

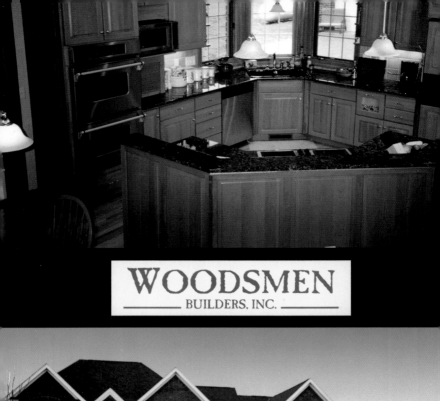

WOODSMEN
BUILDERS, INC.

TAKING YOUR IDEAS AND CREATING A HOME

WOODSMEN
BUILDERS, INC.

12755 Heimberger Rd NW

Baltimore, Ohio

Business/Fax
740.862.5609

ARLINGTON BUILDERS
CUSTOM HOMES

Our art form is creating a place of origin for intrinsically interesting people. We do this by transforming your personality and character into a home.

6333 Post Road ~ Dublin, Ohio 43017
Tel. 614.766.4304 ~ Fax 614.766.2215
"We Create with Passion"

Swain Builders

"Homes of Distinction"

788 Lauraland Drive
Columbus, Ohio 43214
(P) 614 451 9907 • (F) 614 457 7999

WILLIAM R. PEPPERNEY, ARCHITECT
ARCHITECTURAL RESOURCE GROUP, INC.
65 East Wilson Bridge Road, Suite 202, Worthington, Ohio 43085

L R

CONSTRUCTION

5223 South Old 3c Highway
Westerville, OH 43082
614.891.0960 Fax 614.891.1488

155 Green Meadows Dr. S. • Westerville, OH 43081
(614) 846-0052 FAX 846-0060

Design
Build

BAKER HENNING..**(614) 280–8900**
47 East Lincoln Street, Columbus   Fax:(614) 280–9015
See ad on page: 46d, 100, 102d, 172
Principal/Owner: Damon Baker, Todd Henning
Website: www.bakerhenning.com e-mail: damonb@netwalk.com
Additional Information: Established in 1986. Began in historic renovation. Today does
a mix of design/build and build with outside architects on major renovation and new custom
home projects.

TRIGLYPH COMPANIES ....**(614) 224–4048**
309 South Fourth Street, 5th Floor, Columbus   Fax:(614) 224–4670
See ad on page: 170
Principal/Owner: Marty Finta
Additional Information: Custom home builder specializing in design/build themed and
waterfront architecture.

BRIAN WILAND AND ASSOCIATES INC. ....**(614) 798–0234**
38 West Bridge Street, Dublin   Fax:(614) 798–0636
See ad on page: 46b, 46c, 171
Principal/Owner: Brian Wiland
Additional Information: Brian Wiland and Associates is a design/build architectural firm
specializing in the design and construction of single family homes and remodeling.

brian wiland

DESIGN/BUILD ARCHITECTS

38 West Bridge Street
Dublin, Ohio 43017

All photography by: Steven M. Elbert

Timberframe

RIVERBEND TIMBER FRAMING ....**(517) 486–4355**
9012 East US 223, Blissfield   Fax:(517) 486–2056
See ad on page: 174, 175
Principal/Owner: Frank Baker
Website: www.riverbendtf.com e-mail: infor@riverbendtf.com
Additional Information: "Since 1979, Riverbend has established a long history of deeply satisfied customers with our award–winning, finely crafted timber frame structures."

Remodeling
Specialists

AURORA INDUSTRIES ....**(614) 876–6734**
4790 Riverwood Drive, Hilliard   Fax:(614) 529–0300
See ad on page: 189
Principal/Owner: Patrick L. Livingston
e-mail: plivins317@prodigy.net Additional Information: Aurora Industries, specializing in
custom remodeling, represents quality and integrity with one of the finest reputations in
custom remodeling.

BIG 8 REMODELING ....**(614) 475–2265**
2900 Ole Country Lane, Columbus   Fax:(614) 475–1999
See ad on page: 183
Principal/Owner: J. Scott Frank, CR

CLEAR CHOICE BUILDING & RENOVATIONS, INC....................................**(614) 836–8302**
5266 Loeffler Drive, Groveport   Fax:(614) 836–0947
See ad on page: 200
Principal/Owner: Robert M. Quayle
Website: www.clear–choice–renovations.com

DAVE FOX REMODELING ....**(614) 459–7211**
1161 Bethel Road, Suite 104, Columbus   Fax:(614) 459–7133
See ad on page: 180, 181
Principal/Owner: Dave Fox (President), Gary Demos
Website: www.davefoxremodeling.com

FRY CONTRACTING COMPANY ....**(614) 486–3002**
1014 Dublin Road, Columbus   Fax:(614) 486–8774
See ad on page: 190, 191
Principal/Owner: Robert S. Fry
e-mail: frycontr@aol.com Additional Information: 25 years in business, Big 50 award by
"Remodeling Magazine", CGR Certified, NAHB Member

Photos by B. Barr Photography

MICHAEL MATRKA, INC
1211 Chesapeake Ave.
PH 614.486.7707   FAX 614.486.7721

KK

KEVIN KNIGHT
& COMPANY
DESIGNERS • BUILDERS

dave fox
REMODELING

1161 Bethel Road - Suite 104, Columbus OH 43220 (614) 459-7211

www.davefoxremodeling.com

Bringing your remodeling dreams to life!

Space · Craft
Architecture and Construction

2781 Olentangy River Rd. Columbus, OH 43202 ph. 614.268.2590

V·I·S·I·O·N

The bridge between concept and creation

Kitchens & Baths • Room Additions • Specialty Projects

Over 35 years of award-winning remodeling & design experience.

Big 8
Since 1965
REMODELING COMPANY
www.big8remodeling.com

NARI
NATIONAL ASSOCIATION OF
THE REMODELING INDUSTRY

4 Certified Remodelers on Staff
475-2265

2900 Ole Country Lane (Off Stelzer Rd. - North of Airport)

QUALITY &
Specializing in Kitchens

PHOTOGRAPHY BY KEVIN MAYER/THE KW MAYER COMPANY

BEFORE

MARK TROYER
BUILDERS, INC

DESIGN/BUILD   CERTIFIED REMODELER

9720 Lafayette – Plain City Road, Plain City, Ohio 43064
Phone: 614.873.4456 • Fax: 614.873.9697

EXCELLENCE
Bathrooms and Additions

AFTER

Mark Troyer Builders, Inc.
has been partnering with
homeowners in the Columbus
Metropolitan area since 1986.
Combining high quality
workmanship with knowledgeable,
respected, and creative expertise,
Mark Troyer Builders will take
your design concepts and turn
them into reality.

CELEBRATING OVER
15 YEARS
OF EXCELLENCE

GEORGETOWN BUILDERS, INC. ....**(614) 488–0752**
1429 King Avenue, Columbus   Fax:(614) 486–0694
See ad on page: 193
<u>Principal/Owner:</u> J. Robert White
<u>Website:</u> www.georgetownbuilders.com <u>e-mail:</u> getownbldr@aol.com

H.K. & S.A. PHILLIPS RESTORATION INC. ....**(614) 443–5699**
972 Harmon Avenue, Columbus   Fax:(614) 443–9040
See ad on page: 188
<u>Principal/Owner:</u> Spike Phillips
<u>Website:</u> www.phillipsrestoration.com <u>e-mail:</u> kevin@phillipsrestoration.com
<u>Additional Information:</u> Since 1959, Commercial & Residential Masonry Restoration.

H.T. BUILDERS ....**(614) 873–3138**
9402 Lafayette Plain City Road, Plain City   Fax:(614) 873–3138
See ad on page: 194, 195
<u>Principal/Owner:</u> Howard Troyer
<u>e-mail:</u> ht_builders@msn.com
<u>Additional Information:</u> We are a small company committed to quality construction and
craftsmanship. Owner is directly involved in all phases of construction.

JS BROWN...**(614) 291–6876**
1522 Hess Street, Columbus   Fax:(614) 291–7090
See ad on page: 198, 199
<u>Principal/Owner:</u> Jeffrey S. Brown
<u>Website:</u> JSBROWNCOMPANY.COM

KEVIN KNIGHT & COMPANY ....**(614) 885–2400**
70 West Olentangy Street, Powell   Fax:(614) 885–1610
See ad on page: 112, 113, 114, 115, 116, 178
<u>Principal/Owner:</u> Kevin Knight
<u>e-mail:</u> kk2400@aol.com

E.L. MACIOCE GENERAL CONTRACTOR, LLC ....(614) 239–9250
2929 Switzer Road, Columbus   Fax:(614) 252–7051
See ad on page: 197
<u>Principal/Owner:</u> Edward Macioce
<u>e-mail:</u> elmgc@bcol.net

MCR SERVICES ....(614) 421–0860
638 East 5th Avenue, Columbus   Fax:(614) 421–0865
See ad on page: 187
<u>Principal/Owner:</u> Wade Hungerford

186

H.K & S.A. Phillips Restorations Inc.

Quality Masonry Restoration

SINCE 1959

*Commercial, Industrial, Residential
Historical*

972 Harmon Ave. Columbus, OH 43223
614.443.5699 PH   614.443.9040 FAX
www.phillipsrestoration.com

AURORA
INDUSTRIES

Patrick Livingston
General Contractor

4790 Riverwood Drive • Hilliard, OH 43026
Tel: 614.876.6734 • Mobile: 614.395.3700 • Fax: 614.529.0300

HOME

It is your refuge from the world, your sanctuary—the center of your family and all that you love.

It's not just a house, it's your home.

At Fry Contracting, every home we remodel or build is as distinctive as the individuals who work with us. While every client is different, each is looking for a contractor who listens, is considerate of their time, and is attentive to every detail. That's our mission at Fry Contracting. You'll find that the homes we've remodeled throughout the city are testaments to our craftsmanship and quality service.

We turn houses into homes.

Fry CONTRACTING

where quality lasts a lifetime

25 years of experience · member of the Building Industry Association
licensed · bonded · insured

Fry Contracting Co.
Robert Fry, President, CGR
1014 Dublin Road · Columbus Ohio 43215
tele 614.486.3002 fax 614.486.8774 eMail frycontr@aol.com

MICHAEL MATRKA, INC...**(614) 486–7707**
1211 Chesapeake Avenue, Columbus
See ad on page: 177
Principal/Owner: Michael Matrka
e-mail: mmatrka@aol.com Additional Information: 20 year old company. High level detail.
Small to very large project capability. Highly interactive management systems.

Fax:(614) 486–7721

RIVERSTONE CONSTRUCTION, INC. ....**(614) 882–1340**
6295 Maxtown Road, Suite 200, Westerville
See ad on page: 179
Website: www.riverstoneconstruction.com e-mail: riverstone@ee.net

Fax:(614) 882–4562

SHORTY'S REMODELING COMPANY, INC....**(614) 481–9474**
1601 West 5th Avenue, #205, Columbus
See ad on page: 196
Principal/Owner: Curtis Frabott
e-mail: cfrabott@columbus.rr.com

Fax:(614) 481–9485

SPACE CRAFT ARCHITECTURE AND CONSTRUCTION ....**(614) 268–2590**
2781 Olentangy River Road, Columbus
See ad on page: 182
Principal/Owner: Bradley A. Dean
e-mail: brad@spacecraftonline.com

Fax:(614) 268–2599

MARK TROYER BUILDERS, INC. ....**(614) 873–4456**
9720 Lafayette–Plain City Road, Plain City
See ad on page: 184, 185, 193
Principal/Owner: Mark Troyer
e-mail: jeff@marktroyerbuilders.com
Additional Information: Established in 1986. Certified remodeler. Member of NARI, NKBA, BBB
and Dublin and Upper Arlington Chambers of Commerce.

Fax:(614) 873–9697

GEORGETOWN BUILDERS

Combining Excellence in Design with Quality Craftsmanship

Georgetown Builders Inc., has been remodeling homes in the Central Ohio area since 1982 and offers a complete project package. The goal of Georgetown Builders is to work with homeowners to bring their construction dreams to life.

With emphasis on quality, regardless of the project size, Georgetown Builders focuses on retaining architectural integrity to ensure the new project blends with the original structure. Your dreams and vision can be fulfilled with Georgetown Builders.

1429 KING AVE. COLUMBUS, OH 43212
PH: (614) 488-0752   FAX: (614) 486-0694
E-MAIL: getownbldr@aol.com / www.georgetownbuilder.com

H.T. Builders, Inc.
Home Improvement Specialist

9402 Plain City-Lafayette Road
Plain City, Ohio
614-873-3138

H.T. Builders, Inc.

Home Improvement Specialist

Beauty is in the eyes of the beholder.
Quality is in the hands of the craftsman.

QUALITY
+SERVICE
VALUE

Randall Lee
Scheiber
Photography

Clear Choice Building & Renovations Inc.

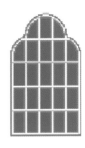

The Clear Choice For All Your Renovations
5266 Loeffler Drive Groveport, Ohio 43125
General Contractor - Design/Build Renovations

If you're thinking about improving your home, please give us a call to talk about your ideas. From a gallery of styles for your kitchens and baths, to elegant home expansions, we can help you develop ideas that will give you the best value for each dollar you invest and the highest quality money can buy.

614-836-8302

Visit our website at www.clear-choice-renovations.com

Roofing
Specialists

DURABLE SLATE COMPANY, THE ....**(614) 299–5522**
1050 North Fourth Street, Columbus   Fax:(614) 299–7100
See ad on page: 202
<u>Principal/Owner:</u> Cherie Downey

Basements

BASEMENTS UNLIMITED ....**(614) 554–5779**
2210 Edgevale Road, Upper Arlington   Fax:(614) 457–8352
See ad on page: 206
<u>Principal/Owner:</u> Alan J. Cloern
<u>Additional Information:</u> Upscale basement remodeling for 15 years. Owner of company highly involved in all aspects of job.

OWENS CORNING BASEMENT FINISHING ....**(614) 737–9000**
619 Reynolds Avenue, Columbus   Fax:(614) 737–9001
See ad on page: 204, 205

A Revolutionary New Product From Owens Corning

Recreation Room • Home Office • Dens
Full/Half Bathrooms • Wet & Dry Bar

BASEMENTS
UNLIMITED

"Space for the entire family"
Rec rooms, home office, bathrooms, wet bars, entertainment centers.

BASEMENTS UNLIMITED
Upper Arlington, OH

Since 1987

614-554-5779

INTERIOR
DESIGNERS

Dennis R. McAvena & Associates, Inc.

12338 Morse Road SW
Pataskala, Ohio 43062
740 / 927-4470
Fax: 927-4480

Complete

Interior Design

Services

Photography by Bryan Barr Design by ozone studios

309 S. Fourth St., Suite 100 • Columbus, OH 43215
614/228-4900 • Fax 614/228-5110
www.granddesigngroup.com

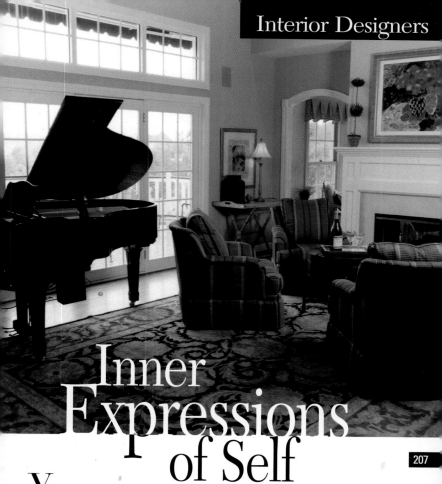

Inner
Expressions
of Self

207

Y̲ou know that something has to be done about your
home's interior. You know what styles you like and what
styles you couldn't possibly live with. You may even have
your mind on a certain furnishing or piece of art that you
want to be a central part of a particular room. But beyond
that, you haven't the foggiest idea of how to bring everything
together. That's where an interior designer comes in.

There are many good reasons to work with an interior
designer, not the least of which is you will most likely save
time and money. It's so easy to get bogged down in the many
small details of home decorating, and lose track of the big
picture. An interior designer has the training and experience
to help you define your style, and keep your project
focused, minimizing costly decorating mistakes. With their
years of professional experience and the tools that they have
at their fingertips, designers can orchestrate, layer by layer,
design elements that compose an inviting and harmonious
décor. Best of all, designers often have access to the best
decorating resources in the area, from furniture showrooms
to the most coveted interior painter. They'll handle the
myriad details while you enjoy the results.

Photo courtesy of **Creations, Interior Design by John Wilson**

Photo by **Al Laus**

WHERE STRUCTURE MEETS INSPIRATION

A great interior designer, like a great architect or builder, sees space creatively, applying years of education and experience to deliver a distinguished residence at the highest level of quality in an organized, professional manner. Intensely visual, these talented individuals imprint a home with the spirit and personality of the family living there.

A top quality interior designer who is licensed by the state is educated in the field of interior design, usually holding a bachelor's or master's degree in the subject. In addition to creating interiors, your interior designer also handles the "nuts and bolts" business end of the project. With skill and experience in placing and tracking orders, scheduling shipping, delivery and installation, the designer can bring your project to its perfect conclusion.

AN INTERIOR DESIGNER IS A TEAM MEMBER

Choose an interior designer when you select your architect, builder, and landscape architect. A skilled designer can collaborate with the architect on matters such as window and door location, appropriate room size, and practical and accent lighting plans. In new construction and remodeling, try to make your floor plan and furniture choices simultaneously, to avoid common design problems, such as traffic corridors running through a formal space or awkward locations of electrical outlets.

CREATE THE BEST CLIENT-DESIGNER RELATIONSHIP

Talk to the best interior designers in the area and they'll tell you how exciting and gratifying it is for them when a client is involved in the process. This is happening as more homeowners turn their attention to hearth and home, dedicating their time and resources to achieve a style they love.

Define your needs, in terms of service and the end result. Have an interior designer involved during the architectural drawing phase of a new or renovation project, and get the process started early. Be clear about how much help you want from a designer. Some homeowners have a strong sense of what they want and simply need a consultant-type relationship. Others want significant guidance from a professional who will oversee the entire process.

Set up a relationship that encourages an open exchange of ideas. In pursuit of personal style, you need to trust a professional designer to interpret your

---

FIVE THINGS YOU SHOULD KNOW

1. Know what level of guidance you want: a person to handle every detail, someone to collaborate with you or simply an occasional consultation.
2. Know what you're trying to achieve. Start an Idea Notebook, filling it with pictures of rooms you like and don't like. This will help you define your style and stay true to your goal.
3. Know your budget. Prices of high-end furnishings know no upper limit. Adopt a "master plan" to phase in design elements if your tastes are outpacing your pocketbook.
4. Know what's going on. Always ask; don't assume. Design is not a mystical process.
5. Know yourself. Don't get blinded by beauty. Stay focused on what makes you feel "at home," and you'll be successful.

thoughts and needs. You must be comfortable saying, "No, I don't like that," and receptive to hearing, "I don't think that's a good idea."

Be forthcoming about your budget. Not all interiors are guided by a budget, but the majority are. Your designer must know and respect your financial parameters and priorities. If a gorgeous dining room table is a top priority, objets d' art can be added later as you find them. Prices of exquisite furniture, custom-carved cabinets, and other high-end furnishings know no upper limit. Be realistic about what you will spend and what you expect to achieve. Do some research in furniture stores and specialty shops, starting with those showcased in this book.

Be inquisitive as the design unfolds. This is a creative effort on your behalf, so let yourself enjoy it, understand it and be stimulated by it.

START THINKING VISUALLY: STOP, LOOK AND CLIP

Before you start scheduling initial interviews with interior designers, start compiling an Idea Notebook – it's the best tool for developing an awareness of your personal style. Spend a weekend or two with a pair of scissors, a notebook, and a stack of magazines, (or add a section to the Idea Notebook you made to inspire your architecture and building plans). Make this a record of your personal style. Include pictures of your favorite rooms, noting colors, fabrics, tile, carpet, fixtures, the way light filters through a curtain, anything that strikes your fancy. On those pictures, circle the design elements that you'd like to incorporate into your own home décor and make comments regarding those elements you don't care for. Think hard about what you love and loathe in your current residence. Start to look at the entire environment as a rich source of design ideas. Movies, billboards, architecture, clothing – all are fascinating sources for visual stimulation.

Then, when you hold that initial meeting, you, too, will have a book of ideas to share. Although a smart designer will be able to coax this information from you, it's tremendously more reliable to have visual representations than to depend on a verbal description. It also saves a tremendous amount of time.

THE INTERIOR DESIGN PROCESS: GETTING TO KNOW YOU

Give yourself time to interview at least two interior designers. Invite them to your home for a tour of your current residence and a look at items you wish to use in the new environment. If you're building

TIME TO REDESIGN

The example below gives a general estimate of the costs involved in redesigning a 15 x 22 sq. ft. living room in a mid-scale price range.

Initial consultation: $500
Cost per hour (5 hour minimum): $100/hr
New rug (oriental or custom): $8,000
Furniture: Transitional (contemporary upholstery, traditional wood pieces)
Sofa, $3,000
Chairs (2), $1,000 ea.
Coffee table, $2,000
End tables (2), $1,000 ea.
Sofa table, $2,000
French Be'rgre chair, $3,000
Lamps (1 bronze, 2 porcelain): $1,200
Lighted wall sconces: $1,000
Artwork: $2,000
New paint (labor and paint): $1,500
Accessories: $3,000

Total: $31,700

or remodeling, an interior designer can be helpful with your overall plans when he or she is given the opportunity to get involved early in the building process.

During the initial meeting, count on your intuition to guide you toward the best designer for you. Decorating a home is an intimate and very personal experience, so a comfortable relationship with a high degree of trust is absolutely necessary for a good result. You may adore what a designer did for a friend, but if you can't easily express your ideas, or if you feel he or she isn't interested in your point of view, don't pursue the relationship. Unless you can imagine yourself working with a designer two or three homes from now, keep interviewing.

You may wish to hire a designer for one room before making a commitment to do the whole house.

Some designers maintain a high degree of confidentiality regarding their clients, but if possible, get references and contact them, especially clients with whom they've worked on more than one home. Be sure to ask about the quality of follow-up service.

Be prepared to talk in specific terms about your project, and to honestly assess your lifestyle. For a home or a room to work well, function must be considered along with the evolving style. Designers ask many questions; some of them may be:

• What function should each room serve? Will a living room double as a study? Will a guest room also be an exercise area?

• What kind of relationship do you want to establish between the interior and the landscape?

• Style: Formal, casual or a bit of both?

• Are you comfortable with color?

• Are you naturally organized or disorganized?

• What kind of art do you like? Do you own art that needs to be highlighted or displayed in a certain way? Do you need space for a growing collection?

• Do you feel at home in a dog-eared, low maintenance family room or do you soothe your soul in an opulent leather chair, surrounded by rich cabinetry and Oriental rugs?

• What kind of furniture do you like? Queen Anne, Contemporary, American Arts and Crafts, casual wicker, or eclectic mixing of styles?

• What words describe the feeling you want to achieve? Cheerful, cozy, tranquil, elegant, classic?

PROFESSIONAL DESIGNATIONS

ASID (American Society of Interior Designers)
Ohio/North
3528 Tuttle Ave.
Cleveland, OH
44111
Phone:
216-941-3714
Fax: 216-941-3503
www.asidohn-chapter.org

ASID (American Society of Interior Designers)
Ohio/South/
Kentucky
P.O. Box 498748
Cincinnati, OH
45249
Phone:
800-530-ASID
Fax: 800-530-ASID
www.asidohky.org

IIDA (International Interior Design Association)
International Headquarters
998 Merchandise Mart
Chicago, IL 60654
312.467.1950
www.iida.org
email:
IIDAhq@iida.org
Offers referrals to Central Ohio homeowners.

Designers who add ASID or IIDA after their names are certified members of the organization.

COMPUTING THE INTERIOR DESIGN FEE

Designers use individual contracts, standard contracts drawn up by the American Society of Interior Designers (ASID), or letters of agreements as legal documents. The ASID contract outlines seven project phases – programming, schematic, design development, contract documents, contract administration, project representation beyond basic services, and additional services. It outlines the designer's special responsibilities, the owner's responsibilities, the fees agreed upon, and the method of payments to the designer, including reimbursement of expenses.

Payment deadlines vary. Payments may be due at the completion of each project phase, on a monthly or quarterly basis, or as orders are made. You can usually expect to pay a retainer or a 50 percent deposit on goods as they are ordered, 40 percent upon the start of installation, and the balance when the job is completed.

Design fees, which may be based on "current market rate," are also computed in various ways. They may be charged on a flat fee or hourly basis, or may be tied to retail costs. Expect fees of approximately $100 an hour, varying by experience, reputation and workload. A designer's fee may also be commission-based, which is when a percentage of the cost of the project is added to compensate the designer. When charging by the fixed or hourly fee methods, designers may also add commission to items they purchase for the project. A designer's fees may also be based on the square footage of the area to be designed or decorated. Make sure you understand your fee structure early on.

If you work with a designer at a retail store, a design service fee ranging from $100 to $500 may be charged and applied against purchases.

FROM THE MIND'S EYE TO REALITY

Once you've found a designer who you like and trust, and have signed a clear, specific agreement, you're ready to embark on the adventure.

A good designer knows his or her way around the masses of products and possibilities. Such a person will guide you through upscale retail outlets and to craftspeople known only to a fortunate few in the trade. You can be a "kid in a candy store."

Just as you've allowed time to carefully consider and reconsider architectural blueprints, temper your enthusiasm to rush into decisions regarding your interiors. Leave fabric swatches where you see them day after day. Look at paint samples in daylight,

IMMERSE YOURSELF

The more exposure you have to good design, the easier it becomes to develop your own style.
• Haunt the bookstores that have large selections of shelter magazines and stacks of books on decorating, design and architecture.
• Attend show houses, especially the Designer Showcase homes presented twice annually by ASID, and visit model homes, apartments or lofts.

211

EMBRACE THE MASTER PLAN

Gone are the days when area home-owners felt the need to move into a "finished" interior. They take their time now, letting the flow of their evolving lifestyle and needs guide them along the way.

evening light and artificial light. If possible, have everyone in the family "test sit" a kitchen chair for a week before ordering the whole set, and play with furniture placement. This small investment of time will pay handsomely in the end.

Be prepared to wait for your interiors to be installed. It's realistic to allow eight months to complete a room, and eight to 12 months to decorate an entire home.

Decide if you want your interiors to be installed piecemeal or all at once. Many designers recommend waiting for one installation, if you have the patience. Homeowners tend to rethink their original decisions when pieces are brought in as they arrive. By waiting for one installation, they treat themselves to a stunning visual and emotional thrill. ■

Interior
Designers

CHRISTY ROMOSER INTERIORS ....**(614) 798–1900**
6482 Fiesta Drive, Columbus   Fax:(614) 798–1130
See ad on page: 214, 215
Principal/Owner: Christy Romoser
Website: www.christyromoserinteriors.com e-mail: crinterior@aol.com
Additional Information: Over twenty–five years in the profession, being the interpreter of people's dreams and imaginations.

CREATIONS INTERIOR DESIGN ....**(614) 291–9234**
765 Summit Street, Columbus   Fax:(614) 291–9254
See ad on page: 220
Principal/Owner: John Wilson
e-mail: creationsinteriors@earthlink.net Additional Information: Specializing in artistic, comfortable interiors that are everything but ordinary.

DARRONS OF ARLINGTON ....**(614) 486–4322**
1325 West Lane Avenue, Columbus   Fax:(614) 486–1883
See ad on page: 218
Principal/Owner: Ron & Darryl Haas
Website: www.darrons.com e-mail: mail@darrons.com

DAVID FRANKLIN LTD. ....**(614) 338–0833**
2216 East Main Street, Columbus   Fax:(614) 338–1702
See ad on page: 230, 231, 492b, 492c
Principal/Owner: David J. Franklin Kelley
Website: www.davidfranklinltd.com e-mail: dfltd@aol.com

DESIGN STUDIO, THE ....**(614) 488–7263**
1409 West Third Avenue, Columbus   Fax:(614) 488–7264
See ad on page: 234, 235
Principal/Owner: Dennis Blankemeyer
Website: www.americanfurnishings.com e-mail: amerfurn@aol.com
Additional Information: The Design Studio is an architectural & interior design firm specializing in well crafted residential projects across the Midwest.

DEBORAH DISTELHORST INTERIORS, INC. ....**(614) 268–0710**
2607 Glen Echo Drive, Columbus   Fax:(614) 268–0904
See ad on page: 216
Principal/Owner: Laura J. Casella

ELEGANT REFLECTIONS..**(614) 792–1154**
10869 Buckingham Place, Powell   Fax:(614) 792–1996
See ad on page: 229
Principal/Owner: Laura Jackson

213

christy
romoser
interiors

allied ASID
6482 fiesta drive
columbus, OH 43235
614-798-1900
614-798-1130 Fax

www.christyromoserinteriors.com

Interior Photos by Christopher Casella.

Everyone has their own unique taste and style. Deborah Distelhorst Interiors, Inc. will focus on guiding you in turning your house into a comfortable and functional home. We cater to the needs of our clients, from a simple consultation to a total design project. For our 25 years we have been helping our clients feel proud to share their home with family and friends.

Deborah Distelhorst Interiors, Inc.
Laura J Casella
614-268-0710
ASID, Allied Member

Dennis R. McAvena & Associates, Inc.

Dennis McAvena, Allied ASID
Gayle Schaffer Kreutzfeld, FASID

BLT Productions,
Brent Turner, Cols, OH

12338 Morse Road SW • Pataskala, Ohio 43062
Tel: 740-927-4470 • Fax: 740-927-4480

We Make Your Dreams Come True.

Joan Ball

Betty Carter

Van Shephard
Allied A.S.I.D

Gloria Gephart

Lombards has been making home furnishing dreams come true for three generations of satisfied customers. We can do the same for you.

Bea Foster
Allied A.S.I.D

Lombards' talented staff of experienced designers looks forward to assisting you with your home furnishings needs-whether it's an accessory, a single room or your entire home. At Lombards, sharing fresh thoughts and original ideas with you is our specialty. Lombards' designers skillfully weave your needs and lifestyle with their artistry and talents to create a home that's uniquely yours-functional, flexible and fashionable. So come into Lombards today. We'll help you create a home that's a visual delight and a source of unending pride.

Mary Kay Piras
Allied A.S.I.D.

Tracey Estell-Horton
Allied A.S.I.D

Sharon Danyi
Allied A.S.I.D

David Mc Kiernan
Allied A.S.I.D.

Lombards
FURNITURE GALLERIES

2060 Bethel Rd., Two mile West of Route 315 • Columbus, Ohio 43235 •
(614) 459-2989 • Mon, Wed, Thu 10-9; Tue, Fri, Sat 10-6

CREATIONS
Interior Design
by
John Wilson

765 Summit Street

Columbus, OH 43215

614•291•9234

614•291•9254 F

Specializing in Artistic, Comfortable Interiors

that are Everything but Ordinary

DEBORAH DISTELHORST INTERIORS, INC.

Laura J. Casella: "Our client's pre – teen daughter wanted a comfortable room to grow with. We brought the outdoors in by using a floral wallcovering and painting clouds on the ceiling. Using an existing quilt, we selected coordinating fabrics with many colors, including everything from soft pastels to vibrant splashes. She had her heart set on a canopy bed, but the clipped ceiling did not allow for it, so we created our own, by attaching a custom – built canopy to the ceiling. Now her room is a relaxing place to study as well as 'hang out' with friends. It's this girl's favorite room in the house."

Photo by **Christopher Casella**

Desi

DENNIS R. MC AVENA & ASSOCIATES, INC.

Dennis McAvena: "These particular clients reside in an older home, and asked that we honor the traditional architecture and symmetry. They enjoy a wide variety of styles and accessories. Our challenge was a dual one – create a setting for their sophisticated taste, and provide a scheme for winter and summer months. This photo shows the room during the warm summer months, where rugs are removed to expose the simple, but beautifully toned wood floors. The window coverings are treated simply with Chinese grass shades to diffuse light. The upholstered pieces have been slip covered in soft white cotton fabric and accessories are simple, to contribute to the tranquil order."

ners

Photo by **Brad Simmons Photography**

224

CHRISTY ROMOSER INTERIORS

Christy Romoser: "Hot, intense, torrid — the fiery hues add an exotic character to this comfortable reading area. The high — gloss lacquered cabinet contrasts with the generously proportioned leather upholstery. Hand — carved artifacts from Indonesia and Africa introduce a primitive influence."

Desi

DAVID FRANKLIN, LTD.

David Franklin: "This urban library is a very pleasing blend of distinct architectural motifs. The antique furniture and accessories are fine examples from England, France and China. I think the room reveals, in a quietly eloquent manner, a happy combination of different styles and periods."

CREATIONS, INTERIOR DESIGN BY JOHN WILSON

John Wilson: "The best thing about doing children's rooms is the ability to use lots of color, and this little girl's room is a perfect example of that. The bright blue walls were enhanced with playful bugs, and pink accents were used to tie everything together. Her doll collection is housed in a beautiful case that looks like a house, while all of her Madelines watch carefully from the shelf. This little girl can't help but feel happy every time she closes her eyes."

225

Photo by **Al Laus**

ners

GRAND DESIGN GROUP

Pamela Vost: " 'A quiet retreat' was the direction we were given for designing this room. We chose a soft color palette of pale yellow, taupe and white to provide an overall serene feeling, and added luxury bedding and a collection of original artwork to entice the senses. We dressed the oversized window with a fluid treatment of plaid silk that frames the beautiful view, and placed a chaise lounge nearby for the perfect place to read or enjoy the view."

Photo by **Bryan Barr**

226

Desi

LOMBARD'S FURNITURE GALLERIES

Bea Foster: "Small rooms can be fun and cozy, with the right mix of texture and style. The Empire style chairs, with double caning and a soft red striped silk fabric, were combined with an elegant yet simple hand-carved loveseat. The velvet accent pillows, detailed with hand-beading, add a touch of whimsy to the room. The richly carved detailing of the wood occasional tables enhances the beauty of the room. The emphasis here is on quality and comfort, with warmth and interest added to a very elegant retreat."

LOMBARDS FURNITURE GALLERIES

Sharon Danyi: "This room was designed with livability in mind. Comfort was a must, with French styling updated for today's home. Larger scaled pieces were used to create a clean look, in proportion with the home's architecture. The soft textures of velvet and tapestry combine for a look of casual elegance. Subtle greens and corals were used with a neutral background to create a pleasing ambiance. This room emits a warmth and welcome, inviting you in for a glass of wine with guests, or alone time with a favorite novel."

Finally...
Central Ohio's Own
Home & Design
Sourcebook

The **Central Ohio Home Book** is your final destination
when searching for home remodeling, building and decorating
resources. This comprehensive, hands-on sourcebook to building,
remodeling, decorating, furnishing and landscaping a luxury home
is required reading for the serious and discriminating homeowner.
With more than 500 full-color, beautiful pages, the **Central Ohio
Home Book** is the most complete and well-organized reference
to the home industry. This hardcover volume covers all aspects of
the process, includes listings of hundreds of industry professionals,
and is accompanied by informative and valuable editorial discussing
the most recent trends. Ordering your copy of the **Central Ohio
Home Book** now can ensure that you have the blueprints to
your dream home, in your hand, today.

O R D E R   F O R M

THE CENTRAL OHIO HOME BOOK

☐ YES, please send me _____ copies of the CENTRAL OHIO HOME BOOK at $39.95 per book, plus $4 Shipping & Handling per book.

Total amount enclosed: $_____   Please charge my: ☐ VISA   ☐ MasterCard   ☐ American Express

Card # _____   Exp. Date _____

Signature: _____

Name _____   Phone: (_____) _____

Address _____   E-mail: _____

City _____   State _____   Zip Code _____

Send order to: Attn: Book Sales – Marketing, The Ashley Group – Reed Business, 2000 Clearwater Drive, Oak Brook, IL 60523
Or Call Toll Free: 888.458.1750 Fax: 630.288.7949 E-mail ashleybooksales@reedbusiness.com

All orders must be accompanied by check, money order or credit card # for full amount.

Elegant Reflections

INTERIOR DESIGN

10869 Buckingham Place ~ Pomell, OH 43065
Phone: 614.792.1154   Fax: 614.792.1996

2216 Main Street · Columbus, Ohio 43209 · (614)338-0833

Landa's INTERDESIGN

The Inventive Design Studio

49 East College
Westerville, Ohio 43081
P: 614.899.1773
F: 614.899.2030

Linda Riley Design

design for functional interiors

Building a quality client relationship and offering a range of innovative solutions creates an interior environment meeting your functional needs and aesthetic goals.

817 McDonell Drive   Gahanna, Ohio 43230
tel/fax: 614.475.1502   e-mail: lriley2000@core.com

Residential • Commercial • Specialty Spaces • Historic Restoration

Photos top & bottom left courtesy of Brian T. Schindle/CREATIVE MOMENTS

GRAND DESIGN GROUP ....**(614) 228–4900**
309 South Fourth Street, Suite 100, Columbus   Fax:(614) 228–5110
See ad on page: 206d
Principal/Owner: Pamela Yost, Allied ASID
Website: www.granddesigngroup.com   e-mail: gdgpamyost@aol.com

LANDA'S INTERDESIGN ....**(614) 899–1773**
49 East Collage Avenue, Westerville   Fax:(614) 899–2030
See ad on page: 232
Principal/Owner: Landa Masdea Brunetto IDS
e-mail: labru7@juno.com
Additional Information: Winner (COTY) Regional Contractor of the Year Award 1999–2002
through NARI. President Central–Ohio (NARI) National Association of the Remodeling Industry
2001–2002 Specializing in New Build Consultations & Tile Design.

LOMBARDS FURNITURE GALLERIES ....**(614) 459–2989**
2060 Bethel Road, Columbus   Fax:(614) 459–3925
See ad on page: 219, 452
Principal/Owner: Judy & Fred Heer
Website: www.lombardsinteriors.com   e-mail: lombards1@ameritech.net

DENNIS R. MCAVENA & ASSOCIATES, INC. ....**(740) 927–4470**
12338 Morse Road SW, Pataskala   Fax:(740) 927–4480
See ad on page: 206b, 206c, 217
Principal/Owner: Dennis R. McAvena
Additional Information: Dennis McAvena & Associates is a nationally recognized interior design
studio. We have been in business 10 years and take pride in our ability to
accommodate many design styles.

MILLER VAN ORDER INTERIOR DESIGN ....**(614) 224–0001**
527 North Park Street, Columbus   Fax:(614) 224–0844
See ad on page: 221
Principal/Owner: Richard Miller

LINDA RILEY DESIGN ....**(614) 475–1502**
817 McDonell Drive, Gahanna   Fax:(614) 475–1502
See ad on page: 233
Principal/Owner:
e-mail: lriley2000@core.com   Additional Information: Design for functional interiors.

Photo courtesy of **James Burkart Associates, Inc.**

LANDSCAPING

Transform your landscape vision into beautiful reality with Urban Environments' site development professionals.

Landscape Design,

Installation,

Renovation and

Estate Gardening...

Beyond the Expected!

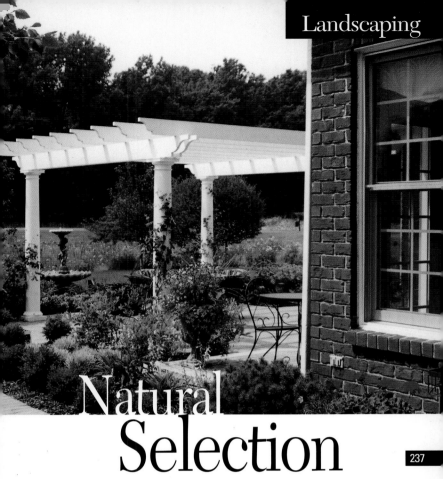

Natural
Selection

Landscaping is the only design area that is, by nature, intended to evolve over time. The philosophy behind landscape design has evolved as well. There are various styles for your unique landscape design statement. These include traditional European formality, the naturalism of Prairie Style or the simplicity and order of Far Eastern influences.

More and more people are blurring the divisions between inside and outside environments, with expanses of windows, patios designed to act as "outdoor rooms," and various types of glass and screened enclosures to enjoy the outdoors whatever the weather. Landscape becomes almost an architectural element at times, creating an interplay and synthesis of indoors and outdoors.

Water gardens are growing in popularity as people learn that these are ecosystems in their own right, requiring little additional time or attention once they are established. Think of it: the soothing splash of a waterfall or babbling brook right in your own backyard!

Photo courtesy of **Finlandscapes, Inc.**

GETTING BACK TO THE GARDEN

Think of the land as a canvas for a work of environmental art. Think of the landscape professional as an artist who uses nature to translate your needs and desires into a living, breathing reality. A formal English garden or seemingly artless arrangements of native plantings, a winding cobblestone walkway leading from a hand-laid brick driveway – these are the kinds of possibilities you can explore. When you work with a professional who is personally committed to superior work and service, designing a landscape is full of creativity, new ideas and satisfying results.

GETTING A LANDSCAPE STARTED

Selecting a landscape professional to create and maintain a distinctive landscape is one of the most important decisions you'll make as a homeowner. In making your decision, consider these questions:

• Do you want to hire a landscape architect or a landscape designer? Landscape architects have met the criteria to be registered by the state. Many hold university degrees in landscape architecture. A landscape designer generally has had training and/or experience in horticulture and landscaping and may also have a background in art.

• Do you want full service? If you want to work with one source, from design to installation to maintenance, only consider those who offer comprehensive service.

Allow approximately one month to interview at least two professionals before making a decision. Start even earlier if you plan to install a swimming pool, which should be dug the same time as the foundation of a new home.

Invite the professional to your home to acquaint him or her with your tastes and personality. Be prepared to answer questions like:

• Do you prefer a formal or informal feel? The formality of symmetrical plantings or the informal look of a natural area?

• Is there a place or feeling you'd like to recreate? Summers spent at the cottage? Your childhood home?

• What colors do you like? Your answer may impact the flowers chosen for your gardens.

• Are you a gardener? Would you like to be? If you're fond of flower, herb or vegetable gardening, your landscape professional will plan and build the appropriate garden.

THE VISION

First you choose your views, then you build your home. To create a harmonious balance between your home and its surroundings, your architect should be invited to visit the site of your new home, and to meet with your landscape architect. The site can often serve as a catalyst, inspiring a design that responds to the uniqueness of the site. When all the team members are included, important details can be discussed and settled, leading to best results for you and your family.

A PARTY OF GARDENS

As gardening attracts more devotees, people are rediscovering the satisfaction of creating imaginative gardens. Some ideas: butterfly gardens, fragrance gardens, moonlight gardens and Japanese gardens.

• How will you use the space? Will children use the backyard for recreation? Will you entertain outdoors? If so, will it be during the day or at night? Do you envision a pool, spa, gazebo or tennis courts there?

• Are you fond of lawn statuary, fountains or other ornamental embellishments?

• What architectural features must be considered? A wrap-around porch, large picture windows? Brick or stone exteriors?

• To what extent will you be involved in the process? Most landscape architects and designers are happy to encourage your involvement in this labor of love. There is a great deal of pleasure to be derived from expressing your personality through the land. A lifelong hobby can take root from this experience. Landscapers say their clients often join garden clubs after the completion of their project, and that many of their rehabbing jobs are done for clients who are already avid gardeners.

Landscape professionals expect that you will want to see a portfolio and inquire about their styles and experience. You may wish to request permission to visit sites of their installed landscapes. If you have special concerns, such as environmental issues, ask if the landscape professional has any experience in such areas.

COMPUTING LANDSCAPE FEES

It's easy to be caught off guard when you get a landscape proposal – it is a significant investment. Therefore, be sure you create a workable budget with your landscape professional before the project begins.

To give the outside of your home the appropriate priority status, plan to invest 10 to 25 percent of the cost of a new home and property in the landscaping. Although landscape elements can be phased in year after year, expect that the majority of the cost will be incurred in the first year. Maintenance costs must also be considered.

Billing practices vary among professionals and depend on the extent of the services you desire. Some charge a one-time fee for a contract that includes everything, some charge a flat design fee up front, others charge a design fee which is waived if you select them to complete the project, and still others build a design fee into the installation and/or maintenance cost.

THE PRICE OF BEING GREEN

What might it cost to create a new paver patio and walk, retaining wall and 600 sq. ft. of new planting beds along the front foundation? Design contract fees - $500 Cut Lanonstone retaining wall (85 face sq. ft.) - $4,130 Concrete paver patio and walkway (480 sq. ft.) - $7,785 Planting development (600 sq. ft.) - $9,000 Includes shrubs, four mid-size trees, perennials, annual beds and sod. Landscape management of one-half acre site for one season - $3,648 Weekly mowing, trimming and disposal; monthly pavement edging; monthly cultivation of open beds; preventative weed control; granular fertilization of beds; pruning; weekly dead heading of faded flowers, groundcover maintenance, turf fertilization.

Total - $25,063

A PROFESSIONAL DEVELOPS AN ENVIRONMENT

While you're busy imagining glorious gardens, your landscaper will be assessing practical issues like grading and drainage, the location of sewers, utility lines and existing trees, where and when the sun hits the land and the quality of the soil.

This important first step, the site analysis, should take place before construction has even begun, in the case of a new house. Site work helps ensure that the blueprints for your house won't make your landscape dreams impossible to achieve, and vice versa. If you've told your builder you want a breakfast nook, you'll probably get one regardless of the fact that it requires taking out a tree you value.

If you're considering installing a custom driveway or sidewalk, this early stage is the time to inform your builder. Ask your builder not to do construction outside the building envelope. You and your landscape professionals should design and build your driveway and walkways.

Expect the design process to take at least six weeks. During this time, the designer is developing a plan for the hardscape, which includes all of the man-made elements of your outdoor environment, and the many layers of softscape, which are the actual plantings. You can expect to be presented with a plan view that is workable and in harmony with your home, as well as your budget.

Hardscape elements, like irrigation systems and pavements, will be installed first, before a new house is completely finished. Softscape will go in later.

At the end of the first phase of your project, do not be surprised if the land does not look "complete." A landscape should be given time in the hands of nature to mature: three years for perennials, five years for shrubs and 15 years for trees.

LUXURY LIVING WITH A CUSTOM-DESIGNED POOL

The beauty and value of a custom-designed swimming pool are unmatched. A welcome design element to the landscape, a pool adds to the overall property value of the residence and creates greater use and enjoyment of the yard. As area families spend more of their leisure time at home, a pool answers their dreams of living well at home.

Deciding to build a swimming pool is best done as a new home is being designed so the pool can enhance the home and landscape architecture. By integrating the pool into the overall scheme, you'll be able to establish a realistic budget. One of the biggest mistakes homeowners make when purchasing

LIGHTING YOUR LOT

"Less is more" is the best philosophy when designing an outdoor lighting system. Today's beautiful, functional fixtures are themselves worthy of admiration, but their purpose is to highlight the beauty of your home while providing safe access to your property. Well-established lighting companies and specialty companies offer extensive landscape lighting product lines.

THE FINAL EVALUATION

When the landscape is installed, conduct a final, on-site evaluation. You should evaluate the finished design, find out what elements will be installed later and learn more about how the plan will evolve over time. You, the landscape designer or architect, project manager, and maintenance manager should be involved.

a pool is not initially getting all the features they want. It's difficult and costly to add features later.

The design process is time consuming. You may have four or more meetings with your pool professional before finalizing the design. Pool projects can be started at almost any time of year, so avoid getting caught in the busy season, spring to summer. Start getting approvals in January if you want to be enjoying your pool in the summer. The building process takes about two months, after obtaining permits. You should plan to have your pool dug at the same time as the home foundation. Pools are often accompanied by surrounding decks, so make sure your landscape architect, pool builder and hardscape contractor are coordinating efforts to construct both.

OUTDOOR LIVING

Today's homeowners, having invested the time and resources to create a spectacular environment, are ready to "have it all" in their own backyards.

Popular features of today's upscale homes include outdoor living rooms, screened rooms, gazebos and custom-made jungle gyms that will grow with your children. The extended living space perfectly suits our "cocooning" lifestyle, offering more alternatives for entertaining, relaxation and family time at home. Many new homes tout outdoor living space as a most tantalizing feature.

Multi-level terraces and decks offer extra living space and are functional enough to host almost any occasion. With thoughtful and proper design, they fulfill our dreams of an outdoor getaway spot. A multi-level deck built up and around mature trees can feel like a tree house. A spa built into a cedar deck, hidden under a trellis, can give you the feel of being in a far-off paradise.

Landscaping features that will compliment your outdoor living space include Koi ponds and imaginative theme gardens, such as moonlight, Zen, butterfly, fragrance, two-color and native plant gardens.

With so many options available, outdoor living provides a unique opportunity for homeowners to give their creativity free. However, consult with your landscape architect and contractor before deciding on these outdoor features. Some outdoor living space and garden options will function better than others, depending on what area of the country you reside in.

THINKING ABOUT OUTDOOR LIVING

If you're interested in pursuing any of the ideas mentioned above, then the first step is to arrange an on-site meeting with a landscape architect or a

EVERY KID'S FANTASY

In a yard with plenty of flat area: A wood construction expandable play system with: several slides, bridges to connect structures, a tic-tac-toe play panel, three to four swings, climbing ropes, fire pole, gymnastics equipment (trapeze, turning bar), sandbox pit, and a built-in picnic table with benches. Price Tag: around $26,000

In a smaller yard: a wood construction expandable play system with: a small fort, three swings, climbing ropes and two slides. Price Tag: around $6,500

241

GARDENER'S EDENS

Visit these artistic gardens for ideas and inspiration.

Franklin Park Conservatory
1777 E. Broad St.
Columbus, OH
43202
614.645.1800
www.fp
conservatory.org

Topiary Garden
480 E. Town St.
Columbus, OH
43215
614.645.0197

A TYPICAL LANDSCAPE DESIGN TIMETABLE

- **One to two weeks to get the project on the boards**

+

- **One to two weeks to do the actual site and design work and prepare plans**

+

- **One week to coordinate calendars and schedule presentation meeting**

+

- **One to two weeks to leave the plans with the client and get their feedback**

+

- **One week to incorporate changes, create and get approval on a final design**

=

FIVE TO EIGHT WEEKS

WHY YOU NEED AN ARBORIST

It's not just your kids, dogs and the neighborhood squirrels trampling through your yard during construction. Excavation equipment, heavy trucks and work crews can spell disaster for your trees. Call an arborist before any equipment is scheduled to arrive and let him develop a plan that will protect the trees, or remove them if necessary.

licensed contractor who is an expert in landscape building. An experienced professional will guide you through the conceptualization by asking questions like these:

- Why are you building the structure or specialty garden? For business entertaining, family gatherings, child or teen parties, private time?

- Do you envision a secluded covered area, a wide open expanse or both?

- Do you want a single level or two or more levels (the best option for simultaneous activities)?

- Will it tie in with current or future plans?

- How do you want to landscape the perimeter?

- Do you want a chiminea to be included in your outdoor living room, a certain variety of sand for your Zen garden or specific wood used in creating your gazebo?

Don't let obstacles block your thinking. Your gas grill can be moved. Decks are often built around trees and can convert steep slopes into usable space.

Once a design has been settled upon, expect at least three to four weeks to pass before a gazebo or other living space is completed. In the busy spring and summer months, it most likely will take longer. The time required to get a building permit (usually two to four weeks) must also be considered.

If you're landscaping during this time, be sure to coordinate the two projects well in advance. Building can wreck havoc on new plantings and your lawn will be stressed during construction.

DISTINCTIVE OUTDOOR SURFACES

Driveways, walkways, patios and hardscape features were once relegated to "last minute" status, with a budget to match. Today they are being given the full and careful attention they deserve. A brick paver driveway can be made to blend beautifully with the color of the brick used on the house. Natural brick stairways and stoops laid by master crafters add distinctive detail and value. Custom-cut curved bluestone steps, hand selected by an experienced paving contractor, provide years of pride and pleasure.

Hardscape installation doesn't begin until your new home is nearly complete, but for your own budgeting purposes, have decisions made no later than home mid-construction phase.

To interview a paving or hardscape contractor, set up an on-site meeting so you can discuss the nature of the project and express your ideas. Be ready to answer questions like:

• Will the driveway be used by two or three cars, or more? Do you need it to be wide enough so cars can pass? Will you require extra parking? Would you like a circular driveway? A basketball court?

• Will the patio be used for entertaining? Will it be a family or adult area, or both? How much furniture will you use? Should it be accessible from a particular part of the house?

• Do you have existing or future landscaping that needs to be considered?

• Would you like to incorporate special touches, like a retaining wall or a stone archway?

If you're working with a full service landscape professional, and hardscape is part of the landscape design, be certain a hardscape expert will do the installation. A specialist's engineering expertise and product knowledge are vital to the top quality result you want. ■

SOURCES

Ohio Chapter, American Society of Landscape Architects
1555 Lake Shore Dr.
Columbus, OH 43204
614.224.7145
www.ocasla.org

Columbus Chapter, Wild Ones Natural Landscapers, Ltd.
614.939.9273
www.for-wild.org/columbus

Landscape
Contractors

BENCHMARK LANDSCAPE CONSTRUCTION INC. ....**(614) 462–8080**
9600 Industrial Parkway, Plain City   Fax:(614) 873–8060
See ad on page: 258, 259
Principal/Owner: Mark Chamberlain, Ed Veley
Website: www.benchmarkohio.com

BETTERWAY GARDENING, INC. ....**(614) 492–8733**
3325 Williams Road, Columbus   Fax:(614) 492–0709
See ad on page: 266, 267
Principal/Owner: John Pabst
Website: www.betterwaygardening.com e-mail: betterway@earthlink.net
Additional Information: Design build contractors of distinguished outdoor living spaces.
Renovation, new construction, patios, water gardens, low voltage lighting.

BLENDON GARDENS / POLARIS IRRIGATION ....**(614) 840–0500**
9590 South Old State Road, Lewis Center   Fax:(614) 840–0504
See ad on page: 268, 269
Principal/Owner: Nancy Brelsford

BUCK & SONS LANDSCAPE SERVICE, INC....**(614) 876–5359**
7147 Hayden Run Road, Hilliard   Fax:(614) 876–4991
See ad on page: 256, 257
Principal/Owner: Charles Buck, Steven Buck
Website: www.buckandsons.com e-mail: sales@buckandsons.com
Additional Information: Today, Buck and Sons has a staff of over seventy–five employees
and service clients located throughout central Ohio.

CD BROWN & DESIGN ....**(614) 486–0122**
1287 King Avenue, Suite 202, Columbus   Fax:(614) 485–0403
See ad on page: 263
Principal/Owner: C. Daniel Brown

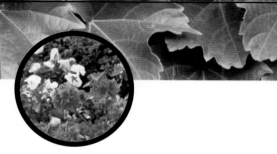

Landscape Design, Installation, Renovation and Estate Gardening...

Beyond the Expected!

Kinman Associates, Inc.
A Landscape Design/Build Firm
7300 Industrial Parkway
Plain City, Ohio 43065

Kinman Associates is trained and founded in the rich tradition of classical Landscape Garden Design. We at Kinman Associates will create your distinctive landscape with the unparalleled sensibility of the beauty and flawless design inherent in nature.

Experience our Design Studio
You are invited to call us for a consultation at our "Idea Center"
at 614-764-8733

KINMAN
ASSOCIATES
THE NATURAL EXTENSION OF ARCHITECTURE

These annuals & more can be found at our retail location:

6470 Lithopolis Rd.
888-652-9551

CROSS CREEK GARDENS

- Gift Shop

- Bulk Top Soil & Mulch

- Custom Potting & Florals

- Full Line of Aquatic Plants & Aquatic Products

- Large Selection of Annuals, Shrubs, Trees & Perennials

- Installations Available & Design Work

- New lines of Pottery, Fountains, Bird Baths

182 N. Sunbury Road • Westerville, OH • P: 614-895-8020 F: 614-895-8464
5211 Johnstown Road • New Albany, OH • P: 614-939-0054

CROSS CREEK GARDENS..**(614) 895–8020**
182 North Sunbury Road, Westerville   Fax:(614) 895–8464
See ad on page: 250
Principal/Owner: Chuck Annis

DRAKE'S LANDSCAPING ....**(614) 761–7880**
8050 McKitrick Road, Plain City   Fax:(614) 873–4228
See ad on page: 274
Principal/Owner: Jim Drake
Additional Information: Established 1986, Landscape design/build, brick/paver patios
and driveways, water features, lighting.

EASTSIDE NURSERY ....**(614) 836–9800**
6723 Lithopolis Rd, Groveport   Fax:(614) 836–0121
See ad on page: 282, 283

ECOSYSTEMS MANAGEMENT ....**(800) 905–5470**
512 Trade Road, Columbus   Fax:(614) 545–0136
See ad on page: 280
Principal/Owner: Shawn Potts

ENVIRONMENTAL MANAGEMENT INC...**(614) 876–9988**
Post Office Box 175, Dublin   Fax:(614) 876–9986
See ad on page: 254
Principal/Owner: Mark Wehinger
Website: www.landscapepros.com

EVERGREEN LANDSCAPING ....**(614) 486–8188**
3235 McKinley Avenue, Columbus   Fax:(614) 486–7178
See ad on page: 278
Principal/Owner: Marc Lerdon

✚ FINLANDSCAPE INC.

Landscape Designers & Builders since 1984

Specializing in European and American Gardens

Telephone 740-927-1994 • www.finlandscape.com

Landscape Structures

Theme Gardens

Hardscaping

Softscaping

"Excellence is the only acceptable outcome"

EMI
Environmental
Management
Inc.

Landscape & Irrigation Construction
Landscape Architecture

P.O. Box 175 • Dublin, Ohio 43017
614.876.9988 • Fax 614.876.9986
www.landscapepros.com

THE
P·A·G·U·R·A

C·O·M·P·A·N·Y

8101 Corporate Boulevard   Plain City, OH 43064
614.873.4007   fax 614.873.0104
www.pagura.com

design, build, maintain

The Pagura Company makes every effort to ensure your relationship
with us is enjoyable and long lasting. We want you to continue
to enjoy your landscapes as they continue to grow and mature
through the years. The materials we use are of the highest quality
and with proper maintenance will provide years of natural beauty.

BUCK & SONS
LANDSCAPE SERVICE, INC.

BENCHMARK

LANDSCAPE CONSTRUCTION INC.

Design & Consultation
Brick Patios, Driveways & Walks
Plant Installation
Water Features
Stone & Timber Walls
Boulder Outcroppings
Flagstone Walks & Patios
Custom Decks, Gazebos & Fences
Low Voltage Lighting
Edging and Mulching
Fertilization Program
Mowing
Annuals and Seasonal Color
On-going Bed Maintenance
Fall Clean Up

9600 INDUSTRIAL PARKWAY
PLAIN CITY, OH 43064
(614) 462-8080

WWW.BENCHMARKOHIO.COM

B.S. Landscape Architecture • The Ohio State University
B.S. Landscape Horticulture • The Ohio State University

FINLANDSCAPE INC. ....**(740) 927–1994**
14352 Clark State Road, Pataskala   Fax:(740) 927–1554
See ad on page: 253
Principal/Owner: Arvo Pikkarainen
Website: www.finlandscape.com e-mail: arvo@finlandscape.com
Additional Information: Landscape designers and builders since 1984 specializing in
European and American gardens.

GREENSCAPES LANDSCAPE COMPANY, INC. ....**(614) 837–1869**
4220 Winchester Pike, Columbus   Fax:(614) 837–2393
See ad on page: 272, 273
Principal/Owner: William Gerhardt
Website: www.greenscapes.net e-mail: info@greenscapes.net
Additional Information: Greenscapes is a full service award winning landscape
design/build/maintenance company serving the greater Columbus area since 1975.

HIDDEN CREEK LANDSCAPING, INC. ....**(614) 542–4254**
1670–B Harman Avenue, Columbus   Fax:(614) 542–4255
See ad on page: 281
Principal/Owner: Jason Cromley

KELLER FARMS ....**(614) 866–9551**
3909 Graves Road, Columbus   Fax:(614) 866–9602
See ad on page: 248, 249
Principal/Owner: Bernard W. Fleming
Website: www.kellerfarmslandscaping.com e-mail: kfleming@kellerfarmslandscaping.com

KINGSCAPES, INC. ....**(740) 965–5464**
4900 Redbank Road, Galena
See ad on page: 284
Principal/Owner: Daniel King
Website: www.kingscapes.com e-mail: dan4king@earthlink.net

TIMBERWOOD
LANDSCAPE COMPANY
Tel: 614.799.0555

c.d. brown design

Landscape Design

Consulting

Contracting

1287 King Avenue
Suite #202
Columbus, Ohio 43212
(614) 486-0122

Peabody
landscape construction

Your home is the
most valuable
personal investment
you will ever make.
By careful planning
we will create a more
pleasant outdoor
living environment
which you and your
family will enjoy for
many years. As well,
proper maintenance
with our professional
services assures that
your colorful landscape
will always be looking
its best throughout
the year.

Quality
is
Our
Priority!

Creative
Residential
Design Build
&
Detailed
Environmental
Site Management

Consumers' Choice
Award™
2001
For
Business Excellence

Better
Way
Gardening
614.492.8733
www.betterwaygardening.com

Stroll Through our

POLARIS
IRRIGATION

(614) 781-9575

<u>Polaris Design Offices:</u>

9590 South Old State Road
Lewis Center, Ohio 43035

Display Gardens

KINMAN & ASSOCIATES, INC..**(614) 764–8733**
7300 Industrial Parkway, Plain City   Fax:(614) 793–0104
See ad on page: 236d, 246, 247
<u>Principal/Owner:</u> Gary Kinman
<u>e-mail:</u> kinman1@aol.com

M & I LANDSCAPES ....**(740) 964–2770**
4311 Dixon Road, Blacklick   Fax:(740) 964–2768
See ad on page: 261
<u>Principal/Owner:</u> Anthony Mampieri

MEYERS LANDSCAPE SERVICES & NURSERY ....**(614) 785–0926**
7719 Holderman Street, Lewis Center
See ad on page: 279
<u>Principal/Owner:</u> Michael L. Meyers
<u>Additional Information:</u> Services provided to resident and commercial owners. We provide free estimates. Services rendered linclude, lawn care, pavers, annuals, landscape design.

PAGURA COMPANY ....**(614) 873–4007**
8101 Corporate Boulevard, Plain City   Fax:(614) 873–0104
See ad on page: 255
<u>Principal/Owner:</u> Steve Pagura
<u>Website:</u> www.pagura.com <u>e-mail:</u> mrpagura@pagura.com
<u>Additional Information:</u> Established in 1979. Over 75 Landscape awards.

PEABODY LANDSCAPE CONSTRUCTION..**(614) 488–2877**
2253 Dublin Road, Columbus   Fax:(614) 488–3543
See ad on page: 264, 265
<u>Principal/Owner:</u> David G. Peabody
<u>Website:</u> www.peabodylandscape.com <u>e-mail:</u> dgpeabody@peabodylandscape.com
<u>Additional Information:</u> Since 1982 we have provided central Ohio with award winning landscape projects. Simply stated "quality is our priority!"

GreenScapes Landscape Co.
Landscape Architects and Contractors
4220 WINCHESTER PIKE • COLUMBUS, OHIO 43232-5612
(614) 837-1869 • Fax (614) 837-2393
w w w . G r e e n S c a p e s . n e t

GreenScapes

- LANDSCAPE ARCHITECTURE
- LANDSCAPE CONSTRUCTION
- LANDSCAPE MAINTENANCE
- WATER FEATURES
- LANDSCAPE LIGHTING
- IRRIGATION SERVICES
- GARDEN STRUCTURES
- HARDSCAPE CONSTRUCTION

Creating beautiful landscapes since 1978.

Drake's Landscaping

Design / Build

At Drakes, our philosophy is simple: Do the job right the first time. Don't cut corners, pay close attention to detail, and treat our customers and their property with respect.

CRAFTSMEN WHO TAKE PRIDE IN QUALITY WORKMANSHIP

614-761-7880

Terra Horticultural Services, Inc.

Landscape Design • Installation

Construction • Maintenance

Tree Service

11515 Taylor Road • Plain City, Ohio 43064
Phone: (614) 470-2543 • Fax: (614) 873-2468

PHARAZYN LANDSCAPING & CONSULTING, INC. ....**(614) 873–4098**
10927 Jerome Road, Plain City   Fax:(614) 873–5980
See ad on page: 251
<u>Principal/Owner:</u> Frank and Jeff Pharazyn
<u>e-mail:</u> pharazynland@mindspring.com <u>Additional Information:</u> Established in 1988

RIEPENHOFF LANDSCAPE, LTD. ....**(614) 876–4683**
3872 Scioto–Darby Creek Road, Hilliard   Fax:(614) 876–4862
See ad on page: 271
<u>Principal/Owner:</u> Steven Purcell
<u>Website:</u> www.riepenhofflandscape.com <u>e-mail:</u> riep@megsinet.net
<u>Additional Information:</u> We are a design–build firm of landscape architects and builders setting the standard since 1975.

STONELEAF LANDSCAPE SERVICES, INC. ....**(614) 261–7233**
508 Chatham Road, Columbus   Fax:(614) 261–9690
See ad on page: 277
<u>Principal/Owner:</u> David Caroselli, Tim Hill
<u>e-mail:</u> stoneleaf@msn.com <u>Additional Information:</u> We specialize in high end custom projects that demand more creativity and hands–on attention to detail.

TERRA HORTICULTURAL SERVICES, INC. ....**(614) 470–2543**
11515 Taylor Road, Plain City   Fax:(614) 873–2468
See ad on page: 275
<u>Principal/Owner:</u> Jeff Stroupe / Kyle Mercer
<u>e-mail:</u> jeffstroupe@peoplepc.com <u>Additional Information:</u> Full service landscape design, construction, installation and tree service company.

TIMBERWOOD LANDSCAPE COMPANY, INC. ....**(614) 799–0555**
4233 Penrith Court, Dublin   Fax:(614) 799–0444
See ad on page: 262
<u>Principal/Owner:</u> Sam Duff

URBAN ENVIRONMENTS INC...**(614) 478–2085**
3001 Innis Road, Columbus   Fax:(614) 478–2086
See ad on page: 236b, 236c, 245
<u>Principal/Owner:</u> Joel Korte
<u>Website:</u> www.urbanenvironments.com <u>e-mail:</u> jkorte@urbanenvironments.com
<u>Additional Information:</u> Urban Environments is a professional contractor providing landscape and irrigation design, installation, renovation and estate gardening services for residential estates.

Design & Construction
Plantings • Stone • Pavers

... A joining of Form, Function, and Life.

Stoneleaf Landscape Services, Inc.
508 Chatham Road
Columbus, Ohio 43214
Phone: (614) 261-7233
Fax: (614) 261-9690
E-Mail: Stoneleaf@msn.com

Stoneleaf Landscape Services, Inc.
satisfies our customers with unique
and interesting solutions, which
promise to fulfill their landscape
goals by incorporating their visions,
inspirations, and anticipating their
needs all while maintaining the
highest standards of service and quality.

OHIO
NURSERY &
LANDSCAPE
ASSOCIATION

Creating Distinctive Outdoor Environments

EVERGREEN
LANDSCAPING

Landscape Design   Construction   Maintenance

3235 McKinley Avenue, Columbus, Ohio 43204

Plants are our Specialty,

Service and Quality are our Priority.

ECO
SYSTEMS
MANAGEMENT
Horticultural & Turfgrass Services

614.545.0135   1.800.905.5470

A TRIUMPH

NO LIMITS

A MOOD FOR EVERY SEASON

SPLENDID

A MAGICAL SPACE

KINGSCAPES, INC.

CUSTOM DESIGN, INSTALLATION & MAINTENANCE

ENHANCE THE VALUE AND BEAUTY OF YOUR HOME
WITH A CUSTOMIZED LANDSCAPE.

REFERENCES AVAILABLE

WE LOVE TO INSTALL, PONDS, WATERFALLS & STREAMS
VISIT OUR WEB SITE AT: **KINGSCAPES.COM** FOR FURTHER
INFORMATION AND PHOTOS OF OUR WORK.

FOR A FREE CONSULTATION, CALL **740.965.5464**

Landscape
Architects

JAMES BURKART ASSOCIATES INC. ....**(614) 486–7186**
1819 West Lane Avenue, Columbus   Fax:(614) 481–7852
See ad on page: 288
Principal/Owner: James Burkart
Website: www.jburkart.com e-mail: jburkart@radar.net

KINZELMAN KLINE, INC. ....**(614) 224–6601**
444 South Front Street, Columbus   Fax:(614) 224–6607
See ad on page: 286
Principal/Owner: Richard McBride
Website: www.kinzelmankline.com e-mail: dmcbride@kinzelmankline.com
Additional Information: Award winning multi–disciplinary firm dedicated to providing superior
professional landscape architecture, architectural and planning services to our clients.

M.J. DESIGN ASSOCIATES, INC. ....**(614) 799–8555**
5634 Claire Court, Dublin   Fax:(614) 760–9883
See ad on page: 289
Principal/Owner: Joel John, Molly John
Website: www.mjdesignassociates.com e-mail: mollyjohn@mjdesignassociates.com

SCHIEBER & ASSOCIATES, INC. ....**(614) 478–7381**
457 D. Waterbury Court, Gahanna   Fax:(614) 478–8028
See ad on page: 287
Principal/Owner: Mark A. Schieber
Website: www.schieberassociates.com e-mail: schieber@lwaynet.net
Additional Information: A studio of landscape architecture & horticulture dedicated to
providing unique, "evolutionary " & practical landscapes that withstand the test of time.

285

KINZELMAN KLINE
landscape architecture and planning

444 South Front Street Columbus, Ohio 43215
P 614 224 6601 F 614 224 6607
www.kinzelmankline.com

BURKART

DISTINCTIVE LANDSCAPE ARCHITECTURE

JAMES BURKART ASSOCIATES, INC.

1819 West Lane Ave.
Columbus, Ohio 43221
Tel 614.486.7186
Fax 614.481.7852
www.jburkart.com   jburkart@radar.net

CREATING CUSTOM SITE ENVIRONMENTS AS
DISTINCTIVE AS THE CLIENTS WE SERVE

Hardscape,
Masonry & Water

COFFMAN STONE ....**(614) 861–4668**
6015 Taylor Road, Gahanna
Fax:(614) 861–4665
See ad on page: 294, 295
Principal/Owner: Tom Coffman
Website: www.coffmanstone.com e-mail: tomc@coffmanstone.com
Additional Information: Where creativity begins. Products Include: Aggregates, Pavers, Boulders, Slabs, Concrete Products, Flagstone, Retaining Walls, Wall Stone and more.

CUSTOM CONCRETE PLUS, INC. ....**(740) 549–2603**
8318 Oak Creek Drive, Lewis Center
Fax:(740) 549–2603
See ad on page: 298
Principal/Owner: Art Mynes

DECORATIVE PATIO CONCEPTS ....**(614) 792–7899**
94 Village Pointe Drive, Powell
Fax:(614) 792–1180
See ad on page: 302, 303
Principal/Owner: David Newcomer

DESIGN CRETE, INC. ....**(614) 861–6677**
1195 Technology Drive, Gahanna
Fax:(614) 861–6779
See ad on page: 296, 297, 422
Principal/Owner: Larry Jones
Website: www.designcreteinc.com

KING CONCRETE ....**(614) 279–6533**
2824 B Fisher Rd., Columbus
Fax:(614) 279–4181
See ad on page: 291

MR. MULCH ....**(614) 792–8686**
2721 West State Route 161, Columbus
Fax:(614) 792–1686
See ad on page: 300
Principal/Owner: Craig Schweitzer
Website: www.mrmulch.com Additional Information: Specializing in man–made and natural retaining walls, walkways and patios. We also design custom ponds and water features.

OBERFIELD'S INC. ....**(614) 252–0955**
528 London Road, Delaware
Fax:(740) 363–7644
See ad on page: 299
Principal/Owner: William R. Oberfield
Website: www.oberfields.com e-mail: info@oberfields.com
Additional Information: Oberfield's manufactures an elite collection of concrete pavers and retaining walls. Ask your builder or landscape contractor about our selection for your dream home.

WELLNITZ LANDSCAPE PRODUCTS ....**(614) 220–9419**
975 McKinley Avenue, Columbus
Fax:(614) 220–9425
See ad on page: 292, 293
Principal/Owner: Michael Thompson
Website: www.wellnitz.com e-mail: mthompson@wellnitz.com
Additional Information: Supplier and manufacturer of concrete products for residential, commercial and industrial landscaping.

ZEN CRETE ....**(614) 844–4849**
1049 Pebblebrook Drive, Columbus
See ad on page: 301
Principal/Owner: Jim Hartsough

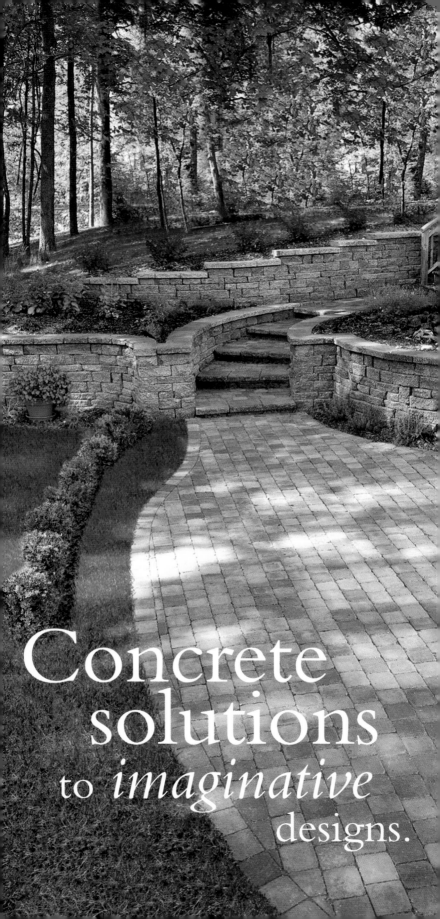

Concrete
solutions
to *imaginative*
designs.

Go ahead.
Let your *imagination*
run wild.

Wellnitz

Your beautiful home deserves only the best laid plans. At Wellnitz we've been satisfying our customers with concrete solutions for over 75 years. It's no wonder that Wellnitz hardscape products are found in some of the most elite neighborhoods in Columbus.

Our customers know that at Wellnitz, their needs are understood. Our staff of highly trained experts can work comfortably with landscape designers, contractors, builders or directly with homeowners.

Our inventory of quality concrete paving products — the largest selection in Central Ohio — consists of a myriad of colors, shapes, textures and sizes. So whether one chooses the Old World look of natural stone, the traditional feel of clay brick paving, or something altogether unique, Wellnitz provides landscape solutions that fit together beautifully.

It's a fact: for driveways, patios, walkways, pool decks and retaining walls, there simply isn't a more durable product line available. Our concrete pavers are guaranteed for life, weathering the tests of time and temperature, and are virtually maintenance free. Considering flexibility and durability, this means significant long-term savings over poured concrete, asphalt and timber.

Let Wellnitz pave the way for your imagination.

975 McKinley Ave.
Columbus, Ohio 43222
614-220-9419   www.wellnitz.com

Wellnitz
Landscape Products

The Standard of Excellence

6015 Taylor Road
Gahanna, OH 43230

Office: 614-861-4668
Fax: 614-861-4655
Toll-free: 1-866-COFFMAN
        (1-866-263-3626)

www.coffmanstone.com

Where creativity begins.

ate Residence –
rinted Front Walk with
orative Borders

Private Residence - Upper Arlington, OH
Water Feature with Concrete Fountain Walls and Cap

Longaberger Tea House
- Dresden, OH
Slate Texture Walks with
"Carved Stone" Entry Walls

DESIGNCRETE

CUSTOM CONCRETE PLUS, INC.
Concrete Stamping and Pavers

740.549.2603

What Outdoor Living Should Be

OBERFIELD'S INC®

www.oberfields.com
740-369-7644 • 614-252-0955
Classic Collection of Tumbled Pavers & Retaining Walls

Decorative Patio Concepts
94 Village Pointe Drive
Powell, Ohio 43065
Ph: 614-792-7899 Fax: 614-792-1180

Stamped Concrete Patios, Driveways, Walkways, & Pool Decks

Wood Decks, Trellises, 3 & 4 Season Rooms & Fences

Swimming
Pools & Spas

COMMERCIAL POOLS, INC. ....**(614) 766–0050**
2888 Bethel Road, Columbus   Fax:(614) 766–6519
See ad on page: 306
Principal/Owner: Charles Lambert
Website: www.commercialpools.com e-mail: clam1947@directvintiernet.com

MIDWEST SPORTS ....**(937) 642–4667**
16191 Hunters Run, Marysville   Fax:(937) 642–8669
See ad on page: 307
Principal/Owner:
e-mail: midwestspts@midohio.net
Additional Information: Sales and installation of indoor and outdoor sports equipment
and athletic surfaces. Retrofit and new construction.

YARD PLAY...**(614) 761–2384**
470 West Olentangy Street, Powell   Fax:(614) 761–2435
See ad on page: 305
Principal/Owner: Kevin Mullins
Additional Information: Featuring premium redwood playsets and recycled safety surfaces.

YARD PLAY
featuring premium redwood playsets

YARD PLAY

470 West Olentangy Street
Powell, Ohio 43065
(614) 761-2384

Play with your kids at home!

TrueTurf Putting Greens

- The finest components available

- Complete design/landscape integration

- Custom-built indoor/outdoor installations

- Fits your lifestyle and your budget

- Professional project management

- Know where your kids are

- Play up to 15 different games

- Promotes teamwork and sportsmanship

- Entertain family and friends

- Adds real value to your property

- Virtually maintenance-free

- 10 year limited warranty

- Easy to upgrade components

- *Just plain fun!*

Midwest Sports

800-858-5446

TrueCourt is a member of the
TrueSports Network

www.truesports.net

Awnings

CAPITAL CITY AWNING, INC. ....**(614) 221–7380**
577 North Fourth Street, Columbus   Fax:(614) 365–9420
See ad on page: 309
<u>Principal/Owner:</u> Timothy Kellogg
<u>Website:</u> www.capitalcityawning.com <u>e-mail:</u> sales@capitalcityawning.com
<u>Additional Information:</u> Retractable awnings, window awnings, patio & deck awnings.
Residential, commercial & new construction.

Landscape
Lighting

NITELIGHTS OF COLUMBUS, INC. ....**(614) 442–1145**
Columbus   Fax:(614) 870–7891
See ad on page: 311
Principal/Owner: Craig Schmidt, Troy Hutter
Website: www.nitelights.com

NiteLights of Columbus, Inc.
Architectural & Landscaping Illumination

EVERY HOME CAN BE SAFER
AND MORE ENJOYABLE
WITH PROFESSIONAL
LANDSCAPE LIGHTING.

Think about how much time, energy and money you have invested in your home. It is probably one of your largest investments. So, why let your beautifully landscaped and stunning home fade into the shadows of darkness when the sun goes down. Let the professionally installed architectural and landscape lighting of NiteLights illuminate your home.

This unique NiteLights system offers:

- Added safety and security for your family and guests

- Beautiful "curb" appeal that will make your home the highlight of the neighborhood

- Increased value and resale of your home

- More hours to use your outdoor areas, including patios, decks, pools and walkways

Call For A Free Demonstration
614.442.1145

Irrigation
Systems

DESIGN ONE IRRIGATION SYSTEMS...**(614) 210–0660**
Dublin   Fax:(614) 873–0699
See ad on page: 314
Principal/Owner: James Judge
e-mail: judge@designoneirrigation.com
Additional Information: Design One is a full service irrigation company specializing
in the most efficient use of our most valuable natural resource, water.

T. CARMICHAEL INC....**(740) 881–6066**
3129 Home Road, Powell   Fax:(740) 881–4501
See ad on page: 313
Principal/Owner: Chris Carmichael

T. CARMICHAEL, INC.

RAIN DRAINAGE & LAWN SPRINKLER SYSTEMS

3129 HOME ROAD
POWELL, OH 43065
740.881.6696 FAX: 740.881.4501

Custom Sprinkler Systems for Luxury Homes

Design One Irrigation Systems, Inc.
Dublin, OH
614.210.0660

Arborists

DAVEY TREE EXPERT COMPANY, THE..**(614) 471–4144**
3603 Westerville Road, Columbus   Fax:(614) 471–9126
See ad on page: 315
<u>Website:</u> www.davey.com

Photo courtesy of **Clive Christian, Columbus**

KITCHEN

&

BATH

IMMERSE

Get up to your neck in serenity with the Sōk Bath™ by Kohler®. Available from Ferguson Bath & Kitchen Galleries.

Hilliard, 4363 Lyman Drive, (614) 876-8555

www.ferguson.com

©2002 MarketFocus Communications, Inc.

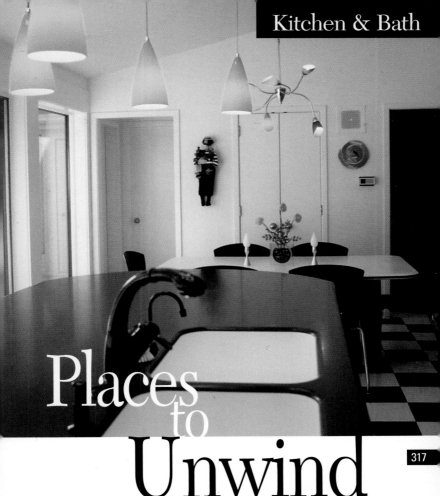

Places to Unwind

Ever notice that when there's a social gathering in a home, people congregate in the kitchen? Today, the kitchen serves not only as a place for preparing food, but also as a place where the party begins and ends, where couples relax over coffee in a cozy breakfast nook, or where delicious buffets await family and guests alike.

Kitchen islands now function as self-serve appetizer stations, fully equipped with range tops, warming bins and microwaves. Open architectural floor plans call for kitchens to flow into areas to gather for conversation or entertainment. Without a doubt, today's larger kitchen is the real family room, the heart and soul of the home.

The bath has evolved into a truly multipurpose "cocooning" area as well. Sufficient room for exercise equipment, spacious master closets and spa features are in high demand, resulting in master suites to allow one to escape from the world. The emphasis on quality fixtures and luxury finishes remains, whatever the size of the room.

Photo courtesy of **Glavan Fehér Architects, Inc.**

DEFINING THE WAY WE LIVE

Homeowners building a new home, or remodeling an existing one, demand flexible and efficient spaces, custom designed to fill their needs. Reaching that goal is more challenging than ever. As new products and technologies race to keep up with the creative design explosion, the need for talented, experienced kitchen and bath designers continues to grow.

The kitchen/bath designer will be a member of your homebuilding team, which also includes the architect, contractor, interior designer and, in new home construction, the landscape architect.

Professional kitchen and bath designers, many of whom are also degreed interior designers, possess the education and experience in space planning particular to kitchens and baths. They can deliver a functional design perfectly suited to your family, while respecting your budget and your wishes. Their understanding of ergonomics, the relationship between people and their working environments, and a familiarity with current products and applications will be invaluable to you as you plan.

SEARCH OUT DESIGN EXCELLENCE

Designing a kitchen or bath is an intimate undertaking, filled with many decisions based on personal habits and family lifestyles. Before you select the kitchen/bath professional who will lead you through the project, make a personal commitment to be an involved and interested client. Since the success of these rooms is so important to the daily lives of you and those around you, it's a worthwhile investment of your time and energy.

Choose a designer whose work shows creativity and a good sense of planning. As in any relationship, trust and communication are the foundations for success. Is the designer open to your ideas, and does he or she offer information on how you can achieve your vision? If you can't express your ideas freely, don't enter into a contractual relationship, no matter how much you admire this person's work. If these rooms aren't conceived to fulfill your wishes, your time and resources will be wasted.

What also is true, however, is that professional designers should be given a comfortable degree of latitude to execute your wishes as best as they know how. Accomplished designers earned their reputation by creating beautiful rooms that work, so give their ideas serious consideration for the best overall result.

Many homeowners contact a kitchen or bath designer a year before a project is scheduled to begin. Some come with a full set of complete drawings they simply want to have priced out. Some take full

INGREDIENTS OF A NEW KITCHEN

What might it cost to design and install a 16 ft. x 33 ft. kitchen?
• Cabinetry: kitchen, island, pantry, desk, 36-42 in. high wall cabinets, maple, modified Shaker styling, custom solid wood construction: $44,000
• Stained glass doors, glass shelves: $3,500
• Granite countertop & tumbled marble backsplash with mosaic: $14,500
• Two electric ovens, 36 in. gas cooktop with hood, 48 in. built-in refrigerator, two dishwashers, under counter refrigerator, warming drawer, microwave, disposal, hot water dispenser: $20,000
• Plumbing fixtures: $2,900
• Porcelain tile flooring: $4,000
• Lighting: low voltage, halogen and xenon: $2,500
• Labor: $7,000
Total: $98,400

advantage of the designer's expertise and contract for plans drawn from scratch. And some want something in between. Be sure a designer offers the level of services you want – from 'soup to nuts' or strictly countertops and cabinetry.

Designers charge a design fee, which often will be used as a deposit if you choose to hire them. If you expect very detailed sets of drawings, including floor plans, elevations, and pages of intricate detail, such as the support systems of kitchen islands, the toe kick and crown molding detail, be specific about your requirements. All contracts should be written, detailed, and reviewed by your attorney.

TURNING DREAMS INTO DESIGNS – GET YOUR NOTEBOOK OUT

The first step toward getting your ideas organized is to put them on paper. Jot down notes, tape photos into an Idea Notebook, mark pages of your Home Book. The second step is defining your lifestyle. Pay close attention to how you use the kitchen and bath. For example, if you have a four-burner stove, how often do you cook with all four burners? Do you need a cook surface with more burners, or could you get by with less, freeing up space for a special wok cooking module or more counter space? How often do you use your bathtub? Many upper-end homeowners are forgoing the tub in favor of the multi-head shower surround and using bathtub space for a dressing or exercise area or mini-kitchen. As you evaluate your lifestyle, try to answer questions like these:

THINKING ABOUT KITCHEN DESIGN

• What feeling do you want to create in the kitchen? Traditional feel of hearth and home? The clean, uncluttered lines of contemporary design?

• Is meal preparation the main function of the kitchen? Gourmet cooks and gardeners want a different level of functionality than do homeowners who eat out often or want to be in and out of the kitchen quickly.

• How does the family use the kitchen? How will their needs change your requirements over the next ten years? (If you can't imagine the answer to this question, ask friends who are a few years ahead of you in terms of family life.)

• Do you want easy access to the backyard, dining room, garage?

• Is there a special view you want preserved or established?

APPLIANCES NOW

New appliances in the kitchen are fun and user-friendly.
• Prep sinks and cooktops located conveniently in the island
• Refrigerators with titanium finishes that don't leave fingerprints
• Monitors that can be built-in or mounted under a cabinet.
• Wireless water-proof keyboards for surfing the Internet while bathing or cooking
• Refrigerator touch screens for pulling up favorite recipes
• Dishwashers with a full-size, flat third rack for broiler pans, cook-ie sheets and other hard-to-wash items
• Recessed light-ing and task light-ing fixtures, such as sleek pendant lamps
• Built-in coffeemakers with electrical lift systems that hide them within a cab-inet after the lattes and espressos have been served.

319

WHAT DESIGNERS OFFER YOU

1. Access to the newest products: With their considerable knowledge of products and solutions, your remodeling or budget limitations can be more easily addressed.
2. Ergonomic design for a custom fit: Designers consider all the measurements - not just floor plan space - but also how counter and cabinet height and depth measure up to the needs of the individual family members.
3. A safe environment: Safety is the highest priority. As kitchens and baths serve more functions, managing traffic for safety's sake becomes more crucial.
4. Orderly floor plans: When an open refrigerator door blocks the path from the kitchen to the breakfast room, or you're bumping elbows in the bathroom, poor space planning is the culprit.
5. Smart storage: Ample storage in close proximity to appropriate spaces is essential.

• Do you want family and friends to be involved and close to the action in the kitchen?

• What appliances and amenities must be included? Warming drawers, refrigeration zones, wine coolers, ultra-quiet dishwashers that sense how dirty the dishes are, cooktops with interchangeable cooking modules, and convection ovens with electronic touchpad controls are all available.

• What are your storage needs? If you own a lot of kitchen items, have a relatively small kitchen, or want personally tailored storage space, ask your kitchen designer to take a detailed inventory of your possessions. Top quality cabinets can be customized to fit your needs. Kitchen designers, custom cabinetmakers, or space organization experts can guide you. Consider custom options such as:
  • Slotted storage for serving trays
  • Pull-out recycling bins
  • Plate racks and wine racks
  • Cutlery dividers
  • Angled storage drawer for spices
  • Pivoting shelving systems
  • Pull-out or elevator shelves for food processors, mixers, televisions or computers

• Is the kitchen also a work area or home office? Do you need a location for a computerized home management or intercom system?

THINKING ABOUT BATH DESIGN

• What look are you trying to create? Victorian, Colonial, Contemporary, whimsical?

• What functions must it fill? Exercise area, sitting room, dressing or make-up area?

• Who will use the bath? Children, teens, guests (and how many)?

• What is the traffic pattern? How do people move in and around a bathroom? (Set up your video camera in the corner one morning to get a realistic view.)

• What amenities are desired? Luxury shower systems, whirlpool tub, ceiling heat lamps, spa, heated tile floors, audio and telephone systems

• What are your storage needs? Linen or clothes closets? Stereo and CD storage? Professionals will customize spaces for your needs.

• Do you want hooks for towels or bathrobes? Heated towel bars or rings?

THE SKY'S THE LIMIT

New high-end kitchen budgets can easily reach the $100,000 range, so it's important to identify your specific needs and wishes. The sky's the limit when designing and installing a luxury kitchen or bath in the 2000s, so don't get caught by surprise by the cost of high quality cabinetry, appliances and fixtures. Know what you're willing to spend and make sure your designer is aware of your budget. Projects have a way of growing along the way. If you've established a realistic budget, you have a solid way to keep the project moving forward and prioritizing your wishes. Think in terms of this general breakdown of expenses:

Cabinets 40%
Appliances 15%
Faucets and Fixtures 8%
Flooring 7%
Windows 7%
Countertops 8%
Labor 15%

TODAY'S KITCHEN-ANTIQUE OR SLEEK, IT'S YOUR CHOICE

Whether your tastes run to classical and traditional European designs, or you prefer contemporary looks, today's imperative is custom. You determine what you want. Gorgeous imported natural stone countertops and floors, and luxury options like dedicated wine coolers, stem glass holders, and plate racks are ever popular and can be accommodated in any style.

Today's refrigerators can now serve as home automation control centers. Plasma screens built into refrigerator doors can serve as touch-screen home automation control centers, running everything from ovens and entertainment centers to security systems. In other modes, they function as TV screens, even Internet portals. Check your e-mail while you're peeling the potatoes – why not!

With advances in refrigeration technology, homeowners now have separate integrated refrigerators and freezer drawers installed near the appropriate work zone – a refrigerated vegetable drawer near the sink, a freezer drawer by the microwave, dedicated refrigerators to keep grains or cooking oils at their perfect temperatures. Ultra-quiet dishwashers with push-button controls hidden on top of the door for a sleek appearance, instant hot water dispensers, roll-out warming drawers and cooktops that can boil water in seconds are just some of the products that meet the demands of today's luxury lifestyle.

"WHAT ABOUT RESALE?"

This is a question designers hear when homeowners individualize their kitchens and baths. It's only prudent to consider the practical ramifications of any significant investment, including investing in a new custom kitchen and bath.

Beautiful upscale kitchens and baths will only enhance the value of your home. Indeed, these two rooms are consistently credited with recouping more than their original cost, estimates range from an increase in value of 10% to 50% over what was spent. The greatest return, however, is in the present, in the enjoyment of the space.

321

TODAY'S BATH – BRINGING THE SPA EXPERIENCE HOME

Imagine it's a Thursday night at the end of a very busy week. You come home, have a great work out while listening to your favorite CDs over the loudspeakers in your private exercise room, then jump into an invigorating shower where multiple shower heads rejuvenate your tired muscles, and a steaming, cascading waterfall pulls all the stress from your body. You wrap yourself in a big fluffy bath sheet, toasty from the brass towel warmer as you step onto the ceramic tile floor that's been warmed by an underfloor radiant heating unit. You grab something comfortable from your lighted, walk-in closet, and then head out of your luxurious bathroom to the kitchen to help with dinner.

Today's master baths are indeed at-home spas. They are a place to de-stress from hectic and active lifestyles, and new designs seek to accomplish this through simplicity, softness of textures and surfaces, and the use of water's soothing nature itself. You've heard about aromatherapy, now there's Chromatherapy-colored lights located in the bathtub. The system cycles through eights hues, and if you like a particular color, you can settle on that one by pushing a button.

For the utmost in minimalist faucet design, how about eliminating the faucet altogether? New faucet designs have the water flowing directly out of the wall. Used with porcelain hand basins, these wet surface lavatories are formulated for a comforting, almost Zen-like washing experience. Water flows onto a raised plateau, with an overflow perimeter reminiscent of disappearing edge pools that catches the water and sends it down the drain. The open-bottom hand basin creates a seal with the lavatory's surface when filled with water, enabling you to use it as a wash basin and then release the contents by simply lifting it. Perfect for those who want the experience of washing in a fountain instead of an ordinary sink.

For those seeking a mega-experience, spa tubs can provide the bathing equivalent of the Jumbotron. Watch a 48-inch color plasma TV screen as you pop in a video and soak to your heart's content (though soaking through a 3-hour movie like Lord of the Rings might be a bit much.)

THE REALITY OF REMODELING

Dollar-smart homeowners know that in cost versus value surveys, kitchen renovations and bath additions or renovations yield a very high return on the original investment. These homeowners

A STEP UP

Custom counter height is an idea whose time has arrived in new and remodeled homes. Multiple heights, appropriate to the task or the people using the particular area, are common. When one permanent height doesn't work as a solution to a problem, consider asking for a step to be built in to the toe kick panel of the cabinetry.

GET TWO DISHWASHERS

Homeowners today are installing extra dishwashers:
1. To make cleanup after a party a one-night affair.
2. To serve as a storage cabinet for that extra set of dishes.
They're also installing dishwashers at a more friendly height to eliminate unnecessary bending.

rarely embark on such remodeling projects with resale in mind. However, knowing their investment is a wise one gives them the freedom to fully realize their dreams of the ultimate sybaritic bath or the friendliest family kitchen that accommodates them now and well into the future.

For more information on remodeling, see "The Second Time's The Charm" in the Custom Home Builders and Remodelers section.

A REMODELING CONTINGENCY FUND

Kitchen and bath remodeling projects are well known for unexpected, unforeseen expenses, so put a contingency fund in your budget from the beginning. This fund can cover anything from structural changes to your sudden desire to install skylights in the kitchen.

THE BEAUTY OF TOP QUALITY SURFACES

Luxury surfaces continue to add astonishing beauty to kitchens and baths in new and remodeled homes throughout the area. Solid surfaces now are available in an ever-widening range of colors, including a granite look, with high degrees of translucence and depth. Granite and stone add a beautiful, natural look, with an abundance of choices and finishes. Tile, stainless steel, laminates, and wood – even concrete – are other possibilities. Each surface has its benefits, beyond the inherent beauty it can add to your design.

Your kitchen designer will advise you on the best choices for your project, based on overall design and budget. Use the professionals showcased in these pages to find the best quality materials and craftsmanship. ■

ELECTRIC VS. GAS

An age-old debate, yes, but today's electric ranges have come a long way. Sleek, scratch-resistant glass cooktops feature simmer settings that hold sauces and stews below the boiling point. And controls can be locked for child-safety. Today's gas ranges feature grates that are dishwasher safe and sealed burners that make cleanup easy. Dual-stacked burners offer greater low-end control for melting or simmering. Electric, gas or both; the choice is yours.

323

Kitchen & Bath
Designers

CLASSIC KITCHENS, INC. ....**(614) 552–5252**
820 Refugee Road, Pickerington
See ad on page: 326, 327
Principal/Owner: Dale Lugar
e-mail: classickitchensohio@juno.com

CLIVE CHRISTIAN..**(614) 899–9716**
110 Polaris Parkway, Westerville   Fax:(614) 899–6555
See ad on page: 332, 333
Principal/Owner: James Madura
Additional Information: Fine English cabinetry in traditional designs. Custom designed in antique painted or wood finishes, hand crafted in England.

D.L. ATKINSON, INC. ....**(614) 875–2380**
3797 McDowell Road, Grove City   Fax:(614) 875–2472
See ad on page: 330
Principal/Owner: Donald L. Atkinson
e-mail: dlatkinson@ee.net Additional Information: Custom made cabinets and furniture from all wood, made to your specifications!

ELLIS KITCHEN & BATH STUDIO, INC........................................**(614) 461–1218**
477 South Front Street, Columbus   Fax:(614) 461–9068
See ad on page: 329
Principal/Owner: David Norton
Website: www.elliskitchens.com e-mail: info@elliskitchens.com

FERGUSON BATH & KITCHEN GALLERY ....**(614) 876–8555**
4363 Lyman Drive, Hilliard   Fax:(614) 876–0156
See ad on page: 314b, 314c, 328
Principal/Owner: Randy Massie
Website: www.ferguson.com

JAE COMPANY, THE ....**(614) 294–4941**
955 West 5th Avenue, Columbus   Fax:(614) 294–6978
See ad on page: 334
Principal/Owner: Mark Humrichouser
Website: www.jaecompany.com

LONDON KITCHENS & BATHS ....**(614) 488–2666**
1065 Dublin Road, Columbus   Fax:(614) 488–2831
See ad on page: 331
Principal/Owner: Daniel J. Atchison
Additional Information: Specialty design services; 16 years in business.
Full service remodeling contractor specializing in kitchen & bath.

MASTER WOOD–WORKS ....**(614) 846–5588**
6323 Busch Boulevard, Columbus   Fax:(740) 363–3878
See ad on page: 335
Principal/Owner: Todd Marker
Website: www.masterwood–works.com

MILLER CABINET COMPANY ....**(800) 983–6455**
6217 Converse–Huff Road, Plain City   Fax:(614) 873–8394
See ad on page: 325, 354b, 354c
Principal/Owner: Nate Yoder

Photographed by J.E. Evans

Kitchen and Bath Design
Hand-Crafted Custom Cabinetry
Professional-Style Appliances

Please visit our showroom
M-F 8-5; Sat 9-12:30
6217 Converse-Huff Road   Plain City, Ohio 43064
614 873-4221   800 983-6455
www.millercabinet.com

THE
MILLER CABINET
COMPANY   Plain City

The finest in custom cabinetry

CLASSIC KITCHENS

SHOWROOM

820 Refugee Rd • Pickerington, OH 43147

(614) 552-5252

www.classickitchens.com

"Set Your Home Apart From The Ordinary"
Expert Design
Professional Installation

GRABILL QUALITY CABINETRY

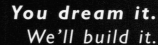

LONDON
Kitchens and Baths
WHERE YOUR DREAMS COME TRUE

NATIONAL KITCHEN
NKBA
& BATH ASSOCIATION

1065 DUBLIN ROAD, COLUMBUS OHIO 43215   (614)488-2666 FAX 488-2831

PRESENTING the traditional, timeless appeal of the English style. Custom designed to fit your needs, made of the finest construction and finished in antiqued wood or hand painted finishes.

MADE IN ENGLAND.

KraftMaid
Cabinetry

There are kitchens and there are Master Wood-Works Kitchens. Wood-Mode cabinetry, customized to meet the most discriminating homeowners, and kitchen designs from Master Wood-Works Kitchens can be traditional or contemporary, painted or plain, but always in style.

When you choose Wood-Mode cabinetry you are assured of quality that can last a lifetime, with maximum storage capabilities, hand rubbed finishes, select woods and superior construction.

Wouldn't you rather have a Wood-Mode kitchen from Master Wood-Works?

Fixtures &
Hardware

BATH AND BRASS EMPORIUM, THE..**(614) 885–8420**
683 East Lincoln Avenue, Columbus   Fax:(614) 885–4470
See ad on page: 340
<u>Principal/Owner:</u> Charles Savko

EASTWAY SUPPLIES, INC. ....**(614) 252–0974**
1561 Alum Creek Drive, Columbus   Fax:(614) 252–0021
See ad on page: 339
<u>Principal/Owner:</u> Keith Sharrock
<u>Website:</u> www.eastwaysupplies.com <u>e-mail:</u> ksharrock@eastwaysupplies.com

SPECIALTY BUILDING PRODUCTS ....**(740) 549–9911**
7699 Green Meadows Drive, Lewis Center   Fax:(740) 549–0215
See ad on page: 337, 383

Specialty
Building Products

ABINET DESIGNS FOR EVERY PERSONALITY

chosen by central Ohio's
leading custom builders

Corsi

Kahle

740-549-9911

7699 Green Meadows Drive
Lewis Center, OH 43035

hansgrohe
Refreshing, Invigorating, Incredible
DECO LAV
INCORPORATED
www.eastwaysupplies.com

Solid Surfaces

HYTEC TOPS ....(614) 251–0383
  2741 East Fourth Avenue, Columbus   Fax:(614) 251–0385
  See ad on page: 314d, 348, 415
  Principal/Owner: Ron Mercer

Appliances

BUILDER APPLIANCE SUPPLY ....(614) 751–4525
  6845 Commerce Court, Blacklick   Fax:(614) 759–4102
  See ad on page: 342, 343, 344, 345
  Principal/Owner: Randy Sickmeier

JOHN TISDEL FINE APPLIANCES ....(513) 339–0990
  7177 Central Parke Boulevard, Cincinnati   Fax:(513) 339–0988
  See ad on page: 346, 347
  Principal/Owner: John Tisdel
  Website: www.johntisdelappliances.com e-mail: john@jtdinc.com
  Additional Information: Distributor of fine luxury appliances including Wolf, Sub–zero,
  Asko and Franke.

341

Countertops

KITCHEN TOPICS.COM ....(614) 989–2744
  6330 Frost Road, Suite C, Westerville   Fax:(614) 895–7070
  See ad on page: 418
  Website: www.kitchentopics.com e-mail: dan@kitchentopics.com

Get in touch with your inner chef.

Viking products are marketed under the Ultraline® brand name in Canada.

Find yourself in the complete Viking kitchen. Professional features like precision controls and convection baking allow you to tune in to your culinary side. While the high-performance products give you the power to cook everything you've been dreaming of. Set the gourmet inside your heart free.

Before you create the perfect meal,
create the perfect kitchen.

The life of the kitchen™

A **KitchenAid**® appliance is more than a product- **its a brand.**

Builder Appliance Supply Inc.

Largest Selection! Lowest Cost!
On Over 25 Brands of Appliances!

Choose from: General Electric, Five Star, Jenn Air, Whirlpool, Viking, Dacor, KitchenAid, Sub Zero, Asko, Monogram, Maytag, Venmar Hoods, GE, Thermador, Blanco, Marvel, Fisher Paykel, Wolf Gourmet, Amana, U-Line, Scotsman, Gaggenau, Bosch, etc.

HOME BUYERS • BUILDERS • REMODELERS

Choice for all tastes... Priced for all budgets.

Builder Appliance Supply
6845 Commerce Ct. • Columbus, OH 43004
614-751-4525

PASSPORT
to a Lifestyle

The Appliances of Choice.

CORIAN & GRANITE

DEAN'S CUSTOM FIXTURES

Alfresco Kitchen: **The Alfresco kitchen is a fresh look at bringing the outdoors in. To keep the space open and render it a gathering place, Alfresco comprises a collection of combination work, storage and entertaining free-standing pieces. For interest and atmosphere, it uses an array of materials and treatments to mimic the light, bright, inspirational feeling of the outdoors. With a built-in cooktop/grill on one end and room for six on the other, the cook can grill it up and dish it out to eager diners sitting opposite.**

350

Photo by **Plain & Fancy**

CLIVE CHRISTIAN, COLUMBUS

Regency Bath: **Elegance and sophistication can only describe the new Regency Bath by Clive Christian English Furniture. Gold leafing highlights the fine detailing of the frieze and pilasters, creating a look of richness fitting for the master bath or powder room. Cabinetry is designed and built in England, to the finest standards. To achieve a truly customized finish, the Classic Cream color and gold leaf detailing is applied by hand in the home.**

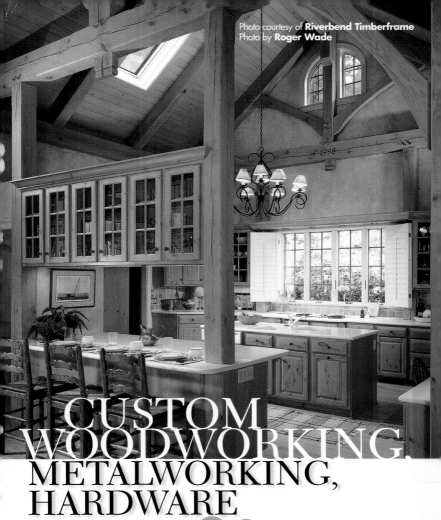

CUSTOM WOODWORKING, METALWORKING, HARDWARE & GLASS

Photographed by J.E. Evans

Please visit our showroom
M-F 8-5; Sat 9-12:30
6217 Converse-Huff Road   Plain City, Ohio 43064
614 873-4221   800 983-6455
www.millercabinet.com

Your Family Deserves the Best.

THE
MILLER CABINET
COMPANY   Plain City

The finest in custom cabinetry

America's Finest Handcrafted Solid Brass Decorative Hardware

Period Brass

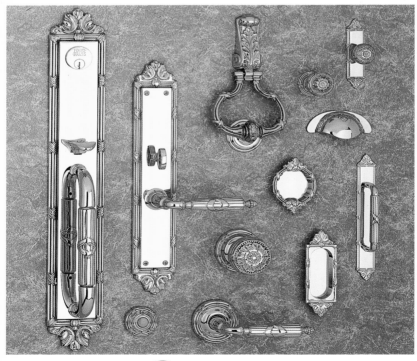

Hardware Creations

Fine Decorative and Builder's Hardware

351

Paying
Attention
to the
Details

W hat is it that makes a home truly original? Interior architectural elements handcrafted by the finest artisans contribute greatly to the uniqueness of a custom home.

Techniques with wood, metal, and glass have evolved over millennia. These ancient crafts are now ready to enhance your home. Cabinetry, moldings, ceiling medallions, chair rails, staircases, mirrors and mantels tell your story and reflect your unique tastes. Doors, windows and hardware should function in accord with the way you live, whether you want bay windows with storage drawers below, double French doors that open up the space between rooms, or hardware that simply reflects your style.

Photo courtesy of **Clive Christian, Columbus**

ELEGANT STORAGE

Nowhere is the commitment to elegant living through quality materials more apparent than in the selection of cabinets and millwork. Representing a significant percentage of the overall cost of a new or renovated home, sophisticated homeowners use this opportunity to declare their dedication to top quality.

Architectural millwork, made to order according to a set of architectural drawings, is becoming an increasingly popular luxury upgrade. Such detailing creates a richly nostalgic atmosphere that reminds homeowners of the comfort and security of a grandparents' home or the elegance of a club they've been in.

Elegant libraries, dens or sitting rooms dressed with fashionable raised panel cabinetry and special moldings are often included in the plans for new homes and remodeling projects. As a homeowner considering how and where to install millwork, ask yourself questions like these:

• How is the room used? Will a study be used for work or for solitude? Entertaining or a second office? Will it have to function as both a working office and an elegant room?

• How are the cabinets and shelves used? Books, collectibles, audio-video equipment, computer, fax or copy machines?

• What look do you want? You may want to consider "dressing" your rooms in different woods. You may like the rich look and feel of cherry paneling in your library, mahogany in the foyer, oak in a guest room and plaster in a dining room.

• Will the interior millwork choices work with the exterior architecture? A colonial home reminiscent of Mount Vernon should be filled with authentic details, like "dog-ear" corners, that create classic luxury. Using millwork inside a modern home can add interest and warmth to one or many rooms.

TAKE TIME TO MAKE A STATEMENT

Handcrafted high quality woodwork cannot be rushed. Millwork specialists encourage clients to contact them as early as possible with a clear idea of what kind of architectural statement they wish to make. The earlier you plan these details, the more options you'll have. Wainscoting with raised panels has to be coordinated with electrical outlets, window and door openings; beamed ceilings with light fixtures, and crown moldings with heating vents.

Hold a preliminary meeting before construction begins while it's early enough to incorporate innovative or special requirements into your plans. The more time you can devote to design (two to three weeks is

---

PRICING
A POWER
LIBRARY

• A 15 ft. x 16 ft. library, fully paneled in cherry, mahogany or oak, some cabinets, with moldings, desk with hidden computer, coffered ceilings: $20,000 to $30,000.
• In a 16 ft. x 24 ft. two-story study, less paneling and more cabinetry of cherry, mahogany or oak, heavy with moldings, and radius work, desk with more pull out and hidden compartments for fax machine, small copier, bar with leaded glass cabinet fronts and a marble top, built-in humidor, and heavily coffered ceilings with multiple steps: $40,000.

352

HOW TO
RECOGNIZE
CUSTOM
CABINET QUALITY

1. Proper sanding which results in a smooth, beautiful finish.
2. Superior detail work, adding unexpected elegance.
3. Classic application of design features and architectural details.
4. Beautiful, functional hardware selections.
5. High-quality hinges and drawer glides.
6. Superior overall functionality.

recommended), the better your result will be. You're creating a custom millwork package that's never been designed for anyone before. Investments made on the front end are the most valuable. Ask about design fees, timelines and costs per revision. Keep your builder up to date on all of your millwork plans.

Drawings can be as detailed as you require. If you want to see the intricacies of a radius molding before you contract for it, let the millwork specialist know your requirements. Ask to see wood samples, with and without stain or paint.

Try to visit installed projects to get a firsthand feel for the quality of a specialist's work and to develop clearer ideas for your own home.

Changes made after an order is placed are costly. Therefore, if you're unsure, don't make a commitment. Add accessory moldings and other details as you see the project taking shape.

Expect a heavily laden room to take at least five to eight weeks to be delivered, about the time from the hanging of drywall to the installation of flooring. Installation takes one to three weeks, depending on the size and scope of the project.

THE SIGNATURE STATEMENT OF CUSTOM CABINETRY

Handcrafted custom cabinets are a recognizable standard of excellence which lend refinement and beauty to a home. Built in a kitchen, library, bathroom, or closet, or as a freestanding entertainment system or armoire, custom cabinets are a sophisticated signature statement.

DESIGNING HANDSOME CABINETRY

Cabinetry is a major element in your dream home, so let your imagination soar. Collect pictures of cabinets, noting the particular features you like. Cabinet makers appreciate visual examples because it's easier to interpret your desires from pictures than from words. Pictures crystallize your desires.

When you first meet with a cabinet maker, take your blueprints, and if possible, your builder, architect or designer. Be prepared to answer questions like:

• What is the exterior style of your home and do you want to continue that style inside?

• How will you the use the cabinets? Cutlery trays, pullout bins? Shelves for books, CDs, computer software, collections?

• What styles and embellishments do you like? Shaker, Prairie, Country English, Contemporary? Fancy moldings, wainscoting, inlaid banding?

WHY YOU WANT A PROFESSIONAL DESIGNER

• They rely on experience to deliver you a custom product. Computer tools are great, but nothing replaces the experienced eye.
• They have established relationships with other trades, and can get top-quality glass fronts for your cabinets, or granite for a bar top.
• Their design ability can save you significant dollars in installation.
• They know how to listen to their clients and help them get the results they dream of.

353

PRICING OF CUSTOM KITCHEN CABINETS

• Deluxe Kitchen - Face frame-style cabinets of oak, maple or pine, with raised panel doors; crown molding on upper cabinetry, decorative hardware, wood nosing (cap) around counter tops: $10,000 - $20,000
• Upgrade to - Shaker inset-style cabinets in cherry-wood, painted finish: $20,000 additional.

Use your Idea Notebook to communicate your preferences.

• Do you prefer particular woods? Cherry, oak, sycamore, or the more exotic ebony, Bubinga or Swiss pearwood? (Species must be selected on the basis of the finish you want.)

• Will cabinetry be visible from other rooms in the house? Must it match previously installed or selected flooring or countertops? (Take samples.)

MANAGING THE LENGTHY PROCESS OF A CUSTOM CABINET PROJECT

With plenty of unhurried time, you can be more creative, while allowing the woodworkers the time they need to deliver a top quality product. Take your blueprints to a cabinet maker early. Although installation occurs in the latter part of the construction, measuring usually takes place very early on.

If your project is carefully thought out, you won't be as likely to change your mind, but a contingency budget of 10 to 15 percent for changes (like adding radiuses or a lacquered finish) is recommended.

Custom cabinets for a whole house, (kitchen, butler's pantry, library, master bath, and three to four additional baths) may take 10 to 15 weeks, depending on the details involved (heavy carving adds significant time). Cabinets for a kitchen remodeling may take two months.

EXCEPTIONAL STAIRCASES

Take full advantage of the opportunity to upgrade your new or remodeled home with a spectacular staircase by contacting the stairmakers early in the design phase. Their familiarity with products, standards and building codes will be invaluable to you and your architect, contractor or interior designer.

Visit a stair showroom or workroom on your own or with your architect, interior designer or builder during the architectural drawing phase of your project. Discuss how you can achieve what you want at a cost-conscious price. Choosing a standard size radius of 24 inches, in place of a custom 25 ½ inch radius, for example, will help control costs.

Although your imagination may know no bounds in designing a staircase, hard and fast local building codes may keep your feet on the ground. Codes are not static, and stairmakers constantly update their files on local restrictions regarding details like the rise and run of a stair, and the size and height of rails.

USING PLASTER DETAILING

Plaster architectural detailing and trim add a distinctive look to any home. Most often used in out-of-the-way places, like in ceiling medallions or crown moldings, the high relief detailing is especially impressive.

PRICES OF CUSTOM STAIRS

Stairs can cost anywhere from $200 to $95,000, depending on size, materials and the complexity of design:
• Red Oak spiral staircase, upgraded railing: $10,000
• Red Oak circle stairs, standard railings on both sides and around upstairs landing: $13,000
• Six flights of Red Oak circle stairs stacked one atop the next, with landings at the top of each stair: $95,000
• Walnut or mahogany adds 50 percent to the overall cost.

THE STAIR-BUILDING PROCESS

The design of your stairs should be settled in the rough framing phase of the overall building project. If you work within this time frame, the stairs will be ready for installation after the drywall is hung and primer has been applied to the walls in the stair area.

Stairs can be built out of many woods. The most popular choice is red oak, but cherry, maple, walnut and mahogany are also used. If metal railings are preferred, you'll need to contact a specialist.

A top quality stair builder will design your stairs to your specifications. Consider the views you want of the house while on the stairs, and what kind of front entrance presentation you prefer. You may want to see the stairs from a particular room. An expert also can make suggestions regarding comfort and safety, and what styles will enhance the overall architecture.

Plans that are drawn on a computer can be changed with relative ease and can be printed at full size. This is very helpful to homeowners who want to see exactly what the stairs will look like in their home. The full-size plans can be taken to the job site and tacked to the floor to be experienced firsthand.

LOOKING AT THE BEAUTY OF CUSTOM GLASS AND MIRROR

A room can be transformed through the use of custom decorative glass and mirrors. Artists design intricately patterned, delicately painted glass to add light and architectural interest in all kinds of room dividers and partitions. Glass artistry can be based on any design, playing on the texture of carpet, the pattern of the brick, or repeating a fabric design. A glass block wall or floor panel can add the touch of distinction that sets a home above the others. Stained glass, usually associated with beautiful classic styling, can be designed in any style – from contemporary to art deco to traditional.

Top specialists, like those presented in the following pages, take great care in designing and delivering unique, top quality products. They work with top quality fabricated products, with the highest quality of beveling and edge work.

THE ARTISTIC PROCESS

Glass specialists will visit your home or building site to make recommendations and estimate costs and delivery time. Study their samples and if they have a showroom, go take a look. Perhaps you could visit an installed project. Seeing the possibilities can stimulate your imagination and open your eyes to new ideas in ways pictures simply cannot.

DOOR #1, #2, OR #3?

- Door #1 - Six panel oak door with sidelights of leaded glass: $1,700 - $2,000
- Door #2 - Six panel oak door with lead and beveled glass: $3,000
- Door #3 - Oversized, all matched oak, with custom designed leaded glass and brass, sidelights, elliptical top over door: $15,000
- Allow $500 to $1,500 for door-knobs, hinges and other hardware.

355

LUXURY GLASS & MIRROR

- **Mirrored Exercise Room: Floor to ceiling, wall to wall mirrors, on two or three walls. Allow at least a month, from initial measuring, to squaring off and balancing walls, to installation. Price for polished mirror starts around $9 per square foot. Cutouts for vent outlets cost extra.**
- **Custom Shower Doors: Frameless, bent or curved shower doors are popular luxury upgrades. Made of clear or sandblasted heavy glass - 1/2 in. to 3/8 in. thick. $2,000 and up.**
- **Stained Glass Room Divider: Contemporary, clear on clear design, with a hint of color. Approximately 4 ft. x 6 ft., inset into a wall. $4,500.**
- **Glass Dining Table: Custom designed with bevel edge, 48 in. x 96 in. with two glass bases. $1,200.**

356

Allow a month to make a decision and four weeks for custom mirror work delivery, and ten to 14 weeks for decorated glass.

In order to have the glass or mirror ready for installation before the carpet is laid, decisions must be made during the framing or rough construction phase in a new home or remodeling job. Mirrored walls are installed as painting is being completed, so touch-ups can be done while painters are still on site.

Expect to pay a 50 percent deposit on any order after seeing a series of renderings and approving a final choice. Delivery generally is included in the price.

THE BEAUTY AND CHARM OF CUSTOM WINDOWS AND DOORS

Just as we're naturally drawn to establish eye contact with each other, our attention is naturally drawn to the "eyes" of a home, the windows, skylights and glass doors.

These very important structural features, when expertly planned and designed, add personality and distinction to your interior while complementing the exterior architectural style of your home.

After lumber, windows are the most expensive part of a home. Take the time to investigate the various features and qualities of windows, skylights and glass doors. Visit a specialty store offering top of the line products and service and take advantage of their awareness of current products as well as their accumulated knowledge.

Visit a showroom with your designer, builder or architect. Because of the rapidly changing requirements of local building codes, it's difficult for them to keep current on what can be installed in your municipality. In addition, the dizzying pace of energy efficiency improvements over the past five years can easily outrun the knowledge of everyone but the window specialist. Interior designers can help you understand proper placement and scale in relation to furnishings and room use.

As you define your needs ask questions about alternatives or options, such as energy efficiency, ease of maintenance, appropriate styles to suit the exterior architecture, and interior.

Top quality windows offer high-energy efficiency, the best woodwork and hardware, and comprehensive service and guarantees (which should not be prorated). Good service agreements cover everything, including the locks.

Every home of distinction deserves an entry that exudes a warm welcome and a strong sense of homecoming. When we think of "coming home," we envision an entry door first, the strong, welcoming look of it, a first impression of the home behind it. To get the best quality door, contact a door or millwork specialist with a reputation for delivering top quality products. They can educate you on functionality, and wood and size choices and availability, as well as appropriate style. Doors are also made of steel or fiberglass, but wood offers the most flexibility for custom design.

Since doors are a permanent part of your architecture, carefully shop for the design that best reflects the special character of your home. Allow two to three weeks for delivery of a simple door and eight to 12 weeks if you're choosing a fancy front door. Doors are installed during the same phase as windows, before insulation and drywall.

DESIGN FLAIR HINGES ON FANTASTIC HARDWARE

Door and cabinet hardware, towel bars and accessories add style and substance to interiors. Little things truly do make the difference – by paying attention to the selection of top quality hardware in long-lasting, great-looking finishes, you help define your signature style and commitment to quality in a custom home. There are hundreds of possibilities, so when you visit a specialty showroom, ask the sales staff for their guidance. They can direct you towards the products that will complement your established design style and help you stay within the limits of your budget. When a rim lock for the front door can easily cost $500, and knobs can be $10 each, the advice of a knowledgeable expert is priceless.

Most products are readily available in a short time frame, with the exception of door and cabinetry hardware. Allow eight weeks for your door hardware, and three to four weeks for cabinetry selections. Since accessory hardware is usually in stock, changing cabinet knobs, hooks and towel bars is a quick and fun way to get a new look.

If you're looking to add a creative touch, blacksmithing as decorative art has come to the fore as a way for homeowners to express their personal style. Whether reproductions of period pieces or a new, original design, ornamental iron combines strong, functional purpose with graceful art. ∎

THREE TIPS FOR DOOR HARDWARE

1. Use three hinges to a door - it keeps the door straight.
2. Match all hardware - hinges, knobs, handles, all in the same finish. Use levers or knobs - don't mix.
3. Use a finish that will last.

Millwork

ARCHED CASINGS, INC....**(614) 873–1196**
    10167 Kimberly Drive, Plain City   Fax:(614) 873–9963
    See ad on page: 359
    <u>Principal/Owner:</u> Jerry Whitmer
    <u>e-mail:</u> archedcasings@copper.net

COLUMBUS WOOD PRODUCTS ....**(614) 486–6040**
    1165 Kinnear Road, Columbus   Fax:(614) 486–6254
    See ad on page: 362, 363
    <u>Principal/Owner:</u> Jeff Davis

P & W MILLWORKS INC. ....**(614) 873–4698**
    8005 B Lafayette–Plain City Road, Plain City   Fax:(614) 873–8633
    See ad on page: 360, 361
    <u>Principal/Owner:</u> Phillip Raber
    <u>Website:</u> www.pwmillworks.com   <u>e-mail:</u> sheldonbeachy@pwmillworks.com

CURVED WOOD

TRADITIONAL SHAPES

ARCHED CASINGS INC.

Curved Wood Mouldings
& CNC Router Specialists

SPECIALITY SHAPES

1-888-273-2567 614-873-3576 Fax 614-873-9963
8490 CARTERS MILL RD. PLAIN CITY, OH 43064
ArchedCasings@copper.net

Photography by Kevin Mayer The KW Mayer Company

COLUMBUS WOOD PRODUCTS

MOULDINGS • DOORS • STAIRPARTS • HARDWARE

614-486-6040

"The Direct Source for Fine Millwork and Hardware."

Quality shows in
the details which is why so many
of the finest builders prefer the
custom craftsmanship of
Columbus Wood Products
trimwork, doors and staircases.

For over 20 years, Columbus
Wood Products' complete
manufacturing facility has been
a direct source for fine
millwork and finish hardware in
the Columbus, Cincinnati and
Pittsburgh areas. A full-service
showroom and professionally
trained staff make it a pleasant
experience to select the
millwork details that will bring
out the best in every home.

When quality, selection and
service matter, call Columbus
Wood Products.

Custom
Cabinets

CABINET–TREND INC. ....**(614) 235–2131**
  3766 April Lane, Columbus   Fax:(614) 235–9962
  See ad on page: 349
  Principal/Owner: Brian K. Martin Sr.
  e-mail: C–Trend@aol.com

Custom
Woodwork

COLONIAL CUSTOM WOODWORKING ....**(614) 519–5399**
  810 Howard Street, Mount Vernon
  See ad on page: 391
  Principal/Owner: Ed Kupiec
  e-mail: dejedd@aol.com Additional Information: My company has provided interior trim
  services in the Columbus area for 12 years. We specialize in raise panel wainscoting,
  mantles, stairways, built–ins, custom cabinets and all other aspects of interior trim.

Photog: Bryan Barr

ANTHONY CONTE'S CABINETS

6298 Lancaster–Circleville Road
Lancaster, Ohio 43130

740–687–3327
fax 740–687–0980

Designed by Judith Kenison Interior Design
614–459–9990

CUSTOM CABINETS
MAKE YOUR HOME AS UNIQUE AS YOU ARE

Decorative Glass
& Mirrors

AMERICAN IMAGE GLASS ....**(614) 471–3770**
4390 Westerville Road, Columbus   Fax:(614) 471–3771
See ad on page: 374
Principal/Owner: Dave Foresta
e-mail: dpf@insight.rr.com

CLASSIC GLASS & MIRROR, INC. ....**(614) 263–0069**
3643 Karl Road, Columbus   Fax:(614) 263–0070
See ad on page: 373
Principal/Owner: Brian N. Taylor

COLUMBUS GLASS BLOCK..**(614) 252–5888**
3091 East 14th Avenue, Columbus   Fax:(614) 252–5661
See ad on page: 372
Principal/Owner: Mike Lange
Website: www.columbusglassblock.com e-mail: mikel@columbusglassblock.com
Additional Information: Your source for professional glass block installations.
Ohio's original and largest glass bock company.

FRANKLIN ART GLASS STUDIOS, INC. ....**(614) 221–2972**
222 East Sycamore Street, Columbus   Fax:(614) 221–5223
See ad on page: 370
Principal/Owner: Gary Helf
Website: www.franklinartglass.com e-mail: info@franklinartglass.com
Additional Information: Fine craftsmanship since 1924.

GLASS HILL DESIGNS..**(614) 284–9307**
See ad on page: 371
Principal/Owner: Samuel G. Hill
Website: www.glasshilldesigns.com

369

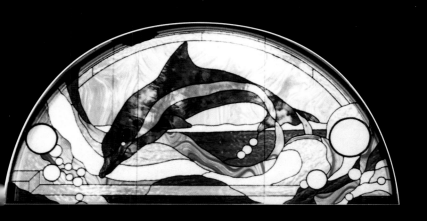

GLASS HILL DESIGNS

Leaded Architectural Glass

Residential ~ Commercial ~ Liturgical

614-284-9307
www.glasshilldesigns.com

Columbus Glass Block- Ohio's original and Largest Glass Block Company: Your Source for professional glass block designs and installations.

Shower Walls - Decorative Walls
Beautiful Windows

Please call for a free design consultation.

3091 East 14th Ave. ~ Columbus, OH 43219
Tel: 614.252.5888 ~ Fax: 614.252.5661
Email: mikel@columbusglassblock.com

CLASSIC GLASS & MIRROR, INC.

3643 Karl Road • Columbus, Ohio 43224
614-263-0069 • 614-263-0070 FAX

"Specializing in Custom Mirror Design & Shower Doors"

American Image Glass

4390 Westerville Road • Columbus, Ohio 43231
P: 614-471-3770 • F: 614-471-3771

Hardware

GOLDEN BEAR LOCK & SAFE, INC. ....**(614) 733–5625**
   7445 Daron Court, Plain City   Fax:(614) 733–0004
   See ad on page: 380, 524
   <u>Principal/Owner:</u> Tim Moore
   <u>Website:</u> www.goldenbearlock.com <u>e-mail:</u> goldenbearlock@cs.com
   <u>Additional Information:</u> Excellent service for 25 years. Retail store/mobile service. Custom door
   hardware, contract sales, installation, locksmithing, electronic access systems, safes.

HARDWARE CREATIONS ....**(614) 294–9944**
   1080 Goodale Boulevard, Columbus   Fax:(614) 294–2323
   See ad on page: 354d, 376, 377, 378, 379
   <u>Principal/Owner:</u> Debbie McCale

VANGUARD HARDWARE, INC. ....**(614) 267–6602**
   3017 Indianola Avenue, Columbus   Fax:(614) 267–8061
   See ad on page: 381
   <u>Principal/Owner:</u> Gary J. Wilkosz

FINE BRASS HARDWARE SINCE 1927

Colonial
BRONZE CO.

HAND-FINISHED, SOLID BRASS HARDWARE
for the kitchen and bath in 35 elegant, durable finishes

Finishes for Life
TARNISH-FREE GUARANTEED®

ROCKY MOUNTAIN

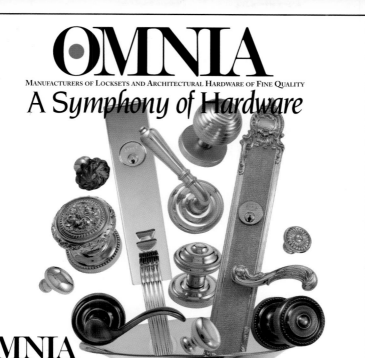

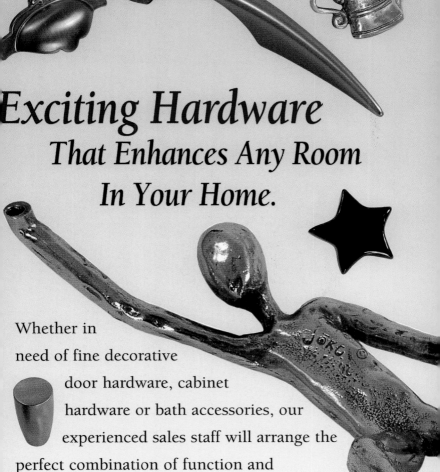

Exciting Hardware
That Enhances Any Room
In Your Home.

Whether in
need of fine decorative
door hardware, cabinet
hardware or bath accessories, our
experienced sales staff will arrange the
perfect combination of function and
style to fit any budget.

Paying attention to detail

Golden Bear has the top names in door hardware for your home. From brass to chrome to brushed bronze, we offer the fine details that enhance the beauty of your decor.

Because in your home the details are important.

Visit our showroom or visit us online.

VANGUARD HARDWARE INCORPORATED

You have already invested time and care to research and decide on a homebuilder. This is the company that will turn your dreams into reality. Now come the fine details! The finishing touches that will truly make this house a distinctive reflection of what you want your home to be. Make the statement you desire, be it one of comfort and tradition, or one of boldness and modern contemporary. When planning and designing these personal details, be sure to contact Vanguard Hardware, Inc. and allow us to work with your builder to insure that the Door, Cabinet, and Bath hardware will reflect the planning that went into every detail throughout your new home. Custom homebuilders and homeowners alike will appreciate the experience and attention to detail that is the benchmark of our company. Founded in 1971 and concentrating on customer service, Vanguard Hardware, Inc. has always strived to be a leader in providing the best values, selections, and services the builder has required. Now offering a showroom, available by appointment for builders, interior decorators, and homeowners.

3017 Indianola Ave. • Columbus, Ohio 43202
614.267.6602

Windows &
Doors

APCO INDUSTRIES ....**(614) 224–3125**
815 Michigan Avenue, Columbus   Fax:(614) 224–1719
See ad on page: 384, 385
Principal/Owner: Mark Mason
Website: www.apco.com e-mail: mark@apco.com

DESIGNER DOORS, INC. ....**(800) 241–0525**
183 East Pomeroy Street, River Falls   Fax:(715) 426–4999
See ad on page: 388
Principal/Owner: Kent Forsland
Website: www.designerdoors.com e-mail: info@designerdoors.com
Additional Information: Complete portfolios available on–line @ www.designerdoors.com.

NORTH AMERICAN WINDOWS..**(614) 529–7050**
3670 Parkway Lane, Hilliard   Fax:(614) 529–7059
See ad on page: 387
Principal/Owner:

PERMA VIEW OF COLUMBUS ....**(614) 436–8226**
561 Schrock Road, Columbus   Fax:(614) 885–4222
See ad on page: 386
Principal/Owner: Phil Megla

SPECIALTY BUILDING PRODUCTS ....**(740) 549–9911**
7699 Green Meadows Drive, Lewis Center   Fax:(740) 549–0215
See ad on page: 337, 383

Specialty
Building Products

WINDOWS THAT DEFINE YOUR HOME

chosen by central Ohio's
leading custom builders

Windsor

740-549-9911

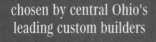

7699 Green Meadows Drive
Lewis Center, OH 43035

WINDSOR
WINDOWS & DOORS

rough
day
?

...here's
a
couple
of
easy
choices.

MARVIN
Windows and Doors

APCO
Windows&Doors

apco.com

Think of the possibilities.®

MARVIN

Windows and Doors

Made for you.®

www.marvin.com

Whether you're planning a major remodeling project or just want to replace a few old windows, no one offers you more shapes, styles or sizes than Marvin. And Marvin offers many glazing options to enhance the energy performance of your home; from single glazing for temperate areas to insulating glass with Low E II coating and filled with argon gas for extreme conditions. So for windows and doors that not only look good but perform beautifully, call or visit our showroom soon.

NA
NORTH AMERICAN
WINDOWS
& MILLWORK

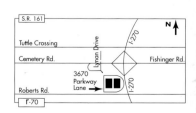

The Marvin Window Showroom
Mon.- Fri. 9 am - 6 pm • Sat. 9 am - 1 pm
Evening Hours & House Calls By Appointment

3670 Parkway Lane • Hilliard
(You Can See Us From I-270)
(614) **529-7050**

Custom
Metalwork

DECORATIVE IRON ....**(713) 991-7600**
10600 Telephone Road, Houston   Fax: (713) 991-0022
See Ad on Page: 386, 387
Website: www.decorativeiron.com
Principal/Owner: Marshall Hoffman

LARA'S ART METAL ....**(281) 405-8289**
610 Raymac Street, Houston   Fax: (281) 405-9884
See Ad on Page: 383
e-mail: melvitero@hotmail.com
Principal/Owner: Jose Emilio Lara Additional Information: Lara's Art Metal has adorned
eclectic homes with the graceful designs of ornamental iron for more than a decade.

Stairs &
Metalworking

VANDYKE CUSTOM IRON, INC. ....**(614) 860–9300**
311 Outerbelt Street, Columbus   Fax:(614) 863–9670
See ad on page: 390
Principal/Owner: John VanDyke
Additional Information: Serving Ohio for more than 30 years.

We can also redesign or upgrade your existing wood or iron rails with elegant new components. We have hundreds of ballusters to choose from.

VanDyke
CUSTOM IRON INCORPORATED

311 Outerbelt Street
Columbus, Ohio 43213
(614) 860-9300

Colonial Custom Woodworking

We specialize in custom cabinets, mantels, stairways, and all aspects of interior trim.

The Ashley Group Luxury Home Resource Collection

The **Ashley Group (www.theashleygroup.com)** is pleased to offer as your final destination when searching for home improvement and luxury resources the following **Home Books** in your local market. Available now: *Chicago, Washington D.C., South Florida, Los Angeles, Dallas/Fort Worth, Detroit, Colorado, New York, Atlanta, Arizona, Philadelphia, San Diego, North Carolina, Boston, Houston, Las Vegas, Connecticut/Westchester County, Central Ohio and Kansas City.* These comprehensive, hands-on guides to building, remodeling, decorating, furnishing, and landscaping a luxury home, are required reading for the serious and selective homeowner. With over 700 full-color, beautiful pages, the **Home Book** series in each market covers all aspects of the building and remodeling process, including listings of hundreds of local industry professionals, accompanied by informative and valuable editorial discussing the most recent trends.

Order your copies today and make your dream come true!

THE ASHLEY GROUP LUXURY HOME RESOURCE COLLECTION

Yes! Please send me the following Home Books! At $39.95 for each, plus $4.00 Shipping & Handling and Tax per book.

☐ Dallas/Fort Worth Home Book *Premier Ed.*	___ # of Copies	☐ Detroit Home Book *Premier Ed.*	___ # of Copies
☐ New York Home Book *Premier Ed.*	___ # of Copies	☐ Colorado Home Book *Premier Ed.*	___ # of Copies
☐ Chicago Home Book *6th Ed.*	___ # of Copies	☐ Los Angeles Home Book *2nd Ed.*	___ # of Copies
☐ Washington DC Home Book *2nd Ed.*	___ # of Copies	☐ South Florida Home Book *2nd Ed.*	___ # of Copies
☐ North Carolina Home Book *Premier Ed.*	___ # of Copies	☐ Las Vegas Home Book *Premier Ed.*	___ # of Copies
☐ San Diego Home Book *Premier Ed.*	___ # of Copies	☐ Philadelphia Home Book *Premier Ed.*	___ # of Copies
☐ Arizona Home Book *Premier Ed.*	___ # of Copies	☐ Atlanta Home Book *Premier Ed.*	___ # of Copies
☐ Boston Home Book *Premier Ed.*	___ # of Copies	☐ Houston Home Book *Premier Ed.*	___ # of Copies
☐ Connecticut/Westchester Cty. Home Book *Premier Ed.*	___ # of Copies	☐ Kansas City Home Book *Premier Ed.*	___ # of Copies
☐ Central Ohio Home Book *Premier Ed.*	___ # of Copies		

I ordered (# Of Books) _____ X $43.95 = $ _____   Total amount enclosed: $ _____

Please charge my: _____ Visa   _____ Mastercard   _____ American Express

Credit Card #: _____   Exp. Date: _____

Name: _____   Phone: _____

Signature: _____

Address: _____   Email: _____

City: _____   State: _____   Zip Code: _____

Send order to: Attn: Book Sales – Marketing, The Ashley Group – Reed Business, 2000 Clearwater Drive, Oak Brook, IL 60523
Or Call Toll Free at: 1.888.458.1750 • Or E-mail ashleybooksales@reedbusiness.com • Visit us on-line at www.theashleygroup.com

All orders must be accompanied by check, money order or credit card # for full amount.

FLOORING & COUNTERTOPS

GRANITE?

style.

elegance.

luxury.

STAINMASTER
Ultra Life®carpet

LEVI'S*4floors*

DUPONT FLOORING CENTER℠

carpet • ceramic • hardwood • laminate • vinyl • area rugs

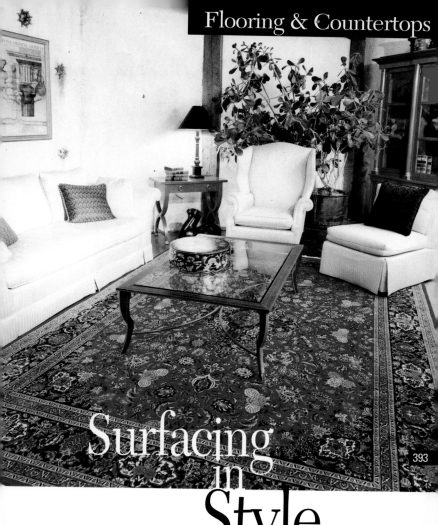

Surfacing in Style

The feel of a home is indelibly tied to the materials that make up its surfaces, and its floors and countertops are two of the most conspicuous. Ceramic tile, red oak, and marble floors, for example, each evoke vastly different responses. Depending on your goals, you can choose materials that make you feel casual and relaxed, cozy and warm, or powerful and prestigious.

As the world becomes smaller due to the ease of global travel, exotic woods, stone and tile are increasingly available. And manmade countertop materials come in an increasing array of colors and styles.

The suppliers and artisans featured in the following pages can offer you a whole new world waiting just below (or on top of) the surface.

Photo courtesy of **Aitken & Assoc./Menendian Oriental Rugs**

Flooring & Countertops

DISTINGUISHED FLOOR COVERINGS...
CARPETS & RUGS

From a room-sized French Aubusson rug to a dense wool carpet with inset borders, "soft" floor treatments are used in area homes to make a signature statement, or blend quietly into the background to let other art and furnishings grab the attention.

Selecting carpeting and rugs requires research, a dedicated search, and the guidance of a well-established design plan. Because the floor covers the width and depth of any room, it's very important that your choices are made in concert with other design decisions – from furniture to art, from window treatments to lighting.

Your interior designer or a representative at any of the fine retail stores featured in the following pages is qualified to educate you as you make your selections.

Rug and carpet dealers who cater to a clientele that demands a high level of personal service (from advice to installation and maintenance) and top quality products, are themselves dedicated to only the best in terms of service and selection. Their accumulated knowledge will be a most important benefit as you select the right carpet for your home.

THE WORLD AT YOUR FEET

Today's profusion of various fibers, colors, patterns, textures, and weights make carpet selection exciting and challenging. Your search won't be overwhelming if you realize the requirements of your own home and work within those boundaries.

Begin where the carpet will eventually end up – that is, in your home. Consider how a carpet will function by answering questions like these:

• What is the traffic pattern? High traffic areas, like stairs and halls, require a stain resistant dense or low level loop carpet for top durability in a color or pattern that won't show wear. Your choices for a bedroom, where traffic is minimal, will include lighter colors in deeper plush or velvets.

• How will it fit with existing or developing decors? Do you need a neutral for an unobtrusive background, or an eye-catching tone-on-tone texture that's a work of art in itself?

• Will it flow nicely into adjoining rooms? Carpet or other flooring treatments in the surrounding rooms need to be considered.

• What needs, other than decorative, must the carpet fill? Do you need to keep a room warm, muffle sound, protect a natural wood floor?

ORIENTAL RUGS

The decision to invest in an Oriental rug should be made carefully. Buying a rug purely for its decorative beauty and buying for investment purposes require two different approaches. If you're buying for aesthetics, put beauty first and condition second. Certain colors and patterns are more significant than others; a reputable dealer can guide you. Check for quality by looking at these features:
• Regularity of knotting.
• Color clarity.
• Rug lies evenly on the floor.
• Back is free of damage or repair marks.

BEYOND TRADITIONAL

Solid surfacing is now being used to make custom faucets, decorative wall tiles, and lots of other creative touches for the home. Their rich colors (including granite), famed durability and versatility are perfect for bringing ideas to life. Check with your countertop supplier for information and ideas.

• How is the room used? Do teenagers and toddlers carry snacks into the family room? Is a finished basement used for ping-pong as well as a home office?

THE ARTISTRY OF RUGS

Nothing compares to the artful elegance of a carefully selected area rug placed on a hard surface. Through pattern, design, texture and color, rug designers create a work of art that is truly enduring. If you have hardwood, marble or natural stone floors, an area rug will only enhance their natural beauty. From Chinese silk, to colorful Pakistanis, to rare Caucasian antiques, the possibilities are as varied as the world is wide.

If you're creating a new interior, it's best to start with rug selection. First, it's harder to find the "right" rug than it is to find the "right" fabric or paint: there are simply fewer fine rugs than there are fabrics, patterns or colors. However, don't make a final commitment on a rug until you know it will work with the overall design. Second, rugs usually outlive other furnishings. Homeowners like to hang on to their rugs when they move, and keep them as family heirlooms.

In recent years, many rug clients have been enjoying a bounty of beautiful, well-made rugs from every major rug-producing country in the world. As competition for the global market intensifies, rugs of exceptionally high caliber are more readily available. Getting qualified advice is more important than ever.

Fine rug dealers, like those showcased in the following pages, have knowledgeable staff members who are dedicated to educating their clientele and helping them find a rug they'll love. Through careful consideration of your tastes, and the requirements of your home, these professionals will virtually walk you through the process. They'll encourage you to take your time, and to judge each rug on its own merits. They'll insist on you taking rugs home so that you can experience them in your own light (and may also provide delivery). And their companies will offer cleaning and repair service, which may well be important to you some day.

WARMING UP TO HARDWOOD

A hardwood floor is part of the dream for many custom homeowners searching for a warm, welcoming environment. Highly polished planks or fine parquet, the beauty of wood has always been a definitive part of luxurious homes and as the design "warming trend" continues, a wood floor figures prominently in achieving this feeling.

FOR SUCCESSFUL CARPET SHOPPING

1. Take along blueprints (or accurate measurements), fabric swatches, paint chips & photos.
2. Focus on installed, not retail price.
3. Take samples home to experience it in the light of the room.
4. Be aware of delivery times; most carpet is available within weeks; special orders or custom designs take much longer.
5. Shop together. It saves time in the decision-making process.

With new product options that make maintenance even easier, wood floors continue to add value and distinction in upscale homes throughout the area and the suburbs. Plank, parquet, and strip wood come in a wide variety of materials, and scores of styles and tones. Consider what effect you're trying to achieve.

Plank wood complements a traditional interior, while parquet wood flooring offers a highly stylized look. Designs stenciled directly on to floorboards create an original Arts and Crafts feel.

Brazilian cherry wood and tumbled travertine quarried from Italy are simply more accessible today, and the door is open to previously obscure materials such as Australian jarrah eucalyptus or American antique red heart cypress (also known as tidewater or bald cypress).

VINYL AND LAMINATES

Vinyl or laminated floor coverings are no longer considered candidates for immediate rehab. As a matter of fact, they're among the most updated looks in flooring. Stylish laminates are made to convincingly simulate wood, ceramic tile and other natural flooring products, and are excellent choices for heavy traffic areas. They come in hundreds of colors and patterns, and offer great compatibility with countertop materials.

THE RENAISSANCE OF CERAMIC TILE

Ceramic tile has literally come out of the back rooms and into the spotlight with its color, beauty and unique stylistic potential. As sophisticated shoppers gain a better understanding of the nature and possibilities of tile, its use has increased dramatically. Homeowners who want added quality and value in their homes are searching out hand painted glazed tiles for the risers of a staircase, quirky rectangular tiles to frame a powder room mirror, and ceramic tiles that look exactly like stone for their sun porch or kitchen. From traditional to modern, imported to domestic, ceramic tile offers a world of possibilities.

It is the perfect solution for homeowners who want floor, walls, countertops or backsplashes made of top quality, durable and attractive materials. A glazed clay natural product, ceramic tile is flexible, easy to care for, and allows for a variety of design ideas. It is easily cleaned with water and doesn't require waxing or polishing. And, like other natural flooring and counter products, ceramic tile adds visible value to a luxury home.

BUDGETING FOR WOOD FLOOR

- 2 ¼ in. strip oak - $10/sq. ft. Wider plank or parquet, glued & nailed - $15/sq. ft. Fancy parquet, hand-finished plank or French patterns (Versailles, Brittany) - $30/sq. ft. and up.
- Estimates include finishing and installation; not sub-floor trim.

THE NUMBER ONE WAY TO DECIDE ON A RUG

Do you like the rug enough to decorate around it? There's your answer.

SELECTING CERAMIC TILE

Not all tile works in all situations, so it's imperative that you get good advice and counsel when selecting ceramic tile for your home. Ceramic tile is wear-rated, and this standardized system will steer you in the right direction. Patronize specialists who can provide creative, quality-driven advice. Visit showrooms to get an idea of the many colors, shapes and sizes available for use on floors, walls and counters. You'll be in for a very pleasant surprise.

If you're building or remodeling, your builder, architect, and/or interior designer can help you in your search and suggest creative ways to enliven your interior schemes. Individual hand-painted tiles can be interspersed in a solid color backsplash to add interest and individuality. Tiles can be included in a glass block partition, on a wallpapered wall, or in harmony with an area rug.

Grout, which can be difficult to keep clean, is now being addressed as a potential design element. By using a colored grout, the grout lines become a contrast design element – or can be colored to match the tile itself.

THE SOPHISTICATED LOOK OF NATURAL STONE

For a luxurious look that radiates strength and character, the world of natural stone offers dazzling possibilities. As custom buyers look for that "special something" to add to the beauty and value of their homes, they turn to the growing natural stone marketplace. A whole world of possibilities is now open to involved homeowners who contact the master craftsmen and suppliers who dedicate their careers to excellence in stone design, installation and refurbishing.

Marble and granite, which have always been options for homeowners, are more popular than ever. With luxurious texture and color, marble is often the choice to add dramatic beauty to a grand entryway or a master bath upgrade. Granite continues to grow in popularity especially in luxury kitchens – there is no better material for countertops. It's also popular for a section of countertop dedicated to rolling pastry or dough. Rustic, weathered and unpolished, or highly polished and brilliant, granite brings elegance and rich visual texture that adds easily recognizable value to a home. Beyond marble and granite, the better suppliers of stone products also can introduce homeowners to slates, soapstone, limestone, English Kirkstone, sandstone, and travertine, which can be finished in a variety of individual ways.

DON'T GET COLD FEET

Stone and tile floors are known for their chilly feel. Electrical products are available now to help warm the surfaces of natural products. Installed in the adhesive layer under the flooring, these warming units are available at the better suppliers and showrooms.

CERAMIC TILE AS STONE

With textured surfaces and color variations, ceramic tile can look strikingly like stone. You can get the tone on tone veining of marble, or the look of split stone, in assorted shapes, sizes and color.

BREAKING IN STONE PRODUCTS IN THE HOME

L ike Mother Nature herself, natural stone is both rugged and vulnerable. Each stone requires specific care and maintenance, and homeowners often experience a period of adjustment as they become accustomed to the requirements of caring for their floors or countertops.

Ask an expert about the different requirements and characteristics. Soapstone, for example, is a beautiful, soft stone with an antique patina many people love. Accumulated stains and scratches just add to the look. Granite, on the other hand, will not stain.

A professional can educate you about the specific characteristics of each stone product so you make an informed decision on what products will best serve the lifestyle of your family.

CHOOSING STONE – A UNIQUE EXPERIENCE

O nce a decision to use a natural stone is made, begin your search right away. By allowing plenty of time to discover the full realm of choices, you'll be able to choose a stone and finish that brings luster and value to your home, without the pressure of a deadline. If you order imported stone, it can take months for delivery. Be prepared to visit your supplier's warehouse to inspect the stone that will be used in your home. Natural stone varies – piece to piece, box to box – a slab can vary in color from one end to the other. If you understand this degree of unpredictable irregularity is unavoidable, it will help you approach the selection in a realistic way.

STRONG AND ELEGANT COUNTERTOPS

T he quest for quality and style does not stop until the countertops are selected. Today's countertop marketplace is brimming with man-made products that add high style without sacrificing strength and resiliency.

As the functions of kitchens become broader, the demand for aesthetics continues to increase dramatically. For lasting beauty with incredible design sensibilities, manmade solid surfaces are a very popular choice. The overwhelming number of possibilities and combinations in selecting countertops makes it vital to work with specialists who are quality-oriented. Countertops represent a significant investment in a custom home, and quality, performance and style must be the primary considerations in any decision. Established professionals, like those introduced in your Home Book, have a reputation for expert installation and service of the top quality products that define luxury.

PRICING FOR NATURAL STONE

As with all flooring and countertop materials, get an installed, not a retail quote. Installation can drive the cost up significantly. Preparing a realistic quote may take days of research, due to the tremendous variety of factors that can influence price. As a general guideline, the installed starting price per square foot:
• Granite: $30
• Tumbled marble, limestone, slate: $20
• Engineered stone/quartzite: $25
• Antique stone, with intricate installation: $75
• Granite slab countertop: $70

SOLID SURFACING SHOWS UP ON TILES

Durable, non-porous solid surface materials are now being used to make decorative wall tiles. Check with your countertop supplier for information and ideas.

MAKE COUNTERTOP CHOICES EARLY

Since decisions on cabinetry are often made far in advance, it's best to make a countertop choice concurrently.

Expect to spend at least two weeks visiting showrooms and acquainting yourself with design and materials. Take along paint chips, samples of cabinet and flooring materials, and any pictures of the look you're trying to achieve. Expect a solid surface custom counter order to take at least five weeks to arrive.

AN ARRAY OF COUNTERTOP CHOICES

You'll face a field of hundreds of colors and textures of solid surfacing, laminates, ceramic tile, natural stone, wood and stainless or enameled steel. Poured concrete counters also are finding their way into luxury kitchens in the area.

Laminate or color-through laminate offer hundreds of colors, patterns and textures, many of which convincingly mimic the look of solid surfacing or granite. Enjoying growing popularity in countertop application, are the natural stones, those staggeringly gorgeous slabs of granite, marble or slate, which offer the timeless look of quality and luxury. Naturally quarried stone is extremely durable and brings a dramatic beauty and texture to the kitchen or bath. For endless color and pattern possibilities, ceramic tile is a highly durable option. Manmade resin-based solid surfacing materials offer many of the same benefits as stone. These surfaces are fabricated for durability and beauty, and new choices offer a visual depth that is astounding to the eye. It can be bent, carved, or sculpted. Elaborate edges can be cut into a solid surface counter and sections can be carved out to accommodate other surface materials, such as stainless steel or marble. Best known for superior durability, solid surfaces stand up to scratches, heat and water.

FINDING THE BEST SOURCE FOR MATERIALS

If you're building or remodeling your home, your designer, builder or architect will help you develop some ideas and find a supplier for the material you choose. Reputable suppliers, like those featured in the Home Book, are experienced in selecting the best products and providing expert installation. Go visit a showroom or office – their knowledge will be invaluable to you. The intricacies and idiosyncrasies of natural products, and the sheer volume of possibilities in fabricated surfaces, can be confounding on your own. ■

BE CREATIVE!

Mix and match counter top materials for optimum functionality and up-to-date style. Install a butcher block for chopping vegetables and slicing breads, a slab of marble for rolling pastry and bakery dough, granite on an island for overall elegance, and solid surfaces for beauty and durability around the sinks and cooktop areas.

399

MAKE IT CONCRETE

This material is a versatile and indestructible choice, available in a variety of colors and textures. Sealed concrete can be made with creative borders, scored, sandblasted or stained. A strong, natural material, it can be made to look like other materials and natural stone.

Marble &
Granite

CHESTER A. SMITH, INC. ....**(614) 294–5271**
1330 Norton Avenue, Columbus
See ad on page: 401
Principal/Owner: Paul C. Smith
e-mail: csmithinc@aol.com Additional Information: Serving Central Ohio for over 70 years in the custom fabrication of natural marble and granite.
Fax:(614) 294–8109

MARBLE & GRANITE WORKS ....**(614) 873–2211**
7635 Commerce Place, Plain City
See ad on page: 402, 403
Principal/Owner: Chris Watson
Fax:(614) 873–8173

NEW MILLENNIUM MARBLE & TILE ....**(614) 206–2417**
6700 Danson Pl, Westerville
See ad on page: 404
Fax:(614) 818–0311

GRANITE • MARBLE • SLATE

CHESTER A. SMITH, INC.

1330 Norton Avenue • Columbus, Ohio 43212
Phone: 614-294-5271 • Fax: 614-294-8109

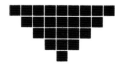

MARBLE & GRANITE WORKS, INC.

MARBLE & GRANITE WORKS

7635 Commerce Place
Plain City, Ohio 43064
Tel: 614-873-2211
Fax: 614-873-8173

Ceramic
Tile

DELTEDESCO TILE & CONSTRUCTION CORPORATION ....**(740) 965–5242**
  38 Evening Street, Sunbury
  See ad on page: 392b, 392c, 406
  <u>Principal/Owner:</u> Sonia DelTedesco
  <u>e-mail:</u> deltile@aol.com
Fax:(740) 965–4030

ROCCO CARIFA TILE COMPANY ....**(740) 549–2244**
  3259 Sunglow Drive, Lewis Center
  See ad on page: 406
  <u>Principal/Owner:</u> Rocco Carifa
Fax:(740) 549–2255

405

Del Tedesco Tile & Construction

38 Evening Street
Sunbury, Ohio 43074
740.965.5242

ROCCO CARIFA

RC

TILE COMPANY

RESIDENTIAL & COMMERCIAL
Tile•Marble•Slate

Phone: (740) 549-2244
Fax: (740) 549-2255
Pager: (614) 730-4606

Email: rcarifa@aol.com

Hardwood

DEIBLE'S HARWOOD FLOORS ....**(614) 499–0118**
    4000 S. High St., Columbus
    See ad on page: 409
    Fax:(614) 497–0545

HARDWOOD SPECIALISTS, LLC ....**(614) 251–9663**
    1574 Old Leanard Avenue, Columbus
    See ad on page: 408a, 408b, 408c, 408d, 408e, 408f, 408g, 408h
    Fax:(614) 251–9669
    Principal/Owner: T.G. Banks
    Website: www.hardwoodspecialists.com e-mail: t.g.banks@hardwoodspecialists.com
    Additional Information: Hardwood Specialists is a full service hardwood flooring company.
    We offer and install the most exclusive & distinctive hardwood flooring available.

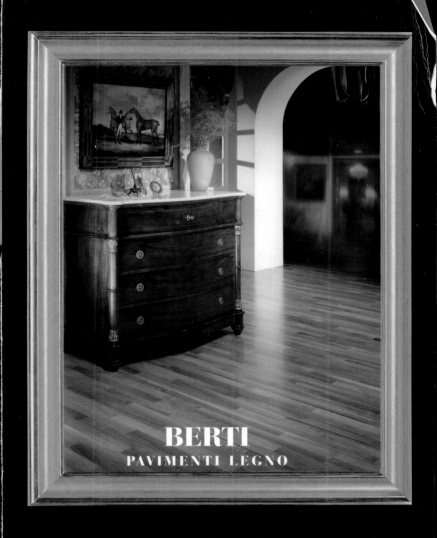

OUR SERVICES

Hardwood Flooring · Floor Inlays · Borders · Medallions

Custom Renovation · Residential & Commercial Remodeling

Detailed Restorations · Expert Installation · Custom Casework

Architectural Millwork · Sanding & Finishing · Maintenance

Protective Floor Coverings · Fire Restorations · Fitness Flooring

Design
Consulting

Quality
Craftsmanship

For custom installation and design of new hardwood floors to refinishing, restoration and maintenance of existing wood floors, we provide a full range of services.

Our quality and craftsmanship are second to none.

EXTRAORDINARY HARDWOOD FLOORING

FINE
ARCHITECTURAL
WOODWORK

Nike World Headquar
Beaverton, Oregon

Hardwood Floor Finishing Systems
Dust Containment • Durable • No Toxic Fumes

Dust Containment System – Virtually eliminates sanding dust.

Durable Waterborne Finishes – The Environmental Choice®
Swedish waterborne finishes provide beauty and the ultimate in
durability without toxic fumes.

Maintenance – Safe, easy-to-use floor care products are all you need to
keep that newly refinished floor looking great for years to come.

Distributed locally by Schafer Hardwood Flooring Company
614-272-6001 • www.schaferhardwoodflooring.com

Bringing out the best in hardwood floors

Hardwood Specialists, LLC

"The Finest in Distinctive Hardwood Flooring"

614.251.WOOD (9663)

www.hardwoodspecialists.com

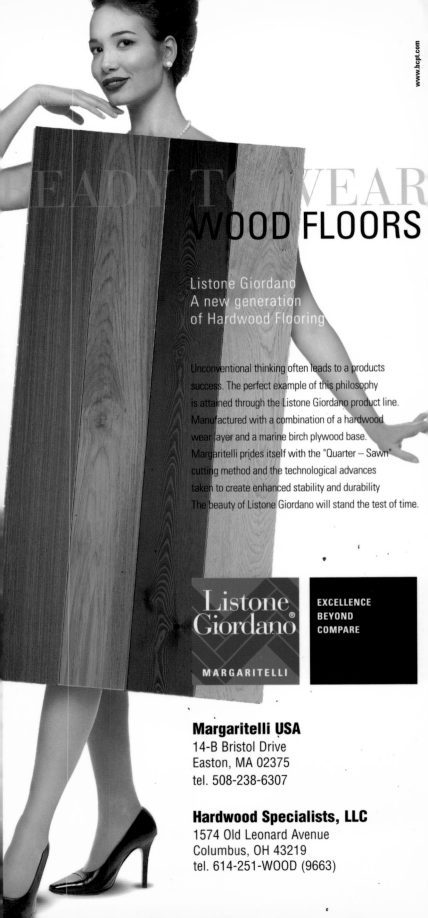

CUSTOM INTERIOR RENOVATION

CUSTOM KITCHENS

"The Finest in Distinctive Hardwood Floorin

Phone 614.251.WOOD (9663) • Fax 614.251.9669

Suppliers

BERTI *Pavimenti Legno*
Traditional flooring patterned designs, inlaid floors

MARGARITELLI
Exceptional engineered flooring

MIRAGE
Engineered prefinished flooring

SHELMAN
African hardwood flooring

HARRIS TARKETT
Australian wood flooring

PATINA
Old world flooring

GRILLWORKS
Hardwood grills for every floor

OSHKOSH
Hardwood medallions, borders, parque

EVERLAST
Specialists in fitness flooring

COVERSPORTS U.S.A.
Protective floor coverings

VERMEISTER
Hardwood floor finishes and adhesives

EQUINOX
Floor d-fenders protective pads

Client List

A small sampling of our distinguished: Commercial & Residential Clien

ANTHROPOLOGIE
Easton: Columbus, Ohio

THE APPLE STORE
Easton: Columbus, Ohio

HILTON HOTEL
Easton: Columbus, Ohio

ZACHARY'S
Easton: Columbus, Ohio

MARC SLUTSKY
Syndicated Columnist

KARL H. SCHNEIDER
Upper Arlington, Ohio

CLOVER VALLEY
Golf Club: Johnstown, Ohio

APDS
Columbus, Ohio

COLUMBUS WOOD
Products: Columbus, Ohio

RICHARD TAYLOR
Architects: Columbus, Ohio

PAUL L. CRAVER
Housewright: Powell, Ohio

DAVID F AXELROD
Westerville, Ohio

Customer Assistance Center

Happy to have made your acquaintance.

We hope this brochure has helped you to get know **Hardwood Speciali
LLC** and given you a better understanding of our product line and servi

If you have any other hardwood-related questions or would like us to se
literature on a specific product or service, call our Customer Assista
Center at 1-888-833-3773. We also invite you to visit our web site
www.hardwoodspecialists.com

Of course, there's still only one way to satisfy your curiosity about
exclusive collection of hardwood floors: Visit our showroom and experie
the finest selection bar none.

Hardwood Specialists, LLC

1574 Old Leonard Avenue, Columbus, OH 43219
Phone: 614.251-9663/ Fax: 614.251-9669/ Toll Free: 888.833-3773
www.hardwoodspecialists.com

Carpeting
& Rugs

CARPET GRAPHICS ....**(614) 299–2570**
617 East Third Avenue, Columbus   Fax:(614) 299–2570
See ad on page: 413
Principal/Owner: Patrick L. Durkin

FOOTPRINTS RUG COMPANY ....**(614) 336–0447**
6478 Fiesta Drive, Columbus   Fax:(614) 336–0448
See ad on page: 412
Principal/Owner: Steven Cudney
Website: www.footprintsrug.com e-mail: footprintsrug@aol.com
Additional Information: Design sensitive staff, to assist the most discriminating customer in selection and service of decorative floor coverings.

K.A. MENENDIAN..**(614) 294–3345**
1090 West 5th Avenue, Columbus   Fax:(614) 294–3348
See ad on page: 411
Principal/Owner: Phil Menendian
Website: www.karug.com
Additional Information: Central Ohio's only full–service rug washing and repair facility.

You'll Never Have to Put One of Our Rugs Out to Pasture

With proper care, quality, hand-crafted Oriental rugs from K.A. Menendian will last long enough to become treasured family heirlooms.

Oriental Rugs are our only business

- Over 90 years in business
- Over 2000 Oriental rugs in stock
- Guaranteed lowest price
- Free in-home trial
- Central Ohio's only full-service rug washing and repair facility

Est. 1910

K.A.Menendian INC.

Ohio's First Name in Oriental Rugs
1090 West 5th Ave. at Kenny Rd.
Mon.-Sat. 9-5:30, Thurs. 9-8, Closed Sun.
(614) 294-3345 • 1-888-KAM RUGS
www.karugs.com

Footprints Rug Company

Featuring:

★ **Tiger Rug**™ -Authentic handknotted Tibetan Carpets in delicious colors.

★ **Oldeboards**™ -The world's finest hand finished plank and patterned wood floors. New hardwood finished to look olde.

★ *Many other assorted carpets, rugs, cork, bamboo,ceramic tile, marble, leather tiles...*

Footprints Rug Company • 6478 Fiesta Dr • Columbus,OH 43235 • 614-336-0447

Carpet Graphics

Artist • Owner
Patrick L Durkin

Hand Crafted Custom Carpet & Area Rugs

617 East Thrid Avenue • Columbus, Ohio 43201

Countertops

DISTINCTIVE SURFACES, INC. ....**(614) 431–0898**
6296 Proprietors Road, Worthington   Fax:(614) 785–0618
See ad on page: 416
<u>Principal/Owner:</u> Mike Beasley
<u>e-mail:</u> distinctive@ee.net

DUPONT CORIAN / ZODIAQ DISTRIBUTOR
See ad on page: 417, 536b, 536c
<u>Principal/Owner:</u> Cinda Carter
<u>e-mail:</u> Cinda.Carter@ovsco.com   <u>Additional Information:</u> For more information or to inquire about local dealers, contact OVS Manager Cinda Carter, Cinda.Carter@ovsco.com.

HYTEC TOPS ....**(614) 251–0383**
2741 East Fourth Avenue, Columbus   Fax:(614) 251–0385
See ad on page: 314d, 348, 415
<u>Principal/Owner:</u> Ron Mercer

GRANITE & MARBLE

2741 East Fourth Avenue
Columbus, Ohio 43219
Phone 614.251.0383
Fax 614.251.0385

"She knew exactly what she wanted. She just wasn't sure what it was."

A Dazzling New Dimension Of Surfacing Material

From the makers of Corian® comes a material like no other: Zodiaq® Quartz Surfaces, with the dazzling radiance of natural quartz crystals suspended in striking colors. Explore the possibilities at Zodiaq.com.

For more information or to inquire about local dealers,
Contact:
DuPont Corian®/ Zodiaq® Distributors
OVS Marketing Manager
Cinda.Carter@ovsco.com

Flooring

COMPLETE FLOORING ....**(614) 873–1895**
299 South Jefferson, Plain City
See ad on page: 425   Fax:(614) 873–9792
Principal/Owner: Bill Rucker

DESIGN CRETE, INC. ....**(614) 861–6677**
1195 Technology Drive, Gahanna   Fax:(614) 861–6779
See ad on page: 296, 297, 422
Principal/Owner: Larry Jones
Website: www.designcreteinc.com

DURAFLOORS ....**(740) 549–2555**
7750 Green Meadows Drive, Lewis Center   Fax:(740) 657–1595
See ad on page: 424
Principal/Owner: Bob McGlone

LEVI'S 4–FLOORS ....**(614) 846–4441**
6329 Busch Boulevard, Columbus   Fax:(614) 846–2528
See ad on page: 392d, 421
Additional Information: We have been providing the finest quality products and installation of
floor covering for over 16 years. We are proud to be the exclusive Dupont Flooring Center in
central Ohio.

MICHAEL DAVID ....**(614) 416–2000**
4281 Morse Road, Gahanna   Fax:(614) 416–2010
See ad on page: 420
Additional Information: Simply the finest in flooring.

PANEL TOWN & MORE ....**(614) 488–0334**
1063 Dublin Road, Columbus   Fax:(614) 488–0359
See ad on page: 426
Principal/Owner: Homdi Soliman

R.A.P. ....**(614) 873–5866**
7450 Montgomery Drive, Plain City   Fax:(614) 873–0224
See ad on page: 423
Principal/Owner: Rebecca A. Palmer
e-mail: rap.flooring@gte.net

Floors So Good
We're Often Looked Down Upon

_____

...ichael David, our passion is floors. Because no matte...
...s change, your floors remain a constant throughout the ...
...r knowledgeable staff works hard to help you choos...
...ct floor from our extensive selection. And when your new...
...shed, you'll love looking down on our work.

Michael David

100   4281 Morse Rd   Gahanna   OH

Floors
made like
fine
furniture.

MANNINGTON
W O O D · F L O O R S

LEVI'S4floors

DUPONT FLOORING CENTER™

carpet • ceramic • hardwood • laminate • vinyl • area rugs

NORTHEAST	**EAST**	**WEST**	**NORTHWEST**
6329 Busch Blvd.	2765 Brice Rd.	2526 Hilliard-Rome Rd.	400 W. Powell Rd.
846-4441	**577-1111**	**876-6400**	**766-4446**

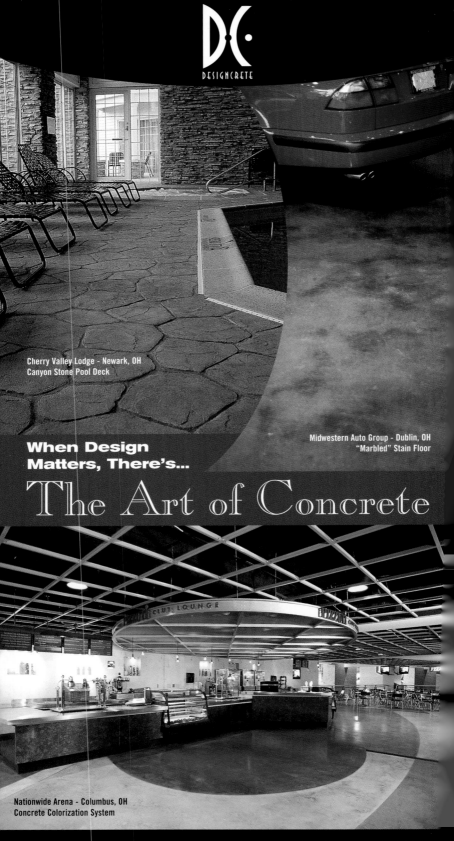

DESIGNCRETE

Cherry Valley Lodge - Newark, OH
Canyon Stone Pool Deck

Midwestern Auto Group - Dublin, OH
"Marbled" Stain Floor

When Design Matters, There's...

The Art of Concrete

Nationwide Arena - Columbus, OH
Concrete Colorization System

INTERIOR/EXTERIOR · RESIDENTIAL/COMMERCIAL

614•861•6677

1195 Technology Dr.   Gahanna, OH 43230   Fx: 614•861•6779

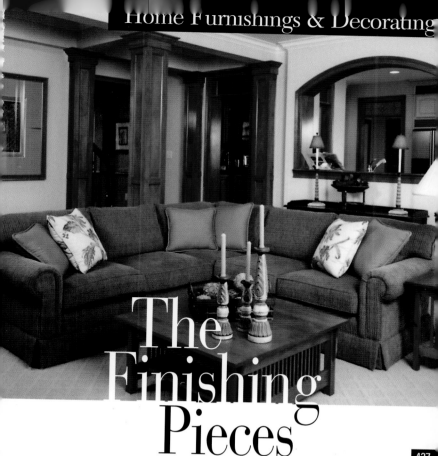

The Finishing Pieces

427

Home furnishings are the frosting on the cake that is your dream home. While your home's location, construction and architecture may be exactly as you have wished, they provide but the stage for your homelife. It is the objects that fill your home, from the furniture to window treatments to lighting, that truly express your personal style and the way you want to live.

Today's homeowners, whether they're in their first or final home, have the elevated taste that comes from exposure to good design. Choice is abundant in the home furnishing industry; one item is more amazingly gorgeous than the next, and anything you can imagine can be yours. This freedom can be overwhelming, even intimidating, if you don't keep a sharp focus.

By visiting the finest stores, specialty shops, and artisans, like those presented in the following pages, you can begin to refine your options and choose the items which best suit your home, tastes and lifestyle. Knowledgeable professionals will be available to guide you. Enjoy.

Photo courtesy of **Amish Country Furnishings**

TAKE TIME TO CHOOSE FURNITURE

Is there an architectural focus point in the room, a fireplace, a skylight or brilliant picture window?
If not, consider creating focus with a significant piece of furniture, possibly custom designed, like an elaborate entertainment center in the family room or an elegant headboard in the master bedroom.

ACHIEVING A BALANCE

428

For a calming, soothing home, consider designing your rooms around the ancient Chinese study of Feng Shui. Not a religion, the science of Feng Shui is used to organize furnishings and decorative accessories in a natural way to balance the energy of the home and create a harmonious environment. Indoor water features, strategic placement of mirrors and open vessels, along with careful consideration of the arrangement of furniture in each room are all part of designing a Feng Shui environment.

You'll be living with your choices for many years to come, so take your time. Try to define why you like what you like. Look through shelter magazines, visit decorator homes and furniture showrooms. When you see a piece or arrangement you like, try to analyze what you like about it. Is it the color, the style of the piece, the texture of the fabric? Recognizing common elements you are drawn to will help you hone and refine your personal style.

As you start out, be sure to ruthlessly assess your current interior. Clear out pieces that need to be replaced or no longer work with your lifestyle, even if you have no clear idea of what you'll be replacing them with. Sometimes empty space makes visualizing something new much easier.

When furnishing a new room, consider creating a focus by concentrating on an architectural element, or selecting one important piece, like a Chinese Chippendale-style daybed or an original Arts & Crafts spindle table. Or, make your focus a special piece you already own.

To make the most of your time when visiting showrooms, take along your blueprint or a detailed drawing with measurements, door and window placements, and special architectural features. If your spouse or anyone else will be involved in the final decision, try to shop together to eliminate return trips. The majority of stores can deliver most furniture within eight weeks, but special custom pieces may take up to 16 weeks.

Be open-minded and accept direction. Rely on your interior designer or a qualified store designer to help direct your search and keep you within the scale of your floor plan. Salespeople at top stores can help you find exactly what you're seeking, and, if you ask them, guide you away from inappropriate decisions toward more suitable alternatives. Their firsthand knowledge of pricing, products and features is invaluable when it comes to finding the best quality for your money.

As you seek these tangible expressions of your personal style, keep these thoughts in mind:

• What are your priorities? Develop a list of "must have," "want to have," and "dreaming about."

• What major pieces will be with you for a long time? Allow a lion's share of your budget for these.

• What colors or styles are already established through the flooring, walls, windows, or cabinetry? Keep swatches with you, if possible.

• Does the piece reflect your tastes? Don't be influenced too strongly by what looks great in a showroom or designer house.

COMPLETE FLOORING

299 S Jefferson Ave.
PLAIN CITY, OHIO 43064

(614) 873-1895

Photo courtesy of **Christy Romoser Interiors**

HOME
FURNISHINGS
&
DECORATING

Distinction

Quality

Value

Howard Brooks, Inc.

7790 Olentangy River Rd. • Columbus, OH 43235
614.888.5353
www.howardbrooksinteriors.com

life, stuff, storage

The home is the heart of life. An ever changing story of ourselves, our family, our friends. A welcome retreat where we protect, nurture and sustain all that is needed and loved. Let California Closets share 25 years experience with you to create the finest custom storage solutions for all the areas of your home.

In central Ohio, California Closets has been voted "The Best" by consumers, by more than 2 to 1, over our closest competitor.

Call for a free design consultation and see why we're NUMBER ONE

614.431.0011

Visit our showroom at
761 Busch Ct., Columbus, OH 43229
www.calclosets.com

CALIFORNIA CLOSETS®

• Does the piece fit the overall decorating scheme? Although the days of strict adherence to one style per room are over, it's still necessary to use coordinated styles.

• Is the piece comfortable? Before you buy, sit on the chair, recline on the sofa, pull a chair up to the table.

• Can you get the furnishings through the doorway, up the elevator, or down the stairs?

• Will a piece work for your family's lifestyle? Choose upholstery fabrics, colors and fixtures that will enhance, not hinder, your everyday life.

DESIGNED FOR YOU

The ultimate in expression of personal style, a piece of custom designed furniture is akin to functional art for your home. A custom furniture designer can create virtually any piece you need to fill a special space in your home and satisfy your desire for owning a unique one-of-a-kind.

Some of the most talented, best known designers working in this area today are listed in the following pages of the Home Book. You can contact them directly, or through your interior designer. At an initial meeting you'll see examples of the designer's work and answer questions like:

• What kind of piece do you want? Freestanding entertainment system, dining table, armoire?

• What functions must it serve? It is a piece of art, but the furniture still must function in ways that make it practical and usable. Explain your needs clearly.

• Do you have favorite woods, materials or colors? As with ordering custom woodwork, the possibilities are almost unlimited. Different woods can be painted or finished differently for all kinds of looks. It's best to have some ideas in mind.

• Are you open to new ideas and approaches? If you'd like the designer to suggest new ways of reaching your goal, let him or her know.

Seek out a furniture designer whose portfolio excites you, who you can communicate with, and who you trust to deliver your project in a top quality, professional manner. Ask for a couple of design options for your piece. Make sure you and the designer are in agreement regarding finishes, materials, stain or paint samples you want to see, and a completion date. Most charge a 50 percent deposit at the beginning with the balance due upon completion. If you decide not to go ahead with construction of a piece, expect to be billed a designer's fee. A commissioned piece of furniture

FROM THE FLOOR UP

Your carpets, rugs or flooring set the stage for your design. Whether a simple backdrop or the starring role, it's important to determine which part you want your floor treatments to take at the outset of your decorating project.

'FAUX' FINISH TROMPE L'OEIL?

Any painting technique replicating another look is called a 'faux' (false) finish. There are many methods to achieve wonderful individual effects. Trompe l'oeil (fool the eye) is a mural painting that creates illusion through perspective. A wall becomes an arched entry to a garden.

requires a reasonable amount of time to get from start to finish. If you want an entertainment system for Super Bowl Sunday, make your final design decisions when you take down the Halloween decorations. Keep in mind that the process cannot be rushed.

ILLUMINATING IDEAS

Lighting can be the focal point of a room, or it can be so subtle that it's almost invisible. The trick is knowing what you want to accomplish. Indeed, when we remember a place as cozy and elegant, or cold and uncomfortable, we're feeling the emotional power of illumination.

The industry is filled with options and combinations, from fixtures and bulbs to dimmers and integrated systems. Top lighting retailers in the area employ in-house design consultants to guide you, or you can employ a residential lighting designer.

To deliver a superior lighting scheme, a designer must know:

• What are your needs? Lighting falls into three categories – general, task, and atmospheric. A study/work area, a cozy nook or a kitchen each require different lighting.

• What feeling are you trying to create?

• What "givens" are you working with? Where are your windows or skylights? The use of artificial, indoor light depends to a great degree on the natural light coming in.

• What materials are on the floor and what colors are on the walls and ceiling? This affects how well your lighting will reflect, or "bounce."

• Where is your furniture placed, and how big are individual pieces? This is especially important when you're choosing a dining room chandelier.

• If you're replacing lighting, why are you replacing it? Know the wattage, for instance, if a current light source is no longer bright enough.

• Are there energy/environmental concerns? Lighting consumes 12 to 15 percent of the electricity used in the home. An expert can develop a plan that maximizes energy efficiency.

WINDOW DRESSING

The well-appointed room includes window treatments in keeping with the style of the home and furnishings. Yet it's also important to consider how your window treatments will need to function in your setting. Will they be required to control light,

WHAT'S YOUR STYLE?

Consider these characteristics of different styles: **Formal**-Dark, polished woods; smooth, tightly woven fabrics; symmetrically placed furnishings. **Casual**-Lighter woods; textured, loosely woven fabrics, asymmetric placement. **Contemporary**-Artistic, sculptural furnishings with smooth, clean lines; bold splashes of color and carefully placed artwork. **French Country**-Aged, carved wood furnishings; textiles feature earth-tones mixed with intense colors; accessorized with wrought iron, pottery and baskets. **Rustic**-Sturdy, extremely textural furnishings of polished logs, softened with cushions and pillows in colorful fabrics. **Shabby Chic**-White furniture and accents, slipcovers, overstuffed upholstery and "old" looking accessories. **Tuscan**-Sturdy heavily distressed wood furnishings with terra cotta tile, stone or marble accents; bright fabrics; washed or faux-finished painted surfaces.

or provide privacy as well? Some windows in your home may need just a top treatment as a finishing touch, while a soaring window wall might require sun-blocking draperies or blinds to minimize heat build-up or ultraviolet damage.

How window treatments will be installed is another design question to consider – inside or outside the window frame, from the top of the window to the sill or from ceiling to floor? Take these points into consideration when designing your window treatments:

• How much privacy do you require? If you love the look of light and airy sheers, remember they become transparent at night and you may need blinds or shades as well.

• Is light control necessary? This is usually a must for bedroom window treatments, as well as for windows with southern or western exposures

• Do you want to take advantage of a beautiful view of the landscape or hide an unsightly view of the building next door?

• Are there any structural elements such as built-in cabinets, outlets or vents near the window to consider?

• Are your windows a focal point of the room or the background that puts the finishing touch on your room design?

• What role will the choice of fabric play? The fabric can unify the whole, standout as the focus, or add another note to the rhythm of the room.

PAINTING OUTSIDE THE FRAMES

Through their travels, reading and exposure to art and design, sophisticated homeowners are aware of the beauty that can be added to their homes with specialty decorative painting. They see perfect canvases for unique works of art in walls, furniture and fabrics. The demand for beautiful art applied directly to walls, stairs or furniture has created a renaissance in decorative painting. Faux finishes, trompe l'oeil and murals have joined the traditional finishes of paint, wallpaper and stain for consideration in outstanding residential interiors.

Specialty painters can help you fine-tune your idea, or develop a concept from scratch. At your initial meeting, discuss your ideas, whether they're crystal clear or barely there. Don't be apprehensive if you don't have a clear idea. Artists are by profession visually creative, and by asking questions and sharing ideas, you can develop a concept together.

Ask to see samples of his or her other work, and if possible, visit homes or buildings where the work has been done. Ask for, and call, references. Find out

CUSTOM DESIGNING A CHERRY WOOD TABLE

What might it actually cost to have a custom designed piece of furniture made for you?
Here is a general estimate of the costs involved in the custom design and construction of a 48 in. x 96 in. dining room table.
• Trees harvested (felled) ($30/hr x 2 hours):
  $60
• Trees sawn and dried:
  $175
• Design (included in the project cost)
• Labor cost (fine sanding, construction, varnishing):
  $5,000
• Special materials (included in cost)

Total:
$5,235

431

RECLAIMING CHARACTER

Magnificently unique custom-designed furnishings can be made of wood reclaimed from building renovations or demolitions. Another option is to use new wood, hand-distressed to lend it the character of an older piece.

THE PRICE OF GETTING ORGANIZED

• An 8 ft. closet, round steel chrome plated rods, double and single hang, with a five-drawer unit: $800 to $1,000
• His-and-Hers walk-in closet, full length and double hang rods, two five-drawer units, foldable storage space, mirrored back wall, shoe rack: $1,000 to $4,000
• Conversion of a full-size bedroom into closet area with islands, custom designed cabinets with full extension drawers and decorative hardware, mirrors, jewelry drawers, and many other luxury appointments: $15,000
• Customized desk area, with file drawers, computer stand and slide shelves for printer, keyboard and mouse pad, high pressure surface on melamine with shelves above desk: $3,000
• Average garage remodel, with open and closed storage, sports racks for bikes and fishing poles, a small workbench, and a 4 ft. x 8 ft. pegboard, installed horizontally: $2,500

if the work was completed on time and on budget. Based on your initial conversations, a painter can give you a rough estimate based on the size of the room and the finish you've discussed. You can expect the artist to get back to you with sample drawings, showing color and technique, usually within a week.

Surface preparation, such as stripping and patching, is not usually done by the specialty painter. Ask for recommendations of professionals to do this work if you don't have a painter you already use.

THE GREAT OUTDOORS

As homeowners strive to expand comfortable living space into their yards, top quality outdoor furniture manufacturers respond with new and innovative styles. Before you shop for outdoor furniture, think about:

• What look do you like? The intricate patterns of wrought iron? The smooth and timeless beauty of silvery teak wood? The sleek design of sturdy aluminum?

• What pieces do you need? Furnishing larger decks and terraces requires careful planning.

• Will you store the furniture in the winter or will it stay outdoors under cover?

• Can you see the furniture from inside the house? Make sure the outdoor furnishings won't distract from the established inside or outside design.

TICKLING THE IVORIES

A new or professionally reconditioned piano makes an excellent contribution to the elegance and lifestyle of a growing number of area homes. Pianos add a dimension of personality that no ordinary piece of furniture can match. They are recognized for their beauty, visually and acoustically.

First time piano buyers may be astonished at the range of choices they have and the variables that will influence their eventual decision. Go to the showrooms that carry the best brand name pianos. Not only will you be offered superior quality instruments, but you'll also get the benefit of the sales staff's professional knowledge and experience. Questions that you need to answer will include:

• Who are the primary players of the instrument?

• What level of players are they (serious, beginners)?

• Who are their teachers?

• What is the size of the room the piano will be placed in?

• What are your preferences in wood color or leg shape?

• Are you interested in software packages that convert your instrument into a player piano?

Pianos represent a significant financial investment, one that will not depreciate, and may actually appreciate over time. If a new piano is out of your financial range, ask about the store's selection of reconditioned instruments that they've acquired through trades. The best stores recondition these pieces to a uniformly high standard of excellence and are good options for you to consider. These stores also hold occasional promotions, when special pricing will be in effect for a period of time.

THE HOME OFFICE COMES INTO ITS OWN

The home office has become a "must have" room for many homeowners. More businesses are being operated from home, and increasing numbers of companies are allowing, even encouraging, telecommuting. Spreading out on the dining room table or kitchen table is no longer an efficient option.

Because the home office often requires specific wiring and lighting, be sure your architect, designer and builder are involved in the planning process. If you're simply outfitting an existing room to be your home office, designers on staff at fine furniture stores can guide you. However, it's still most practical to get some architectural input for optimum comfort and functionality of the space.

While some aspects of home furnishings may be easy to overlook, such as storage and lighting, you should give great attention to all of them. The construction of your dream home will give you a place to live, but the way it is furnished will let you live in the style you want. ■

PROJECT FILE

A project file with carpet, fabric, wallpaper and paint samples, floor plans, a tape measure, a calendar, and a phone list of everyone working on your project can really enhance your decorating experience. With your file in hand, decisions can be made on the spot without having to check if the piece matches or fits into your overall plan.

433

Home
Furnishings

AMERICAN FURNISHINGS COMPANY .... **(614) 488–7263**
1409 West Third Avenue, Columbus
                                                        Fax:(614) 488–7264
See ad on page: 442, 443
<u>Principal/Owner:</u> Dennis Blankemeyer
<u>Website:</u> www.americanfurnishings.com <u>e-mail:</u> amerfurn@aol.com
<u>Additional Information:</u> Specializing in handcrafted furniture, lighting, area rugs and pottery.
Recently named top 100 retailer of American Craft.

AMERICAN FURNISHINGS COMPANY .... **(614) 488–7263**
1409 West Third Avenue, Columbus
                                                        Fax:(614) 488–7264
See ad on page: 442, 443
<u>Principal/Owner:</u> Dennis Blankemeyer
<u>Website:</u> www.americanfurnishings.com <u>e-mail:</u> amerfurn@aol.com

AMISH COUNTRY FURNISHINGS .... **(614) 791–8525**
7600 Fishel Drive North, Dublin
                                                        Fax:(614) 791–8595
See ad on page: 448
<u>Principal/Owner:</u> Rod Geitgey
<u>Website:</u> www.amishcountryfurnishings.com <u>e-mail:</u> contactus@amishcountryfurnishing
<u>Additional Information:</u> One of the country's largest selections of Amish–crafted furniture.
We specialize in entertainment centers.

AMISH ORIGINALS FURNITURE COMPANY .... **(614) 891–6257**
8 North State Street, Westerville
                                                        Fax:(614) 523–7427
See ad on page: 441
<u>Principal/Owner:</u>
<u>Website:</u> amish–originals@aol.com <u>e-mail:</u> amishoriginals@aol.com
<u>Additional Information:</u> Second uptown Westerville location now open in Uptown Centre,
38 North State Street. Quality home furnishings since 1992.

CHATEAU LINEN...**(614) 901–3770**
20 K S State Street, Westerville
                                                        Fax:(614) 901–3772
See ad on page: 439
<u>Principal/Owner:</u> Shirley Roe

CLOCK WAREHOUSE...**(614) 262–2222**
3366 Olentangy River Road, Columbus
                                                        Fax:(614) 262–2256
See ad on page: 459
<u>Principal/Owner:</u> Tom Hlasten
<u>Additional Information:</u> The largest distributor of fine clocks in the midwest.

EDINBURGH GARDENS ....**(614) 488–0998**
1439 Grandview Avenue, Columbus
                                                        Fax:(614) 488–3045
See ad on page: 453
<u>Principal/Owner:</u> Joanie Johnson
<u>Website:</u> www.edinburghgardens.com <u>e-mail:</u> woodputt@aol.com

FUNCTIONAL FURNISHINGS ....**(614) 228–3463**
601 North High Street, Columbus
                                                        Fax:(614) 228–0298
See ad on page: 456
<u>Principal/Owner:</u> Matthew Unger, Jeff Unger
<u>Website:</u> www.functionalfurnishings.com <u>e-mail:</u> sales.main@functionalfurnishings.com

HOWARD BROOKS ....**(614) 888–5353**
7790 Olentangy River Road, Columbus
                                                        Fax:(614) 888–1247
See ad on page: 427b, 427c, 440
<u>Principal/Owner:</u> Peg Smith
<u>Website:</u> www.howardbrooksinteriors.com <u>e-mail:</u> help@hbrooksinteriors.com

Chateau Linens

20 K South State Street • Westerville, OH 43081
Tel: 614.901.3770 Fax: 614.901.3772

Howard Brooks, Inc.

7790 Olentangy River Rd. • Columbus, OH 43235
614.888.5353
www.howardbrooksinteriors.com

With just one visit you'll see how Howard Brooks, Inc. has helped to create many of Central Ohio's most beautiful interiors for over 65 years. We display a diverse collection of timeless styles from the work's finest makers in one of the most beautiful and inspiring retail showrooms in the country.

Howard Brooks welcomes walk-in clients with excellent service and great values, showing 13,000 sq. ft. of hand-selected merchandise available for immediate delivery. Many of our clients choose to special order and we offer more than 350 manufacturers of furniture, upholstery, lamps, mirrors, wallcoverings, window treatments, carpets, custom rugs, accessories and more...Howard Brooks is the premier retailer in Ohio.

For design projects, our talented and attentive staff is available for in-home visits, providing professional design plans as part of the service, with an eye toward your needs. For the committed design client, we draw room plans and present a full range of possibilities based on individual tastes and budget.

Whether you're looking for that one beautiful lamp or to furnish a complete home, the staff of Howard Brooks is here, as we have been since 1936. Our daily commitment is to ensure that you get the quality...value...distinction...comfort and beauty that you deserve.

"Our contemporary American Craft furniture and furnishings reflect the ideals of the American Spirit; honesty, rugged individualism, and unparralleled refinement."

Dennis and Denise Blankemeyer

American Furnishings Co.

614.488.7263
FAX 614.488.7264
1409 W. Third Ave.
Columbus, OH 43212
www.AmericanFurnishings.com

Finally...
Central Ohio's Own
Home & Design
Sourcebook

The ***Central Ohio Home Book*** is your final destination
when searching for home remodeling, building and decorating
resources. This comprehensive, hands-on sourcebook to building,
remodeling, decorating, furnishing and landscaping a luxury home
is required reading for the serious and discriminating homeowner.
With more than 500 full-color, beautiful pages, the ***Central Ohio
Home Book*** is the most complete and well-organized reference
to the home industry. This hardcover volume covers all aspects of
the process, includes listings of hundreds of industry professionals,
and is accompanied by informative and valuable editorial discussing
the most recent trends. Ordering your copy of the ***Central Ohio
Home Book*** now can ensure that you have the blueprints to
your dream home, in your hand, today.

O R D E R F O R M

THE CENTRAL OHIO HOME BOOK

☐ YES, please send me _____ copies of the CENTRAL OHIO HOME BOOK at $39.95 per book, plus $4 Shipping & Handling per book.

Total amount enclosed: $_____ Please charge my: ☐ VISA ☐ MasterCard ☐ American Express

Card # _____ Exp. Date _____

Signature: _____

Name _____ Phone: ( ) _____

Address _____ E-mail: _____

City _____ State _____ Zip Code _____

Send order to: Attn: Book Sales – Marketing, The Ashley Group – Reed Business, 2000 Clearwater Drive, Oak Brook, IL 60523
Or Call Toll Free: 888.458.1750 Fax: 630.288.7949 E-mail ashleybooksales@reedbusiness.com

All orders must be accompanied by check, money order or credit card # for full amount.

INTERIOR DESIGNERS

BUILDERS & REMODELERS

KITCHEN & BATH

BEAUTIFULLY DESIGNED EDITORIAL PAGES

FLOORING

ARCHITECTS

LANDSCAPERS

NEW IN THE SHOWROOM FEATURE

Just a Sampling of the Spectacular pages in your Home Book

Nurseries, Toddler Rooms, Teen Rooms, Linens, Accessories

Columbus' Largest Selection

My Own ROOM
Children's Furniture
1006 Dublin Road in Grandview   614.487.8992

NUT TREE HANDCRAFTED FURNITURE
Designers & Builders of Solid Oak, Cherry,
Walnut & Maple Furniture for Home & Office
"Fine furniture handcrafted in the Swiss-Mennonite
tradition of quality craftsmanship."

2877 Kidron Rd., Kidron, Ohio
Toll Free 1-888-NUT-TREE

Hrs. Mon.-Sat. 9 a.m. -5:30 p.m
www.nuttreefurniture.com

Amish Country Furnishings

7600 Fishel Dr., N
Dublin, OH 43016
(614) 791-8525
1-800-803-1144

"Your Quality Furniture Alternative!"

Open Buggy Furniture Gallery

"Experience Our Heritage"

Bench Built - Solid Lumber Furniture

Home
Furnishings

LOMBARDS FURNITURE GALLERIES ....**(614) 459–2989**
2060 Bethel Road, Columbus
See ad on page: 219, 452
Principal/Owner: Judy & Fred Heer
Website: www.lombardsinteriors.com e-mail: lombards1@ameritech.net
Fax:(614) 459–3925

MILLER'S FURNITURE...**(614) 873–1932**
300 South Jefferson Avenue, Plain City
See ad on page: 454
Principal/Owner: Harold & Betty Miller
Website: www.millerfurniture.com

MODERN OBJECT CASA, THE ....**(614) 416–7171**
4064 Bond Street, Columbus
See ad on page: 451
Principal/Owner: Nicolge Halmaghi
Fax:(614) 416–7173

MY OWN ROOM...**(614) 487–8992**
1006 Dublin Road, Columbus
See ad on page: 446
Principal/Owner: Steve Hurst
Fax:(614) 487–8948

NUT TREE FURNITURE ....**(330) 857–7685**
2877 Kidron Road, Kidron
See ad on page: 447
Principal/Owner: Ray Nussbaum
Website: www.nuttreefurniture.com e-mail: nuttree@zoominternet.net
Additional Information: Designers and builders of solid oak, cherry, walnut and maple furni-
ture for home and office. Quality constructed to last.
Fax:(330) 857–8815

OPEN BUGGY FURNITURE GALLERY, INC. ....**(614) 873–9800**
9800 U.S. State Route 42, Plain City
See ad on page: 449
Principal/Owner:
Website: e-mail: openbuggy@msn.com Additional Information: Our Amish Heritage
Furniture is solid lumber with hand–rubbed oil finishes. We also offer Smith Brothers sofas &
chairs.
Fax:(614) 873–9801

ROCHE BOBOIS ....**(614) 299–9696**
858 North High Street, Columbus
See ad on page: 455
Principal/Owner: Isabella Grayfer
e-mail: casaisa@aol.com Additional Information: Roche Bobois offers quality, classic,
contemporary home furnishings, rugs and accessories directly from Europe. Enjoy the
experience of our design team.
Fax:(614) 299–0312

THE MODERN OBJECT

Bulthaup: Kitchen Architecture

THE ONE-STOP DESTINATION FOR MODERN DESIGN

REPRESENTING THE WORLD'S LEADERS IN DESIGN

KITCHEN: bulthaup
BATH: agape, boffi
LIGHTING: flos, artimide, ingo maurer
FURNITURE: moroso, kartell, vitra
ACCESSORIES: alessi, rosenthal, hackman, iittala, stelton, mono
DESIGNERS: starck, graves, gehry, castiglione, mendini, newsone,
jongerius, massaud, aalto, nelson, jacobsen, panton

THE MODERN OBJECT
4064 New Bond St. • Columbus, Ohio 43219 • 614.416.7171

Why buy home furnishings from Lombards?

Comparable cost: Based on comparable construction, you can buy quality furniture at Lombards for prices equal to or less than other furniture stores everyday.

Complimentary Interior Design: Our professional staff is available to offer in-store interior design advice and suggestions - absolutely free!

Our Reputation: For over 53 years we have been providing our customers with fine quality furniture and great service. We rely on repeat business and referrals from our clients. That's why we're now doing business with many fourth generation Lombards customers.

Enduring Craftsmanship: Lombards furniture offerings are constructed to last. Solid wood, mortise-and-tendon joinery, truly flush joints, hand-applied finishes create furniture to last a lifetime.

Classic Designs: You may have heard it said "styles change" and while that's true, good designs last forever. Out collections embrace a broad range of styles from antique English reproductions to the contemporary of today.

Personal Service: We take the time to listen. Our staff is always here to offer as much, or as little, assistance as you require. We do not believe in high-pressure sales. We do believe in customer service.

Lombards Was Chosen: By the National Home Furnishing Association as one of the top ten sellers of quality home furnishings in the Midwest. We were the only store in Ohio to earn this honor!

Lombards
FURNITURE GALLERIES

The Plaza®

HABERSHAM®
EST. 1972

Entertainment Centers
Armoires · Cupboards
Chests · Sideboards
Dining Tables

CLAUDE MONET MUSEUM
· GIVERNY ·

Fine Furnishings for the Home & Garden

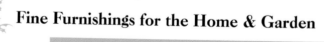

Discover the Difference
Authentic Amish Craftsmanship

You'll find genuine Amish hand-crafted oak & cherry furniture, imported area rugs, upholstered furniture and bedding.

You'll also find an experienced, knowledgeable staff to help you with your decision.

The center unit of this three-piece, mission-style entertainment center features pocket doors and can hold a large TV. The set comes in both oak and cherry.

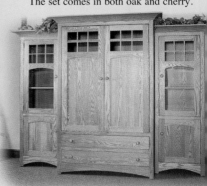

Uniquely beautiful carvings adorn the table legs, chair legs and skirt board of this lovely dining room set available in oak and cherry.

Subtle curves and lines add to the beauty of this bedroom set, available in either oak or cherry. A part of the Delafield Collection, this unique set can be found only at Miller's Amish Wood Shop.

Visit us for quality Oriental rugs from Tibet.

AMISH WOOD SHOP
Miller's FURNITURE
Simple furniture for refined tastes

(614) 873-1932
1-888-456-9898
300 S. Jefferson Plain City
(Just South of Rte. 161 across from Der Dutchman)
Mon.-Thur. 10-6   Fri. 10-8
Sat. 10-5   Closed Sunday
www.millersfurniture.com

Life. Style. Design.

Modern and Contemporary Home Furnishings, Office Furnishings and Accessories.

furniture for the bedroom / youth rooms / dining rooms / office furniture / sofas / leather recliners / lighting / bookcases / barstools / home office / task seating / extensive gift and accessory collections / commercial furnishings for medical and small business / free in-home design service / 90 days same as cash

 FUNCTIONAL FURNISHINGS

Polaris Fashion Place   1500 Polaris Parkway #2220   Columbus, Ohio 43240   614-792-1110
Downtown / Short North   601 North High Street   Columbus, Ohio 43215   614-228-3463
www.functionalfurnishings.com

Accessories

ARTISTICALLY BENT LTD. ....**(614) 298–8966**
718 North High Street, Columbus   Fax:(614) 228–7289
See ad on page: 460
Principal/Owner: Kris Worthington
Website: artisticallybent.com e-mail: kris@artisticallybent.com

BILLIARDS PLUS ....**(614) 760–9797**
5435 Bethel Sawmill Center, Columbus   Fax:(614) 760–9799
See ad on page: 461
Principal/Owner: Kenny Rupp
Website: www.billiards–plus.com e-mail: krupp@billiards–plus.com
Additional Information: Billiards Plus features custom tables and cues, bar stools, lamps and other gaming accessories all at affordable prices.

CARLISLE GIFTS ....**(614) 873–1332**
445 South Jefferson Avenue, Plain City   Fax:(614) 873–1043
See ad on page: 4662, 463
Principal/Owner: Debra Gilpin
Website: www.carlislegifts.com

GARDENS OF SILK ....**(614) 766–4824**
2759 Martin Road, Dublin   Fax:(614) 766–0738
See ad on page: 458
Principal/Owner: Pat Prather

Europe's Finest Clocks

artistically bent, ltd.

• • • • • • •

•

•   a short north gallery

•   featuring

•   contemporary crafts
    for the home

718 north high street columbus,
614.298.8966
www.artisticallybent.com
ohio
43215

5435 BETHEL SAWMILL CTR 760-9797

Custom Pool Tables - Barstools - Custom Cues - Lighting
Pub Tables - Spectator Chairs - Airhockey & Foosball Tables
Slot Machines - Accessories & More - Joss - Sterling
Jerry Pechauer - Mali - McDermott - Slyfoxx
California House - Dynamo - Viking - Pastel - Whitaker
Andrew Gille - Brunswick - AMF - Peter Vitalie - Hilite

BILLIARDS PLUS
5435 BETHEL SAWMILL CENTER
COLUMBUS, OHIO 43235
614.760.9797
www.billiards-plus.com

of Plain City

Conveniently located
beside Der Dutchman
of Plain City.

**Carlisle Gifts of
Plain City**
445 S. Jefferson Rte. 42
Plain City, Ohio 43064
614-873-1332
9 a.m. to 8 p.m.
Monday - Thursday
9 a.m. to 9 p.m.
Friday and Saturday
Closed Sundays

A wonderful blend of elegant treasures, home accessories and the whimsical

Carlisle Gifts is an Authorized Showcase Dealer for Tracy Porter. Featuring the art of Thomas Kinkade, Howard Behrens and Simon Bull.

Carlisle Gifts

of Plain City

Lighting

BERNARD ELECTRIC ....**(614) 221–5195**
253 North Third Street, Columbus
See ad on page: 466
Principal/Owner: Alan Fankhauser
Fax:(614) 221–3581

DESIGNED ILLUMINATION ....**(614) 801–9573**
1205 Holton Road, Grove City
See ad on page: 465
Principal/Owner: David Michael Schad
e-mail: designill@msn.com
Fax:(614) 801–9574

HOME LIGHTING ....**(614) 794–0777**
6055 Cleveland Avenue, Columbus
See ad on page: 467
Principal/Owner: Rick Nathans
Fax:(614) 794–2190

DESIGNED ILLUMINATION

Architectural Lighting Consultants
1205 Holton Road, Grove City, Ohio 43123
614 801 5973

BERNARD ELECTRIC

COMMERCIAL AND
RESIDENTIAL LIGHTING
SPECIALISTS

253 NORTH THIRD STREET
COLUMBUS, OH 43215
614-221-5195

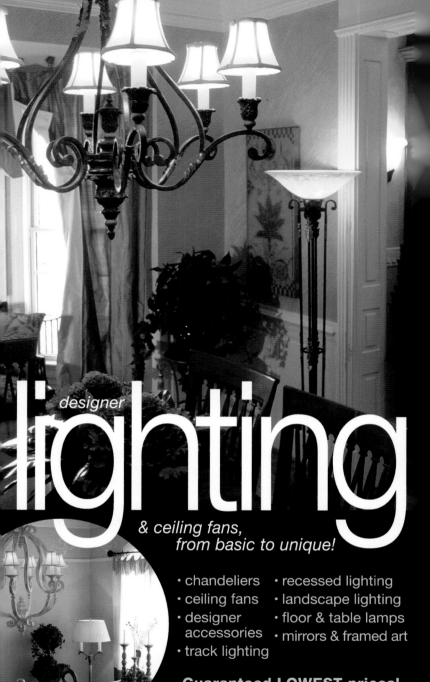

designer lighting
& ceiling fans, from basic to unique!

- chandeliers
- ceiling fans
- designer accessories
- track lighting
- recessed lighting
- landscape lighting
- floor & table lamps
- mirrors & framed art

Guaranteed LOWEST prices!
Central Ohio's Largest Selection
In Store Financing Available
All Major Credit Cards Accepted

MURRAY FEISS

HomeLighting
C E N T E R

614/794-0777
Mon, Fri, Sat: 10-6
Tues, Wed, Thur: 10-8
Open Sun 12 - 5pm

We are located
1 mile south of I-270
at 6055 Cleveland Ave.
Columbus, OH

Finally...
Central Ohio's Own
Home & Design
Sourcebook

The **Central Ohio Home Book** is your final destination
when searching for home remodeling, building and decorating
resources. This comprehensive, hands-on sourcebook to building,
remodeling, decorating, furnishing and landscaping a luxury home
is required reading for the serious and discriminating homeowner.
With more than 500 full-color, beautiful pages, the **Central Ohio
Home Book** is the most complete and well-organized reference
to the home industry. This hardcover volume covers all aspects of
the process, includes listings of hundreds of industry professionals,
and is accompanied by informative and valuable editorial discussing
the most recent trends. Ordering your copy of the **Central Ohio
Home Book** now can ensure that you have the blueprints to
your dream home, in your hand, today.

O R D E R   F O R M

THE CENTRAL OHIO HOME BOOK

☐ YES, please send me _____ copies of the CENTRAL OHIO HOME BOOK at $39.95 per book, plus $4 Shipping & Handling per book.

Total amount enclosed: $_____   Please charge my: ☐ VISA   ☐ MasterCard   ☐ American Express

Card # _____   Exp. Date _____

Signature: _____

Name _____   Phone: (   ) _____

Address _____   E-mail: _____

City _____   State _____   Zip Code _____

Send order to: Attn: Book Sales – Marketing, The Ashley Group – Reed Business, 2000 Clearwater Drive, Oak Brook, IL 60523
Or Call Toll Free: 888.458.1750 Fax: 630.288.7949 E-mail ashleybooksales@reedbusiness.com

All orders must be accompanied by check, money order or credit card # for full amount.

Pianos

GRAVES PIANO AND ORGAN INC. ....**(614) 847–4322**
5798 Karl Road, Columbus   Fax:(614) 847–0808
See ad on page: 473
<u>Principal/Owner:</u> Paul E. Graves
<u>Website:</u> www.gravespianos.com <u>e-mail:</u> pgraves312@aol.com
<u>Additional Information:</u> Ohio's largest piano dealer with over 500 pianos in stock.
Over 40 years in business.

PIANO GALLERY, THE ....**(614) 764–7426**
2829 Festival Lane, Dublin   Fax:(614) 764–1898
See ad on page: 470, 471
<u>Principal/Owner:</u> Jerry L. Wade
<u>Website:</u> www.thepianogallery.com <u>e-mail:</u> jwade@thepianogallery.com

PIANO WAREHOUSE..**(614) 888–3441**
6155 Huntley Road, Columbus   Fax:(614) 985–6522
See ad on page: 472
<u>Principal/Owner:</u> David MacDonald
<u>Additional Information:</u> Since 1981 Columbus' leading purveyor of quality used pianos;
Yamaha, Baldwin, Steinway. New Pianos, Big Discounts.

465

The Secret to Great Entertaining is Great

DGT2

There's nothing like live music to turn an ordinary party into a major social event. The Yamaha Disklavier piano brings famous musicians, like George Gershwin, Christopher Cross, and George Benson, into your home to play exclusive concerts for you and your friends! The Disklavier is not limited to piano music; it can perform the entire orchestral score of a Broadway hit, Mozart concerto, or pop song - complete with vocals! With the Disklavier's unique system, every nuance of the artists' original performances are recreated precisely - down to the smallest detail.

Entertainment!

If you've always wanted to play but never had the chance to learn, Yamaha's exclusive SmartKey will help you sound incredible the very first moment you sit down.

When you own a Yamaha Disklavier, the very best entertainment in town is right in your living room! To experience the Yamaha Disklavier for yourself, call:

THE
PIANO GALLERY
IN DUBLIN
614-764-7426
Sawmill Road south of Route 161 at Martin Road

PIANO WAREHOUSE

*Of all the beautiful expressions with which the fine home is adorned,
none is so indicative of the owners discriminating taste as a piano.*

- ENTRY LEVEL PRE-OWNED TO NEW PREMIUM
  GERMAN AND ITALIAN GRANDS AND VERTICALS.
- DIGITALS AND CD/DISK PLAYERS
- ALL MAJOR BRANDS! BEST VALUES IN COLUMBUS

PIANO WAREHOUSE

WORTHINGTON COMMERCE CENTER
6155 HUNTLEY ROAD
COLUMBUS
614.888.3441

CARLISLE GIFTS OF PLAIN CITY
Tracey Porter Collection Accessories: From wall to floor to tabletop, the Tracey Porter Collection offers many coordinated articles to add warmth and color to your home.

AMISH COUNTRY FURNISHINGS
Signature Bedroom Series - Armoire: By using highly figured Bird's Eye Maple and Natural Cherry, a striking contrast is created. This contrast is only heightened by the beautiful, warm amber color the Cherry develops as it ages. The mixture of classic hardwoods, along with the clean lines and frame and panel construction of this piece make it appealing for traditional or contemporary interiors. This same treatment can be applied to any number of pieces, and other combinations of wood may be used.

470

Photo by Kevin Fitzsimons

Showroom

471

Photo by **William McCarthy**

WHAT ART SAYS
Artistically Bent, ltd.:
"When a piece of art is displayed in the home, its owner, and what the owner sees in the art, is represented to all. Art also brings another dimension to the home, that of the passion of the artist."

MY OWN ROOM
Convertible Crib:
This crib converts to a toddler bed, a daybed and a full size bed. There are dozens of finish options available, and the bed comes in a variety of styles.

Window
Coverings

HANG UPS ....**(614) 239–7004**
3751 April Lane, Columbus   Fax:(614) 239–7668
See ad on page: 479
Principal/Owner: Mark Russell
Website: www.hangupsinc.com

ROMAN SHADES ETC. ....**(614) 235–0157**
687 Kenwick Road, Columbus   Fax:(614) 235–5457
See ad on page: 478
Principal/Owner: Sue Lazerwitz

WINDOW DRESSINGS ....**(614) 476–4597**
150 Crossing Creek Way, Gahanna   Fax:(614) 476–4515
See ad on page: 480
Principal/Owner: Kathleen Nye
Website: windowdressings.info
Additional Information: Specializing in the complete treatment of windows.

WINDOW SHOP, THE ....**(614) 457–0718**
4720 Kenny Road, Columbus   Fax:(614) 457–0720
See ad on page: 477
Principal/Owner: Earl & Mary Corder
e-mail: thewindowshop@aol.com
Additional Information: 32nd year in business. Family owned & operated.

WINDOWS ON THE WORLD ....**(614) 895–7789**
7813 Schott Road, Westerville   Fax:(614) 891–2857
See ad on page: 481

 **the window shop**

Today we see customers purchasing the 2" wood blinds for light & privacy control. Then the window top treatments and draperies to soften the look.

Sheer draperies are becoming very popular again along with decorative trim on top treatments & draperies.

Decorative pillows with trim. Upholstery fabrics to coordinate with total room design.

The window Shop works with all budgets...

Chintz, Silks, upholstery fabrics, floral, tone on tone beautiful colors. CHOICES...

4720 KENNY ROAD
COLUMBUS, OHIO 43220
(614) 457-0718

ROMAN SHADES ETC.

For an Elegant and Creative Difference

Lorraine Curley, ASID

Specializing in: Custom Window Design and Fabrication

Specializing in: **HunterDouglas**
window fashions

687 Kenwick Road • Columbus, OH 43209
614.235.0157

Hang Ups Inc.

Custom Design and Fabrication of Interior Window Coverings

Draperies • Motorized Products • Shutters • Blinds & Shades • Specialty Hardware

By appointment only

3751 April Lane
Columbus, Ohio 43227

Phone:
614.239.7004

Fax:
614.239.7668

Hang Ups Installation Group Inc. offers professional, custom interior window coverings for your home or office. A member of the BBB and serving Columbus proudly since 1978.

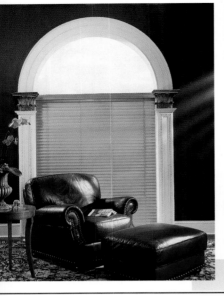 

Specialty Painters
Wall Finishers

APPLEBY PAINTING ....**(614) 847–4451**
See ad on page: 484
Principal/Owner: Troy Appleby
e-mail: applebypainting@columbus.rr.com

BELLALLUSIONS ....**(614) 784–9911**
See ad on page: 483
Principal/Owner: Katy Raine
Website: www.bellallusions.com

PYMER PLASTERING INC...**(614) 252–3737**
1978 East Walnut Street, Columbus   Fax:(614) 258–3258
See ad on page: 485
Principal/Owner: Seth Pymer
Website: www.pymerplastering.com e-mail: info@pymerplastering.com
Additional Information: Quality craftsmanship since 1886, specializing in ornamental,
historical restorations as well as Italian and other old world finishes.

REGENCY WALLCRAFT ....**(614) 865–9370**
5386 Harvestwood Lane, Gahanna   Fax:(614) 865–0947
See ad on page: 486
Principal/Owner: Jim Turner
Website: www.regencywallcraft.com e-mail: jturner@regencywallcraft.com
Additional Information: Regency Wallcraft provides residential & commercial wallcovering
services including wallcovering removal, drywall and plaster repair, surface preparation and
wallcovering installation.

Bellallusions

Decorative Finishes

By

Katy Raine

Unique faux finishing and decorative painting for extraordinary spaces

614.784.9911

www.bellallusions.com

Appleby Painting, Inc. specializing in repairing of exterior and interior of residential homes, apartment buildings, townhouses, and commercial projects. Knowing where you stand is absolutely necessary to any business. We will work with you to prepare accurate **FREE** estimates with detailed specifications

437 Rosslyn Avenue
Columbus, Ohio 43214
Tel: 614-847-4451
Fax: 614-847-1090

 Regency Wallcraft

Old World Craftsmanship
Where Wallcoverings Become Art

614.865.9370   740.549.5039

www.regencywallcraft.com

Home Office,
Garage & Closet

CALIFORNIA CLOSETS ....**(614) 431–0011**
761 Busch Court, Columbus   Fax:(614) 431–1255
See ad on page: 427d, 489
Principal/Owner: Bernie Nagle
Website: www.calclosets.com   e-mail: calclosetsohio@aol.com
Additional Information: Custom storage & organization for every room of the house.

CLOSET IMAGERY..**(614) 755–2344**
271 Schofield Drive, Columbus   Fax:(614) 755–3844
See ad on page: 491
Principal/Owner: Linda Market

ORGANIZED CLOSETS ....**(614) 863–1500**
384 Morrison Road, Columbus   Fax:(614) 863–5211
See ad on page: 490
Principal/Owner:

THOMAS W. RUFF & COMPANY ....**(614) 487–4000**
1114 Dublin Road, Columbus   Fax:(614) 487–4306
See ad on page: 488

life, stuff, storage

The home is the heart of life. An ever changing story of ourselves, our family, our friends. A welcome retreat where we protect, nurture and sustain all that is needed and loved. Let California Closets share 25 years experience with you to create the finest custom storage solutions for all the areas of your home.

In central Ohio, California Closets has been voted "The Best" by consumers, by more than 2 to 1, over our closest competitor.

Call for a free design consultation and see why we're NUMBER ONE

614.431.0011

Visit our showroom at
761 Busch Ct., Columbus, OH 43229
www.calclosets.com

CALIFORNIA CLOSETS®

ORGANIZED Closets

It's not just about closets - it's about organization. And we can help you get there - from the bedroom to the garage and every room in between. Each day just seems to flow a little smoother when you have a plan.

We feature SCHULTE closet systems, the choice of professional installers and designers for their beauty and strength.

Organized Closets

384 morrison road • columbus, ohio 43213

ph: 614.863.1500 | fx: 614.863.5211

www.organizedclosets.com

Beauty

Quality

Photos by Imagemakers Photographic

Integrity

Closet Imagery, Inc.

271 Schofield Drive
Columbus, Ohio 43213
Phone: (614) 755-2344
Fax: (614) 755-3844

CLOSET IMAGERY®

Since 1985

Home Books
12 Tips
For Pursuing Quality

1. Assemble a Team of Professionals During Preliminaries.
Search out and value creativity.

2. Educate Yourself on What to Expect.
But also be prepared to be flexible in the likely event of setbacks.

3. Realize the Value and Worth of Design.
It's the best value for your investment.

4. Be Involved in the Process.
It's more personally satisfying and yields the best results.

5. Bigger Isn't Better – Better is Better.
Look for what produces quality and you'll never look back.

6. Understand the Process.
Be aware of products, prices and schedules, to be a productive part of the creative team.

7. Present a Realistic Budget.
Creative, workable ideas can be explored.

8. Create the Right Environment.
Mutual respect, trust and communication get the job done.

9. There Are No Immediate Miracles.
Time is a necessary component in the quest for quality.

10. Have Faith in Yourself.
Discover your own taste and style.

11. Plan for the Future.
Lifestyles and products aren't static.

12. Do Sweat the Details.
Establish the discipline to stay organized.

HOME BOOK

7654 Crosswoods Drive, Columbus, OH 43235   614-431-2950 fax 614-431-2052

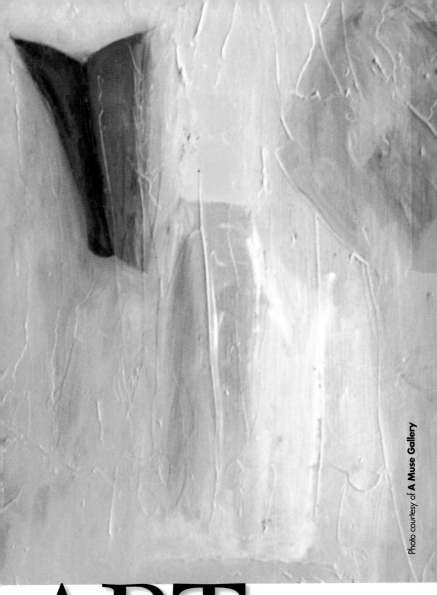

Photo courtesy of **A Muse Gallery**

ART&
ANTIQUES

David Franklin Ltd.
FINE ANTIQUES & INTERIORS
2216 East Main St.
COLUMBUS, OH
43209

(614) 338-0833

2216 Main Street · Columbus, Ohio 43209 · (614) 338-0833

English and European Antiques of the Highest Quality

David Franklin Ltd. offers a varied collection of fine antiques, accessories, and art from the 18th and 19th centuries. With our thirty years of experience in the antiques field David Franklin Ltd. continues to offer the quality and selection our clients have come to expect.

❂

ethniciti™

INTERIORS

residential • commercial • space planning

668 north high street • columbus, oh 43215
tel: 614.222.6700 fax: 614.222.6701
ethniciti@aol.com

489

The Beauty of Rarity

Art and antiques can connect with us in a way that no other objects in our homes can. A favorite piece of art can transport us to another place, set a mood for a room, give visitors a glimpse of our personalities, and provide us with a canvas for the way we feel. Fine art speaks to the soul of the owner. An antique can bring part of the past into our homes, and can bring us thoughts of other times, other places and the people who lived in them. They tell their stories through the generations.

Art and antiques, unlike so many other pieces purchased for the home, have the potential to become a family's heirlooms. Even an inexpensive "find" may someday become a most treasured item because of the warm memories it calls to mind. Truly, these choices are best made with the care and guidance of an experienced professional who understands the significance of these items in your home.

Photo courtesy of **A Muse Gallery**

A PIECE OF THE PAST

LEARN ABOUT ART & ANTIQUES

Part of the pleasure of collecting art or antiques is learning about them. Many homeowners buy a particular painting or sculpture they love, and find that following the art form or the artists becomes a lifetime passion.

The best place to start to familiarize yourself with art is at one of the many wonderful museums in your area. Wander through historic homes in the different historic neighborhoods of the city and get an idea of what the art feels like in a home environment. Go to auctions. Buy the catalog and attend the viewing. At the sale, you'll begin to get an idea of the values of different types of items. Finally, get to know a dealer. Most are pleased to help you learn and want to see more people develop a lifetime love affair with art, similar to their own. If a dealer seems too busy or isn't genuinely interested in helping you, then go to another dealer.

Haunt the local bookstores and newsstands. There are many publications dedicated to these fields.

Homeowners find their way to a love of antiques by many different paths. Some are adding to an inherited collection that connects them with past generations of family or with the location of their birth. Some are passionate about pottery or porcelain, clocks or dolls, and want to expand their knowledge while building a lifetime collection.

Antique furniture, artwork and collectibles also can be used to make a singular statement in an interior. Through a 19th Century English chest, an American Arts & Crafts table, or a beloved collection of Tiffany glass vases, homeowners put a personal signature on their interior design.

Making the right selection is as much a matter of knowledge and experience as it is taste and personal aesthetic. As top quality antique paintings, photographs and other desirable items become more difficult to find, getting expert guidance in identifying good and worthwhile investments is crucial. An interior designer or the knowledgeable professionals at the top galleries in the area can help you determine the value of pieces you are considering by assessing these four characteristics:

• Rarity-In general, the more difficult it is to find similar pieces, the greater the value. Try to determine how many comparable pieces exist. However, it is possible to be too rare. If there are too few similar pieces in circulation, there may be limited demand.

• Quality-The quality of the original materials and workmanship affects the value significantly.

• Provenance-The history of a piece, how many owners it has had, is its provenance. A piece with only a few owners has a better provenance.

• Condition-The more that remains of the original finish, the more valuable the piece. However, in some cases, small imperfections can help to establish authenticity.

When you visit an antique store or gallery, be prepared to seriously consider what type of investment you wish to make and how it will work in a given interior.

If you are pursuing pieces to add to an existing collection, do your research to determine which dealers and galleries in the area cater to your interests. Or, check with a favorite gallery for information. Be open to ideas and suggestions, especially when you're just beginning a collection, or a search for a special antique. There is so much to know about so many different objects, time periods, and design, that it truly does take a lifetime to develop an expertise.

VISITING ART GALLERIES

More than anything else, choosing to make beautiful, distinctive art objects a part of your home brings the joy of living with beautiful things into the daily life of yourself, your family and your guests.

The most important rule to know as your begin or continue to add art to your home is that there truly are no "rights or wrongs." Find what reaches you on an emotional level, and then begin to learn about it.

Use your eyes and react with your heart. Look at art magazines and books. Visit the museums in town, and those in other cities as you travel. Go to the galleries. Visit many of them for the widest exposure to different possibilities. Use the Internet to visit gallery and museum sites from all over the world. Let only your sense of beauty and aesthetics guide you at this point. Consider other constraints after you've identified the objects of your desire.

EXPERT ADVICE

The most reputable art gallery owners and dealers have earned their reputation by establishing an expertise in their field, and serving their clients well.

Buying from these established, respected professionals offers many benefits. Their considerable knowledge of and exposure to art translates into opinions that mean a great deal. You can trust the advice and education they offer you. They've done considerable research and evaluation before any item gets placed in their gallery, and determined that it's a good quality item, both in terms of artistic merit and market value. You can also rest assured that they will stand behind the authenticity of what they present in their galleries. Most offer free consultations, trade-back arrangements, and installation, and will help you with selling your art at some point in the future as your collection grows, you change residences, or your tastes change.

VALUE JUDGMENTS

Buy for love, not money. This is the advice we heard time and again from the best art galleries. Not all art appreciates financially – often it fluctuates over the years according to the artist's career, consumer tastes, and the state of the overall economy. If you love what you own and have been advised well by a knowledgeable professional, you'll be happiest with your investment.

TARNISH OR PATINA?

If your collection includes decorative metal objects like an engraved silver platter or brass handles on an antique chest, tarnish may become an issue. In some cases, the tarnish, caused by oxidation, can add subtle shadings and a beautiful patina to the piece. Before you polish, decide if the piece is more authentic with the tarnish. If so, relax and enjoy.

491

MAKE AN APPOINTMENT

When you have identified a gallery or dealer you admire, call for an appointment to discuss your needs. Most professionals appreciate knowing you will be visiting at a specific time so they can have additional help on hand to attend to other customers.

THE FINESSE OF FINE ART

You know what you like, but how much might it actually cost to fill your home with art? Following is one example, for the analysis, research and procurement of six art pieces.

Before the project begins, a budget is established based on the type of art desired (sculpture, drawings, paintings, tapestry), the quality of the art, scale, and provenance.

The art:
A print for the hallway;
a 4-ft. tall classical bronze sculpture;
a still-life painting;
two tapestries;
a Dufy painting;
Total: $55,000

Additional expenses:
Appraisal services;
framing;
insurance;
consultation fees;
security;
Total; $19,750

Grand Total:
$74,750

Note: a project such as this one usually lasts 12 to 18 months.

Set a working budget (possibly a per-piece budget) and let the gallery know at the outset what the guidelines are. This saves both you and the gallery time and energy. You'll be able to focus on items that are comfortably within the range of your budget. Buy the best quality possible in whatever category you like. You will appreciate the quality for years. Don't hesitate to do some comparison shopping. Although each art object is unique in itself, you may find another piece in the same style that you enjoy equally as well.

The best dealers understand budgets, and respect your desire to get good quality at a fair price. They are happy to work with enthusiastic clients who want to incorporate beautiful art into their lives.

Only deal with dealers who are helpful and present their art fairly. If you feel intimidated in a gallery, or feel the dealer isn't giving you the time and information you deserve to make intelligent choices, visit another gallery. Never buy art under pressure from a dealer, or to meet a deadline imposed by your interior design timetable.

GO TO AN AUCTION HOUSE

Attending an auction is an excellent way to learn about decorative arts, develop and add to a collection, and simply have a good time. Whether you attend as a buyer, seller, or observer, an auction is an experience that will enrich your understanding and enjoyment of the art and antiques world.

If you're a novice, it's important to choose a well-established auction house with a reputation for reliability. Try to be a patient observer and learn about the process as well as the value of items you may be interested in later on.

Buy a copy of the catalog and attend the viewing prior to the beginning of the auction itself. Each item, or "lot," that will be available for sale at the auction will be listed, and a professional estimate of selling price will be included. Professionals will be available during the viewing to answer questions and help you become familiar with the art objects as well as the process.

CHOOSING AN AUCTION

Find out about interesting auctions from the proprietors of galleries you like, or ask to be added to the mailing list of a reputable auction house. With these sources of information, you'll be informed of events that will feature quality items of interest to you. The established auction houses that have earned a reputation for reliability and expertise generally have a single location where they hold their auctions. Sometimes an auction will be held at an estate site, or a seller's location.

Before attending the auction, spend some time researching the art or antique you're interested in bidding on, so you'll be informed about its value and can make an informed decision. Talk to people at the galleries. Visit Internet sites to research your interests, or for information on upcoming auctions and recent auction prices. There also are books available that publish recent auction sales to help you get an idea of price and availability. Check your library or bookseller for publications like Gordon's Price Annual.

There seems to be an air of mystery and sophistication that surrounds auctions, but don't let that discourage you from discovering the auction experience. They are enjoyable and educational for anyone who is interested in obtaining or learning about art and antiques.

BE REALISTIC

For many of us, an auction might seem an opportunity to pick up an item at a bargain price. Realize that there may be bargains to be found, but in general, auctioned items are sold for a fair price. There may be a "reserve price," which is a private agreement between the seller and the auctioneer on the amount of a minimum bid.

If you educate yourself about the category you're interested in, you'll be at an advantage at an auction. It's equally important to research the market value of any lot you may be considering. Remember that there is an auctioneer's commission of 10 to 15 percent of the hammer price, to be paid in addition to the purchase price, as well as applicable sales taxes.

While you won't end up making the top bid simply by tugging your ear, it's important to pay attention when you're bidding. Be aware of the way the auctioneer communicates with the bidders and always listen for the auctioneer's "fair warning" announcement just before the gavel falls. ∎

THE FALL SEASON

Fall signals the beginning of the art season. Galleries will open exhibits and the excitement is contagious. Ask to get on gallery mailing lists to stay informed of fall openings.

VISIT OUR MUSEUMS

As you develop your passion for art and items of antiquity, take advantage of the collections and public education opportunities at some of Ohio's distinguished art museums, like:

493

Columbus Museum of Art 480 E. Broad St. Columbus, OH 43215 614.221.6801

Ohio Historical Society 1982 Velma Ave. Columbus, OH 43211 614.297.2300 www.ohiohistory.org

Pottery

ZANESVILLE POTTERY ....**(740) 872–3345**
7395 East Pike, Zanesville   Fax:(740) 872–3325
See ad on page: 499
Principal/Owner: K.L. Castor

Zanesville Pottery & China
The Designers Choice

An exceptional selection of pottery for Interior, Landscape, and Commercial Professionals

You have just discovered.....

" a wide selection of imported and domestic pottery to add that sensual, old world charm to the home and garden of your dreams."

Art
Galleries

DAVID FRANKLIN LTD. ....**(614) 338–0833**
2216 East Main Street, Columbus   Fax:(614) 338–1702
See ad on page: 230, 231, 492b, 492c
Principal/Owner: David J. Franklin Kelley
Website: www.davidfranklinltd.com e-mail: dfltd@aol.com

A MUSE GALLERY ....**(614) 299–5003**
996 West Third Avenue, Columbus   Fax:(614) 299–5004
See ad on page: 501
Principal/Owner: Caren Petersen
e-mail: musegallery@cs.com Additional Information: Fine art gallery representing over 30
mid–career national and international artists.

ART IMPRESSIONS ....**(614) 421–0838**
714 North High Street, Columbus   Fax:(614) 421–0840
See ad on page: 502
Principal/Owner: Rebecca & Jan Caddell
e-mail: artimpres@aol.com Additional Information: Gallery features living contemporary
artists – American & International, also objects of design & jewelry.

ETHNICITI ....**(614) 222–6700**
668 North High Street, Columbus   Fax:(614) 222–6701
See ad on page: 492d
Principal/Owner: William R. Sands
Website: www.ethniciti.com e-mail: ethniciti@aol.com
Additional Information: Ethniciti celebrates the creation of personal living spaces that express
your originality and individuality through the selection of distinctive home furnishings, creative
interior design and unique fine art.

a muse gallery™

fine art sculpture photography

Caren Petersen Director, Owner & Art Siren

614-299-5003   Toll Free 877-299-5003   Fax 614-299-5004

996 W. Third Avenue, Grandview Heights, OH 43212

art impressions

a contemporary international gallery
714 north high street · columbus · 421-0838

Custom
Framing

ANDERSON'S FRAME DESIGN ....**(614) 848–8116**
652 High Street, Worthington　　　　　　　　　　　　　Fax:(614) 848–4043
See ad on page: 504, 505
<u>Principal/Owner:</u> Matt Anderson
<u>Website:</u> www.afdonline.com　<u>e-mail:</u> framedesign@ad.com

ANDY'S FRAME SETTING ....**(614) 898–7134**
7389 State Route 3, Westerville　　　　　　　　　　　　Fax:(614) 898–1955
See ad on page: 506
<u>Principal/Owner:</u> Andy Dronsfield

HACKMAN FRAMES ....**(614) 841–0007**
502 Schrock Road, Worthington　　　　　　　　　　　　Fax:(614) 841–0445
See ad on page: 508
<u>Principal/Owner:</u> Craig Hackman
<u>Additional Information:</u> Handcrafted and gilded made to order picture frames.

REED ARTS, INC. ....**(614) 291–0253**
909 West 5th Avenue, Columbus　　　　　　　　　　　　Fax:(614) 291–2186
See ad on page: 507
<u>Principal/Owner:</u> Barbara Baker
<u>Website:</u> www.reedarts.com　<u>e-mail:</u> reedart@netwalk.com
<u>Additional Information:</u> In business 16 years; cumulative staff experience of 90 years:
Reed Arts is a name you can trust.

Custom Frames...
Custom Quality.

At Anderson's FrameDesign our quality custom frames are inspired by art. Our goal: to create custom framing that both enhances and protects your treasures. Whether you are a homeowner, a member of the design trade or have a commercial application, we have the expertise and experience to accommodate your needs. Continually educating ourselves on our craft, we stay ahead of the curve. We pride ourselves on listening to our clients first. Only after listening can we put our technical expertise, attention to details and creative artistry to work.

Let us guide you through our tremendous selection of custom picture framing products found only at Anderson's FrameDesign. Visit our studio or contact us to discover what custom picture framing is all about.

652 High Street
Worthington, Ohio 43085
614 848-8116 phone
614 848-4043 fax

AFD

ANDERSON'S FrameDesign

Elegance

Desire

Beauty

Harmonious

Simplicity

Luxurious

Serene

Attitude

Boldness

Design

Extraordinary

Vigorous

Sumptuous

Sophisticated

Andy's
FRAME SETTING
PICTURE FRAMING & GIFT GALLERY

ANDY DRONSFIELD
Owner
andysframe@ee.net
www.andysframesetting.com

7389 State Route 3
Westerville, Ohio 43082
614.898.7134
Fax 614.898.1955

Mon, Wed, Fri, 10-6 Tue-Thu, 10-8 Sat, 10-4

Photo courtesy of **Progressive Audio**

HOME
THEATER
&
TECHNOLOGY

What features won't your husband look for in a home theater?

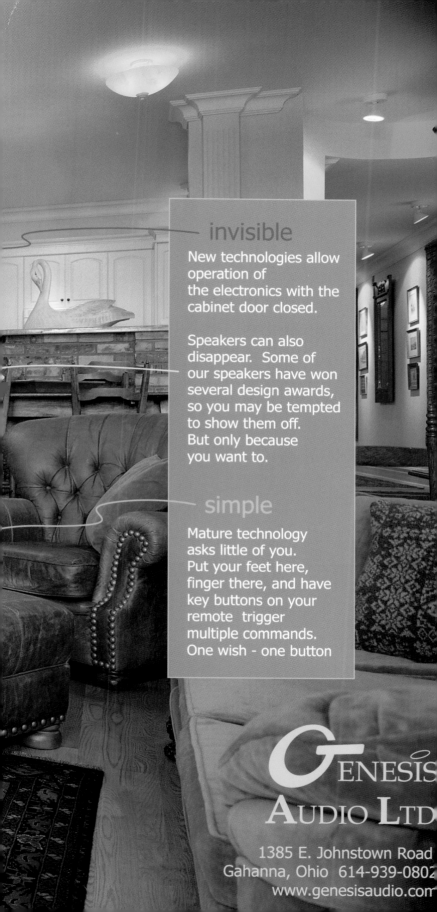

progressiveaudio

1764 N. High Street
Columbus, Ohio 43201
614.299.0565
www.progressiveaudio.com

home theater   audio   custom installation   automation technology

High Tech
Comes
Home

505

The modern home is a hub of technology. Tech wizards continue to deliver better and more powerful products that are less obtrusive and more affordable than ever. From lighting and security systems that can be operated from half-way around the globe to home theaters that rival the quality of commercial movie houses, these once rare luxury items have become priorities for homeowners.

Sophisticated homeowners have had their level of appreciation for quality in sight and sound elevated through the years of experience in concert halls, movie theaters and sports arenas. As they gravitate toward making the home the focus of their lifestyle, and strive to incorporate that high level of performance into their leisure time at home, new technological advances become a more desirable and practical investment.

Photo courtesy of **Franco & Miriello**

THE IMPORTANCE OF A HOME THEATER DESIGN SPECIALIST

Home theater is widely specified as a custom home feature today. The sophisticated homeowner with a well-developed eye (and ear) for quality demands the latest technology in a home entertainment system that will provide pleasure for many years. Because of the fluid marketplace, the vast possibilities of the future, and the complexity of the products, it's crucial to employ an established professional to design and install your home theater.

The experts presented on the following pages can advise you on the best system for your home. They can find an appropriate entertainment center, masterly install your system, and teach you to use it. Their expertise will make the difference.

THE HOME THEATER DESIGN PROCESS

Tell your builder or remodeling specialist early on if you want a home theater, especially if built-in speakers or a ceiling-mounted video projection unit are part of the plan.

Inform the interior designer so proper design elements can be incorporated. Window treatments to block out light and help boost sound quality, furnishings or fabrics to hide or drape speakers, and comfortable seating to enhance the media experience should be considered. If you plan to control the window treatments by remote control, these decisions will have to be coordinated.

When visiting showrooms, be ready to answer these questions:

• What is your budget? There is no upper limit.

• Do you want a High Definition Television (HDTV) or projection video system? A DVD player? Built-in or free-standing speakers?

• Do you want Internet access for your television?

• What style of cabinetry and lighting do you want? Do you want specialized lighting? A built-in bar? How much storage is needed?

• What are the seating requirements? Seating should be at least seven feet from the screen.

• Do you want whole-house control capability so you can distribute and control the system from different rooms of the house?

• How will you incorporate the system with the rest of the room? Must the room meet other needs?

• Do you want extra luxuries, like multiple screens, or a remote control system that allows you to dim the lights and close the draperies?

PLAN AHEAD

Even if you aren't installing a home theater system right away, have a room designed to serve that purpose later. Get the wiring done and build the room an appropriate shape and size. Get the right antenna. Ask for double drywall for noise control.

SAVE AN AISLE SEAT

For the best seat in the house, your home theater will need the following:
A large screen television and/or projection video system (from 32-inch direct view up to 200-inches, depending on the size of the room). New, compact products are available now.
A surround-sound receiver to direct sound to the appropriate speaker with proper channel separation.
A surround-sound speaker system, with front, rear, and center channel speakers and a sub-woofer for powerful bass response.
A comfortable environment, ideally a rectangular room with extra drywall to block out distractions.

• Will this room function in the future? As technology continues to change our lifestyle, plan for this room to grow and change as well. Ask your salesperson for advice.

Home theaters are installed at the same time as security and phone systems, before insulation and drywall. In new construction or remodeling, start making decisions at least two months before the drywall is hung. Allow four weeks for delivery and installation.

AUTOMATED HOME MANAGEMENT

It's like clockwork: Your alarm clock wakes you, and while you are rubbing the sleep from your eyes, a path from your bed to the master bath to the kitchen is lit for you. The stone floor of your bath has warmed and the climates of the rooms you'll be walking through this morning are all in sync. Once your eyes have opened, you walk to the kitchen, where a hot, fresh, pot of coffee is waiting for you and the television is already tuned to your favorite morning news program. Once you've left home, there's no need to worry about whether you've locked all of the doors or have turned the lights off, because those things are also handled automatically. But just in case, for your own peace of mind, you can check on the status of your home's locks, lights and windows from a remote computer or even a cell phone, and lock, close or turn off whatever you may have forgotten about.

Such are the advantages of automated home management. Home automation brings an added, virtually impenetrable layer of ease and security to the home. Energy can be saved by keeping the heat or air-conditioning at a low level while you're out of the house, then as you're on the way home from the office or your daily errands, you can bring the home climate back to your comfort level. Criminals can be thwarted by lighting that not only automatically switches on at night, but comes on at random times, in random rooms, to make it look as if your home is "lived in" when you're away.

You don't have to be a computer wizard to operate these automated home systems. Voice recognition software allows you to simply say "Turn lights on at 7 p.m. for four hours," and it's done. Systems have become smarter: while a direct line to the police department can be activated by an object coming into contact with a door or window at 3 a.m., the homeowner, while at the office or the golf course, can be alerted first when something is detected at 3 p.m. A quick check on any computer, which will give him or her a view from the home's security cameras, can let the homeowner know that the afternoon incident was caused by children who have been told not to play soccer so close to the house.

While it all may have seemed unbelievably futuristic not long ago, modern home technology is making homeowner's lives easier, more peaceful and much more enjoyable. ∎

YOUR PERSONAL SCREENING ROOM

In case you're wondering how much it would cost, here's an example of the costs involved with outfitting a room in the mid- to high-scale price range for a home theater
Labor (at $55/hour): $3,500
50-inch television: $4,000
DVD player: $900
Amplifier with sur-round-sound decoder: $10,000
Six speakers with subwoofer: $10,000
Satellite dish (high definition): $1,000
Delivery/installation: $2,500
Seating: Eight leather mod-ule seats, $15,000
Infrared sensors to control lighting, motorized drapes, security system: $10,000
Total: $57,000

507

BEST TIP:

Have phone lines, DSL or cable modems connected to every TV outlet in the house for Internet access and satellite reception.

Home Theater
Design

ABSOLUTE HOME THEATRE ....**(614) 336–8152**
224 West Olentangy Street, Powell   Fax:(614) 336–8156
See ad on page: 519
Principal/Owner: Dave Robenalt

ARCHITECTURAL VIDEO SYSTEMS, INC. ....**(614) 891–5532**
6591 Blackhawk Circle, Westerville   Fax:(614) 891–5517
See ad on page: 517
Principal/Owner: Gene Lent
Website: architecturalvideo.com e-mail: gene@architecturalvideo.com

AUDIO ENCOUNTERS ....**(614) 766–4434**
4271 West Dublin Granville Road, Dublin   Fax:(614) 766–4589
See ad on page: 520
Principal/Owner: Peggy Deem
Website: www.audioencounters.com e-mail: info@audioencounters.com
Additional Information: Specializing in home theatre design, system integration,
audio/video distribution and pre–wires. Visit our showroom for your personal home
theater demonstration.

GENESIS AUDIO ....**(614) 939–0802**
1385 East Johnstown Road, Gahanna   Fax:(614) 939–0805
See ad on page: 508b, 508c, 521
Principal/Owner: Art DeLorenzo
Website: www.genesisaudio.com e-mail: glowe@byperception.com
Additional Information: We are a custom installation/retail business specializing in all
audio/video applications for the home.

NEWCOME ELECTRONIC SYSTEMS ....**(614) 848–5688**
9005 Antares Avenue, Columbus   Fax:(614) 848–9921
See ad on page: 518
Principal/Owner: Tim Newcome
Website: www.newcome.com e-mail: info@newcome.com

PROGRESSIVE AUDIO ....**(614) 299–0565**
1764 North High Street, Columbus   Fax:(614) 299–6587
See ad on page: 508d, 522
Principal/Owner: Scott Ranney

HOME AUDIO/VIDEO SOLUTIONS
Custom Design • Installation • System Integration

Your home is an expression of your lifestyle. That's why the design of a home audio/video or automation system is so important.

Inspired by your vision, Newcome can design and install an audio/video or automation system to create the ideal atmosphere for your home entertainment.

- ❏ **Home Theater**
- ❏ **Multi-room Audio/Video Systems**
- ❏ **Touch Screen Controls**
- ❏ **Lighting Control Systems**
- ❏ **Home Automation**
- ❏ **Digital Phone Systems**
- ❏ **Computer Networking**

With Newcome, you can improve all the activities you enjoy in your home without compromising the visual ambiance of your interiors.

Call today to schedule an appointment to visit our Demo Room!
866-DIAL-NES • www.newcome.com
Newcome Electronic Systems
9005 Antares Avenue • Columbus, Ohio 43240

Audio Encounters Brings You The Best Home Theater Experience

Audio Encounters has been serving Central Ohio Hi-Fi and Video aficionados since 1985. We are the friendly dealer carrying the best names in audio, video, and home theater products, including McIntosh (the MC602 was voted best home theater amplifier by Audiophile magazine). You don't need to be an expert to own a system that creates a rich theater experience, because we offer personal assistance to match your needs to the right design.

- A quality system to fit your budget
- An unparalleled commitment to service
- Experienced staff to evaluate your needs
- Expert design and installation services
- Pre-wiring for new homes and add-ons for existing installations

Please stop by for a home theater demonstration

Authorized Premier Dealer

4271 W. DUBLIN-GRANVILLE RD.
614.766.4434
www.audioencounters.com

progressiveaudio

1764 N. High Street
Columbus, Ohio 43201
614.299.0565
www.progressiveaudio.com

home theater   audio   custom installation   automation technology

Security
Systems

GOLDEN BEAR LOCK & SAFE, INC...**(614) 733–5625**
7445 Daron Court, Plain City   Fax:(614) 733–0004
See ad on page: 380, 524
<u>Principal/Owner:</u> Tim Moore
<u>Website:</u> www.goldenbearlock.com <u>e-mail:</u> goldenbearlock@cs.com
<u>Additional Information:</u> Excellent service for over 25 years. Retail store/mobile service.
Safe sales & service, locksmithing, CCTV, electronic access systems, safes.

Integrated
Home Systems

SHELTERGUARD SYSTEMS ....**(614) 844–5222**
6665 North Huntley Road, Suite B, Columbus   Fax:(614) 844–5140
See ad on page: 526
<u>Principal/Owner:</u> Nick Kehagias
<u>Website:</u> www.shelterguard.com   <u>e-mail:</u> nkehagias@shelterguard.com

517

LOCATION

NEW ALBANY IS NOT ABOUT
WHERE YOU LIVE.
IT IS ABOUT HOW YOU LIVE.

Welcome To Elegant Living Created By Romanelli & Hughes

Let us create an elegant home for you. Call for information regarding new home locations nearest where you want to live.

Romanelli & Hughes
BUILDING COMPANY
614/891-2042

519

Custom-Tailored Communities

One of the most endearing charms of this area is the wide diversity and individuality of its neighborhoods. Whether your fantasy is to live in a stately, traditional home surrounded by rich foliage, or an ultra-modern custom built home overlooking a golf course, you are sure to find a neighborhood to call you home. To savvy homeowners, location is the most valuable of assets, and has long been their mantra.

Today's state-of-the-art homebuilders have given life to new communities in masterfully planned environments. Visually delightful and diverse, yet cohesive in architectural style and landscape, these communities address with impeccable taste the needs of their residents: proximity to excellent schools, shops, restaurants, favored leisure pursuits, the workplace. Safe havens, often in country or golf course settings, these developments cater to the homeowners' active lifestyles. Artistically designed for ease, these gracious homes welcome family and guests; they are sanctuaries in which to entertain, relax and nourish the spirit.

Photo courtesy of **Architrend Associates**

THE ULTIMATE IN LUXURY LIVING

The builders and developers of custom homes in upscale locations throughout the city and the suburbs realize the value of simplicity and strive to deliver it.

Simplicity is one of the qualities we most desire in our lives. By offering a community designed and built on the philosophy that homeowners deserve a beautiful environment, peaceful surroundings and luxurious amenities to enhance their lives, locations like those featured in the following pages deliver simplicity on a luxury scale.

Homeowners who live in these kinds of communities and locations know what they want. They want an environment where architecture and nature exist in harmony. Where builders have proven dedication to protecting the natural surroundings. They want recreation, like golf, swimming, lakes, walk and biking paths, or tennis courts. They want to live where there is a sense of community, and the convenience of close-by shopping and transportation. Finally, they want the conveniences of a well-planned community – guidelines on buildings and landscaping, strong community identity, and commitment to quality.

FINDING THE PERFECT LOCATION

Think about what kind of location would enhance the lifestyle of yourself and your family:

• Do you need to be near transportation?

• Do you want the security of a gated community?

• What kind of recreational amenities do you want? Golf, tennis or pool? Paths, fishing lakes, or horse trails? Party facilities, restaurants?

• What kind of natural environment do you prefer? Wildlife sanctuary, urban elegance, club luxury?

• What kind of home do you want to build? Determine if your dream house fits the overall essence of a particular community. Some planned communities allow only certain builders at their locations. Find out if these builders create homes that would satisfy your desires.

THE VALUE OF A LUXURY LOCATION

The availability of building sites diminishes with every passing year, and the builders and developers of our finest residential locations know that quality must be established to attract custom home owners. Their commitment to building top quality homes is apparent in the designs and materials used in their projects and in the reputations their locations enjoy.

The demand for homes built in these locations is growing. Their benefits, plus the unique opportunity to build a new custom home in a totally fresh, and new environment, are very enticing. ■

THE COMMUNITY SPIRIT

Enclave neighborhoods developed in luxury locations have the benefit of being part of two communities. The neighborhood identity is strong and so is the larger community spirit. It's the best of both worlds.

THE MASTER PLAN

520

Homes and landscapes in "master plan" locations are as unique and customized as anywhere. However, they are established according to a well-defined overall plan, which gives the homeowners the security of knowing that the high-quality look of their neighborhood will be rigorously upheld.

Communities

NEW ALBANY REALTY, LTD. ....**(614) 939–8900**
220 Market Street, Suite 200, New Albany   Fax:(614) 939–8925
See ad on page: 526b, 526c, 534
Principal/Owner: Lu Klaiber
Website: www.newalbanyrealty.com Additional Information: New Albany Realty, Ltd. preview
center is located at Lampton Park Road and Johnstown Road.

TARTAN FIELDS...**(614) 792–1160**
8070 Tartan Fields Drive, Dublin   Fax:(614) 792–1189
See ad on page: 535

ROOM TO GROW.

Acres of green space. Parks around every corner. A 26-mile trail system. And extensive youth programming at the New Albany Country Club. Yes, children feel right at home here.

New Albany is not about where you live. It is about how you live.   NEW ALBANY REALTY, LTD

The Ashley Group Luxury Home Resource Collection

The **Ashley Group (www.theashleygroup.com)** is pleased to offer as your final destination when searching for home improvement and luxury resources the following **Home Books** in your local market. Available now: *Chicago, Washington D.C., South Florida, Los Angeles, Dallas/Fort Worth, Detroit, Colorado, New York, Atlanta, Arizona, Philadelphia, San Diego, North Carolina, Boston, Houston, Las Vegas, Connecticut/Westchester County, Central Ohio and Kansas City.* These comprehensive, hands-on guides to building, remodeling, decorating, furnishing, and landscaping a luxury home, are required reading for the serious and selective homeowner. With over 700 full-color, beautiful pages, the **Home Book** series in each market covers all aspects of the building and remodeling process, including listings of hundreds of local industry professionals, accompanied by informative and valuable editorial discussing the most recent trends.

Order your copies today and make your dream come true!

Photo courtesy of **Baker Henning Productions, Inc.**

INDEXES

**If you imagine your kitchen
as a canvas for self expression
then Corian® is your palette of
exciting possibilities**

Corian® balances the rhythms of life and work with the harmony of nature. It complements, not competes with, the natural materials that are desirable in today's interior spaces. Corian® offers an extensive palette of colors to embrace any lifestyle, environment or material. Where there is connection, there is harmony and Corian®

For more information or to inquire about local dealers,
Contact:
DuPont Corian®/ Zodiaq® Distributors
OVS Marketing Manager
Cinda.Carter@ovsco.com

CORIAN®
SOLID SURFACES

Alphabetical Index

Professional Index

Architects

529

Art & Antiques

Professional Index

533

Kitchen & Bath

535

Landscaping

Notes

539

Notes

540

541

Notes

543

544